THE ISLAND CALLED PARADISE

THE ISLAND CALLED PARADISE
Cuba
IN HISTORY, LITERATURE, AND THE ARTS

The University of Alabama Press • Tuscaloosa

Copyright © 2014
The University of Alabama Press
Tuscaloosa, Alabama 35487-0380
All rights reserved
Manufactured in the United States of America

Typeface: Minion Pro

Cover photograph: Courtesy of Chip Cooper
Cover design: Michele Myatt Quinn

∞

The paper on which this book is printed meets the minimum requirements of American National Standard for Information Sciences—Permanence of Paper for Printed Library Materials, ANSI Z39.48-1984.

Library of Congress Cataloging-in-Publication Data

Beidler, Philip D.
 The island called paradise : Cuba in history, literature, and the arts / Philip D. Beidler.
    pages   cm
 Includes bibliographical references and index.
 ISBN 978-0-8173-1820-8 (trade cloth: alk. paper)—ISBN 978-0-8173-8743-3 (e book)
 1. Cuba—In popular culture. 2. Cuba—In literature. 3. Cuba—In art. 4. National characteristics, Cuban. I. Title.

F1760.B45 2014
972.91—dc23   2013035328

To the peoples of the United States of America
and la República de Cuba

CONTENTS

Acknowledgments ix
Introduction: Cuba and the Imagination 1

1
Romancing *Cecilia Valdés* 14

2
Un Militar Español de Origen Venezolano 29

3
Mambises in Whiteface 37

4
The Ghost of Walker Evans 50

5
Ignacio Piñeiro, George Gershwin, and the Schillinger System 60

6
The Secret Life of Ricky Ricardo 70

7
Good Neighbor Batista 86

8
The Two Ernestos 99

9
Steverino in Gangsterland 115

10
Why No One in Havana Speaks of Graham Greene 126

11
Inspector Renko on the Malecón 140

12
The Example of Yoani Sanchez 151

Conclusion: The Autumn of the Comandante 164
Source Notes and Reading Suggestions 181
Index 187

ACKNOWLEDGMENTS

For institutional support in the travel, research, and writing that made this book possible, I am indebted to the Cuba Initiative of the University of Alabama and in particular to Dean Robert Olin of the College of Arts and Sciences, who initiated projects and established contacts with Cuban colleagues. In Cuba I am similarly indebted to our sister institution, la Universidad de la Habana and in particular to Professor Jose Vasquez of el Colegio de San Geronimo.

The enumeration of people to whom I owe personal thanks and the description of the particular ways in which I am grateful to each would fill pages. Let me just list them alphabetically. Carmen Burkhalter; Chip Cooper; Catherine Davies; Julio Larramendi; Hank Lazer; Néstor Martí; Dan Ross; Mike Schnepf; Dan Waterman; Shanti Wieland; Tom Wolfe. In every case, the gratitude is anything but pro forma.

Acknowledgment is made for material published in *American Studies* and *Dalhousie Review*.

THE ISLAND CALLED PARADISE

INTRODUCTION

Cuba and the Imagination

Sunday, 28 October 1492: "Esta es la tierra mas hermosa que ojos humanos vieron" ("This is the most beautiful land that human eyes have ever seen").

So Christopher Columbus is said to have spoken on first beholding the island of Cuba.

Nearly five centuries later, according to writer Carlos Eire, at the Christian Brothers Colegio LaSalle de Miramar, the finest primary school in Havana, the lesson had not been lost. "True Ramiro," said a teacher, addressing one of his classmates, "Cuba is a paradise, and it very well might have been the original paradise, the Garden of Eden." "Yes, Cuba is a paradise," he went on, enforcing the point. "There's no other place on earth so lovely as Cuba, and that's why you should be proud of your country. You're all very lucky to live in a paradise."

There is no record of how the idea of a Cuba so imagined may be currently taught in the schools of the post-revolutionary workers' paradise. Still, for anyone who has been to the island, the metaphor remains strikingly apt. This, truly, one says to oneself, is "La Isla Llamada el Paraíso"—the "Island called paradise." It has also been, now for most Americans during more than a half century, a forbidden island—"La Isla Prohibida de Revolución," one might call it; the "Forbidden island of revolution." Accordingly, the book I propose—as in several of the lines above, sometimes written in two languages—is an attempt, albeit mainly from a US and Anglophone cultural perspective, at cultural reconnection. It focuses on the work of artists and entertainers, but also on iconic political, military, historical, and popular-culture figures—Americans, Cubans, and others—playing a major role in creating a Cuba of the cultural imagination. Its premise is that art and imaginative myth perpetually cross the boundaries erected by politics, history, and nationality. Whether on literature, music, painting, movies, television, journalism, and popular-culture history, the individual chapters are meant, all in their ways, to constitute the proof of that premise.

Accordingly, included here, in this book on Cuba and the imagination, will be found a varied cast of characters and/or focal figures, some real, some themselves imaginary, still others—it will be frequently discovered—somewhere in between. One will find essays on a hedonistic British literary cosmopolitan, a doomed, quixotic Venezuelan-Spanish military adventurer, a twentieth-century American jazz composer, a twenty-first-century Havana dissident celebrity blogger, and a Colombian literary master of postmodern fictional experimentalism; a legendary he-man American sportsman novelist and a charismatic Argentine hero-martyr in the cause of world Socialist revolution; a pioneering giant of twentieth-century photography and a well-born political scion from Santiago who, as a singer-bandleader and eventual US television star, became, before the advent of Fidel Castro, the most famous Cuban in the world; the exiled creator of a mid-nineteenth-century Habanera tragic *mulata* heroine whose story became the Cuban national novel and the author of a popular detective series whose fictionalized Russian detective winds up on Havana during the bleak post-Soviet *Período Especial*. Representative legendary figures of a long history make an appearance, in a number of cases, several: the explorer-discoverer Columbus; the brave, defiant Taino chieftain Hatuey; the various Capitanes General and colonial functionaries, Dionisio Vives, Miguel Tacón, Leopoldo O'Donnell, Martinez Campos, Valeriano Weyler; assorted *filibusteros*, brigands, and military exotics such as John Quitman, Narciso López, William Crittenden, Roberdeaux Wheat; the martyrs to the antislavery cause including Jose Antonio Aponte, Gabriel Concepción Valdés (Plácido), José Antonio Saco; the succession of great leaders in the independence struggle, Carlos Manuel Céspedes, José Martí, Antonio Maceo, Máximo Gómez, Calixto García; the American military glory hunters and political outriders of the *Intervención*, Fitzhugh Lee, Joe Wheeler, Theodore Roosevelt, Leonard Wood; the notorious twentieth-century strongmen, Gerardo Machado and Fulgencio Batista; the post–World War II mobsters and high rollers, Lucky Luciano, Meyer Lansky, Vito Genovese, Santo Trafficante; the young heroes of the 26 November Movement, Camilo Cienfuegos, Che Guevara, Raúl Castro; and, of course, him—Fidel Castro, the one they call el Comandante.

I should say from the outset that I am in here, too, as part of my own story of Cuba and the cultural imagination that comprises this book. It is likewise a story that has its own historical and political foregrounding. It begins with a black-and-white memory: on 22 October 1962, I sat in front of the big television in the basement of my college fraternity house and watched the president of the United States speak to the nation about the threat of Soviet strategic nuclear missiles, newly emplaced at operational sites on the island of Cuba. The message to be understood by average Americans such as myself was that the Russians and the Cubans had put the world on the brink of atomic war. Cuba was ninety miles off the coast of Florida; I was a week short of my eighteenth birthday. I seriously wondered if I would make it to eighteen, or, for that matter, if any of us would make it to next week. The unthinkable nuclear apocalypse we had feared since the end of World War II, foreshadowed in the mushroom clouds over Hiroshima and Nagasaki, could happen after all. The world had become profoundly different overnight, a strange, darkened, doomsday place. Half a century later, I would realize that only 11 September 2001 could produce such a corresponding psychological and historical effect of a world profoundly and irrevocably altered.

Now, in a continuation of the story, it is almost fifty years later. The year is 2010. Castro and his people are still there; and, after nearly an adult lifetime, I am going in. I say Castro and his people are there, but I feel like adding "just barely." Those still alive and in public view are mainly old, stooped, and sick, a walking inventory of the gerontology manual. Fidel Castro himself came close to dying in 2006, from a variety of old-age digestive ailments, eventually transferring power in 2008 to his brother, Raul, nearly as ancient, if slightly less decrepit. What will happen when the old revolutionaries finally go is the great question no one in Cuba or elsewhere is prepared to answer. As for me, the college boy myself grown much older, I have survived the missile crisis *and* a combat tour in Vietnam to become a senior research professor at a US university. On an academic visa—the Cubans call it a license—I am now riding into José Martí Airport, just outside Havana, for a ten-day study and writing visit. The plane, a Costa Rican "charter" out of Miami, reminds me of the ones I flew in and out of Panama for jungle warfare school and then in and out of Saigon for my year in Vietnam. So, actually, does the island landscape that I strain to see as the plane breaks through the cloud cover: palm trees; tropical forest; red, laterite clay soil; small streams and canals; scattered agricultural plots; individual houses and farm buildings; dirt roads. Off in the distance I can see the coast and the green ocean; as we pass over Havana, I can see the big bay with Morro Castle on the point. The tension, the foreboding, the strange sense of the unknown: it all reminds me—whether I want it to or not—of flying into Vietnam for the first time forty years ago. It can't be helped. I am a person of my times, carrying within my memory the names and memories of the great, contested, mid-twentieth-century Cold War places of Asia, Africa, Central Europe, Latin America. I recall the stern notation on my first US passport, issued back in 1961 when I was sixteen, about countries forbidden to US travelers. The countries were Albania, Communist China, North Korea, North Vietnam, and Cuba. Now, ninety miles off Miami, I am about to visit one of them. (A year later I will be in Beijing. A year after that, I will find myself back in Havana for the second time. The political travels of my late life years have truly opened to me a world of wonders.) It may be nearly five decades since I saw the Kennedy broadcast about the missiles, but I am still flying into Fidel Castro's Communist Cuba. After all these years, I am about to land on the forbidden island of revolution.

As far as particular memories and imaginings of Cuba over the years are concerned, back in the late 1950s and early 1960s, it so happened that I was the kind of young person who always watched the nightly network television news and read eagerly the great popular magazines of the era—*Time, Life, Look, Colliers,* the *Saturday Evening Post.* I actually won a high school prize once for scoring highest on a test in "current events." For a young person with such interests and preoccupations, it was nearly impossible in those days not to hear or read about Cuba and its besieged dictator, Fulgencio Batista, whose repressive, right-wing, military regime, if unsavory, was at least solidly pro–United States. This was the Cold War after all. I knew further that the regime was being threatened by a romantic, elusive, hit-and-run band of bearded young revolutionaries in combat fatigues holed up in a range of jungle mountains called the Sierra Maestra, somewhere out on the island in a province called at the time Oriente. Finally, like everyone else, I knew the name of the mysterious, charismatic revolutionary leader, Fidel Castro, whose face and image had made him an international media icon. In his signature olive drab combat uniform and fatigue cap, his long, somewhat scraggly beard, his chiseled, intense, handsome features, his dark, soulful, almost hypnotic gaze, he looked like the ultimate Latin American insurgent action hero. When he put on his somewhat nerdy, Buddy Holly–style black-framed glasses he could as easily seem the revolutionary intellectual. In early 1959, the revolution triumphed with the entry of the Castro forces into Havana. News developments followed quickly as the new regime took over the government. Most importantly, the revolution declared itself Communist. Stories followed about executions of Batistianos; expropriations and confiscations of property of the rich; emigration of cultural elites to Miami and other parts of South Florida. An abortive attempt by anti-Castroites to overthrow the revolution, comprising a combined force of right-wing Cuban patriots and various other military adventurers, was repelled at the Bay of Pigs. Not spoken of at all in relation to the debacle was wholehearted US Central Intelligence Agency (CIA) involvement and what turned out to be disastrously halfhearted US military assistance. At the time, the whole episode was considered a national embarrassment, with the new John F. Kennedy presidential administration somehow involved but not involved, assuming responsibility but not assuming responsibility. The Cuban Missile Crisis followed, etched into my consciousness forever as the black-and-white memory described above. For the next five decades, under strict US embargo, Cuba became the forbidden island of revolution.

In retrospect, I should say that what I knew of Cuba during the period—or, perhaps more properly, what I thought I knew—must have been fairly representative of American attitudes. For any American growing up in the 1950s, Batista was a bad guy, and we knew it. We just tended to throw him in with—or, perhaps more properly, get him mixed up with—other American supported tyrants of the Latin American and Caribbean regions, whose names, duly making the news from time to time for one repression or another, somehow ran together with or without their countries: Somoza, Trujillo, Duvalier, Stroessner, Perón. When Batista went down, the general attitude was good riddance. Castro, still a political unknown quantity, certainly looked good: dashing, youthful, charismatic, not unlike our own young presidential aspirant, the soon-to-be elected John F. Kennedy. Although suspected of "Socialist" leanings, as they were called in those days, he also seemed initially full of assurances about US interests, properties, trade, and diplomatic relations. "Cuba Libre" was the watchword: a Free Cuba. For the moment, that was certainly good enough for a lot of young Americans.

Not that any of us had more than the most superficial ideas of how the Batista dictatorship or the Castro revolution or any of the rest of that fit into the island's centuries-old historical or political geography. Had we done something as elementary as look for Oriente Province on a map (it now no longer exists, for some odd reason, broken up into subdistricts), we would have seen that it was nearly as far east (save for Guantanamo) as one could go to the other end of the island from the Florida Straits and Havana—precisely what *oriente* means in Spanish, had anybody taken the trouble to learn it: "east." We would have also known that for centuries it had been the nation's traditional hotbed of revolution, centered on its eastern capital, Santiago de Cuba, the second city of the island. At a stretch, the latter might have been recognized by North Americans as the home of the Bacardi Rum factory; for Cubans, the great historical product of the city and the surrounding regions, however, was insurrection.

As to the larger place called Cuba, by physical and imaginative geography, we would have seen that it is nothing if not an island. By geography, it is in fact a very big island, easily the biggest in the Caribbean, though just seventy miles off the North American land mass. In area, it is actually about the size of Great Britain. In length, around 750 miles, and in width, varying between 20 and 200 miles, with more than 2,000 miles of coastline, it has the distinct feel of a continent. (Indeed, the towering nineteenth-century German natural philosopher, Alexander von Humboldt, the author of *Kosmos*, felt impelled to address an entire free-standing volume to the place, entitled *Essai politique sur l'île de Cuba* (*A Political Essay on the Island of Cuba*). Politically, although an independent modern nation of relative newness—slightly more than a century—it is the home of a people who have thought of themselves in terms of nationality for nearly half a millennium. They are, then, an island nation in the sense that England or Japan are island nations, with a culture closely contained and intimately tied to island geography.

Regarding myths of origin, as with many legendary New World cultures, that of Cuba now can be seen as arising from a convergence of inherited traditional legends: native Taino, African Yoruba, ancient, medieval, and early modern European. Early Atlantic cartographers connected the island with the mythological Atlantis. Columbus believed that it was Cathay. In turn, it became the launching ground for the great continental conquistadores. From the eastern capital, Santiago de Cuba, Cortes in 1518 had set sail for Mexico and de Soto in 1538 for Florida.

The basic facts of early history on the ground followed the standard, lamentable Atlantic world pattern: extirpation of native peoples; introduction of African slavery; rule by colonial elites. After a brief seizure by the British, in 1762–63, the island remained the great, albeit increasingly restive prize domain of a dying Spanish empire. With the rise of the United States as a hemispheric power came annexation efforts by both northern abolitionist/proindependence forces and southern proslavery advocates. At the beginning of the twentieth century, such threats of potential North American domination were fulfilled, as the decades-long native anticolonial military struggle for Cuban independence neared its victorious conclusion, by US intervention and occupation. Through the long first half of the century and beyond, the nation endured a series of client dictators, figurehead presidents, and greedy politicians complicit in exploitation by US business interests. After World War II, the island additionally became a US criminal underworld fiefdom, a pleasure paradise of the Caribbean, with the reputation of supplying sin, sex, and sensation. Slightly more than a half century after the 1902 departure of the US proconsul, Gen. Leonard S. Wood, on 26 July 1953, in Santiago de Cuba, a small insurgent guerrilla band under Fidel Castro made its first major military attack on the main army installation of the Fulgencio Batista dictatorship in the city, the Moncada Barracks, in the process christening the revolution with the name it would carry to the end: the Movement of 26 July. A 1956 reinvasion of Oriente would follow, succeeded by nearly three hard years of fighting in the cause of revolutionary liberation. In the same place, on 1 January 1959, Castro announced victory from the balcony of City Hall before proceeding in triumph to the capital, Havana. The headquarters of celebration there would be the showplace American luxury hotel, the Havana Hilton—shortly to be rechristened the Habana Libre.

Americans puzzled over the train of revolutionary developments. What basically no one knew, save for a handful of academic specialists, was that the island had a five-hundred-year history of revolution. The traditional narrative began with the legend of Hatuey, a Taino cacique/chief fighting a guerrilla war against the Spanish in 1512 who was eventually captured and burned at the stake at Yara, itself to become again a nineteenth-century revolutionary station of the cross. According to a story familiar to most Cubans (from the narrative of a sympathetic Spaniard, Bartolomé de las Casas), the legendary last words of Hatuey were uttered to a priest accompanying the conquistadores, who asked him to accept Catholic rites so as to go to heaven. Hatuey asked if Spaniards went to heaven, to which the priest, of course, replied in the affirmative. According to Las Casas, Hatuey then said without further thought that he did not want to go there but to hell so as not to be where they were and where he would not see such cruel people.

By the mid-sixteenth century, with a final native uprising of the cacique Guamá and his wife Habanaguex, the population of an estimated three million Tainos had been reduced to two thousand. Meanwhile, with new importation of enslaved Africans, a 1533 uprising in the mines at Jobabo began a centuries-long cycle of slave revolts. Accelerated by events associated with the successful slave independence struggle led in nearby Haiti by Toussaint L'Ouverture at the end of the eighteenth century came the Aponte uprising of 1812 and the Escalera conspiracy of 1844, known to history as the Year of the Lash. By 1868, a wealthy white plantation owner, Manuel de Céspedes, issued the "*Grito de Yara*,"—the "shout" or "cry" of Yara—promising freedom to his slaves and calling them to join him in the First War of Cuban Independence. Under the inspirational leadership of the legendary patriot exile Jose Marti and military heroes such as Antonio Maceo, Máximo Gómez, and Calixto García, this was followed by the agonizing Ten Years War of 1868–78 and then two decades later by the successful Third War of Cuban Independence, 1895–98—called by the United States the Spanish-American War and by the Cubans the Intervención. Under the military governorship of Gen. Leonard Wood, a new Cuban government was granted limited independence in 1902. Meanwhile, in the US Congress, a measure called the Platt Amendment imposed heavy American control upon the new island nation, giving the United States unlimited power to intervene in Cuban affairs as deemed necessary. The pre–World War II decades of US politico-economic expansionism came to be called the Dance of the Millions; a postwar investment boom, fueled by new US Mob dollars and dictator greed, turned the island into a floating tourist paradise with all the amenities—hotels, bars, nightclubs, casinos—including a compliant population willing to serve and entertain.

Fidel Castro changed all of that more or less overnight. The land of rum and rumba remade itself into the new land of revolution. Did we think at the time Castro was a Communist? I honestly don't remember. Did we imagine that within ten years the corrupt, thuggish Batista US client regime, which everyone knew was brutal and bloodthirsty even by 1950s Latin American standards, would be replaced by a western hemisphere

Soviet Russian satellite nation, as much an iron curtain country as Poland, Czechoslovakia, or Hungary? I'm sure we didn't have any concrete idea. Maybe we just had too much else on our minds: the Cold War; Korea and the Chinese; Central Europe and the Russians; the Middle East and the Arabs and Israelis; Southeast Asia and the North and South Vietnamese; the ICBM threat; the space race. In the last years of the Eisenhower era, one now has to admit, the victory of the Cuban Revolution and its evolving geopolitical character became second-line news. Vietnam was heating up, the civil rights struggle was at full intensity, and Kennedy was promising Americans a vision of the New Frontier. Somewhere in the Eisenhower-Kennedy handoff, the plans for a Cuban-American anti-Castro invasion and attempted overthrow of the new government turned into a right-wing National Guard weekend. In retrospect, the ignominious Bay of Pigs Invasion of 17–19 April 1961—coming a mere six months before the missile crisis—just didn't register or seemed at a profound disconnect from other, more pressing affairs. News coverage was suppressed about participants including exile Cubans and right-wing American soldiers of fortune. In turn, the Cuban Missile Crisis had its terrifying four weeks in October 1962 and likewise receded into a stunning collocation of what seemed larger events.

How could one know at the time that the ensuing late twentieth-century US relationship with Cuba and Cubans would have its signature in nearly everything that followed? The assassination of John F. Kennedy by Lee Harvey Oswald in Dallas, and in turn the assassination of Lee Harvey Oswald by Jack Ruby, was followed by revelations about Oswald in Russia, Oswald in Cuba, Oswald in New Orleans passing out literature about Cuba. This in turn seemed to play into a new set of almost paranoiac congruencies.

Lyndon Johnson, in his active support of the right-wing, pro-American client government in South Vietnam, would be brought down by a new anti-Communist mission in Asia against a new revolutionary opponent, a force of jungle guerrillas headed by a national hero of revolution, Ho Chi Minh. The latter's mainstream Communist credentials remained a matter of some discussion. Electing to enforce its anti-Communist strategies of aggressive geopolitical containment a hemisphere away from the new Soviet-style regime ninety miles across the Florida straits, the United States, allied to the puppet troops of a compliant military dictatorship, fought a war of virtually unlimited military power against an Asian revolutionary Socialist army of freedom fighters.

Richard Nixon ended the tragic misadventure in Vietnam, only to be brought down by Watergate. Integral to the presidential crisis once again, as with Kennedy, the Bay of Pigs, and the Missile Crisis, were crucial roles played by Cuba and Cubans. Nixon, the beneficiary of Miami real estate investments, hobnobbed at the Key Biscayne Yacht Club with the right-wing exile millionaire businessman Bebe Rebozo. Meanwhile secret operatives recruited by the CIA—among them Cuban Bay of Pigs retreads—were caught burglarizing the headquarters of the Democratic National Committee. Fidel Castro must have looked upon it all with a sense of profound justice. Like Kennedy, who had tried to overthrow him and, failing that, assassinate him, in the ensuing Watergate cover-up, Nixon, arguably the most powerful anti-Communist figure of the American twentieth century, was now forced to vacate the office of US president.

Later presidents Gerald Ford, Jimmy Carter, Ronald Reagan, George H. W. Bush, Bill Clinton, George W. Bush, and Barack Obama, along with Dwight Eisenhower, John F. Kennedy, Lyndon Johnson, and Richard Nixon before them, have all shared one thing as a common precondition of their domestic and foreign policies. Cuba, the forbidden island of revolution, has always been there, ninety miles away. For all of them, *he* has always been there as well: Fidel Castro, el Comandante. It is the autumn of the Comandante, to be sure, as Fidel Castro, the last great world figure of the mid-twentieth century, increasingly alone with his thoughts, endures the long, early twenty-first-century decades of his dying. In death, as in life, he will stand among the Cold War giants: Eisenhower, Kennedy, Khrushchev, Mao Zedong, Ho Chi Minh.

My own account of Cuba and the imagination concludes with a more recent memory, this one in living color. In the year 2010, the nearly eighteen-year-old college freshman of the Kennedy Cuban missile broadcast, having spent a long career as a university professor of language and literature, found himself at last on the way to see that great place of history for the first time. Permitted to visit on an academic/creative arts agreement—a cooperative venture by my university and the University of Havana involving the interchange of students, faculty, administrators, creative writers, musicians, historians, biologists, anthropologists, language teachers—even the odd physicist, helping to design a downtown kids' planetarium—I had been sent to compose the narrative text of an art volume by two photographers. A collaborative enterprise, focused on the "Ciudad Viva" (Living City) project for the restoration of the Old City of Havana, *Habana Vieja*, the book project was itself to be patterned on a reflexive US-Cuban/Cuban-US design, an enactment of the very idea of cultural and artistic exchange. Cuba through American eyes was to be rendered by an established art photographer roughly my age; Cuba through Cuban eyes was to be the province of a younger Cuban art photographer with whom my American colleague had established a professional relationship. Both had been profoundly influenced, it turned out, by the American photographer Walker Evans—who had famously photographed Alabama, the home state of our university, during the Depression, but who had carried out a comparable project in Cuba during the same years.

In final photographic design and production, the result was a stunning art volume, centering on twenty-first century preservationist views of Old Havana as a UNESCO World Heritage Site. In the accompanying narrative, along with essays by eminent Cuban figures including the city historian, Dr. Eusebio Leal, and Magda Resik of Cuban Public Radio, I chose to discuss the art of photography from the standpoint of dual cultural perspective, of artistic collaboration, of cultural exchange, of what might be called worlds and images in translation. The central premise of the essay narrative was the one described at the outset: that art and the creative cultural imagination, at certain crucial moments, transcend historical, political, and even geographic boundaries. In the two years ensuing, the experience of preparing that essay in turn would lead to a separate textual project and a further experiment in that proposition. I envisioned it as a book-length text of representative essays approaching the premise from a wide variety of cross-cultural perspectives, angles, parallaxes, and conflations. From various positionings of history, literature, politics, painting, music, movies, television, and the other popular arts, I would organize a text with discrete clusters of cultural essays on the colonial nineteenth century, the prerevolutionary twentieth century, the mid-twentieth-century period of radical political transition, and the postrevolutionary decades extending from the late twentieth century to the present. Accordingly, the nineteenth-century essays now include texts on *Cecilia Valdés*, the national novel of Cuba; on the legendarily brave but foolhardy midcentury filibustero, Narciso López; and on the nineteenth-century *Mambise* freedom fighters in their cultural representations. Essays on early twentieth-century figures in their relation to Cuban culture and events include studies of the American photographer Walker Evans, the composer George Gershwin, and the Cuban-born US movie and television star Desi Arnaz. Essays on the transitional era eventuating in the Castro revolution include "Good Neighbor Batista"—on the gift of a priceless Cuban art collection by Dictator Fulgencio Batista to Daytona Beach, Florida, his home in exile during the 1940s and 1950s; "The Two Ernestos"—on the persistence of images in Cuba of Ernest Hemingway and Che Guevara as twinned icons of maleness; "Steverino in Gangsterland"—on a bizarre Havana broadcast of the Steven Allen Sunday Night variety show just months before the victory of the revolution; and "Why Nobody in Havana Speaks of Graham Greene"—concerning *Our Man in Havana*, a spy novel published just before the revolution and filmed just afterward. Late twentieth- and early twenty-first-century materials include "Inspector Renko on the Malecón," in which American author Martin Cruz Smith's detective novel provides a rare insight into the period of extreme hardship just after Russian withdrawal called el Período Especial; "The Example of Yoani Sanchez," on the current Havana dissident blogger whose work in the age of the Internet has brought her major international attention; and "The Autumn of the Comandante," an extended epilogue, with the title derived from Gabriel García Márquez's novel of a decaying dictatorship now in a new century serving as at once prophecy and context for a vision of the final years of the current regime.

    The book so envisioned is the one the reader now holds. It is a book on Cuba and the imagination by a writer, once an anxious American college boy watching news on TV of the Soviet Missile Crisis, who fifty years later finally got to go there, and who, like so many others before him, found his critical and creative spirit captured by the island—not to mention a shared history, US and Cuban, Cuban and US, in which the cultures of the two nations have never been anything less than integral to each other. Many of us on both sides of the Florida straits remain entranced by each other's histories; most of us remain equally perplexed by the bizarre intransigence of each other's politics. This is to say that we remain, in many ways, cultures of mutual misinformation. Americans do not want to kill the Comandante; annex the island; wreck the economy; destroy the armed forces. Cubans do not live in some fenced-off latter-day East Germany or Albania. The island today is a welcoming and vibrant destination for visitors from hosts of other nations and cultures, European, Latin American, and North American—in the latter case, mainly Canadians, but also, increasingly, numbers of US citizens. Cuba is not a dour post-Marxist wreck; it is certainly nothing like a conventionally imagined third-world nation. Although the government allows for limited independent economic enterprise and closely monitors political speech and personal expression, the nation can also boast of universal education, widespread common literacy, and comprehensive free medical treatment at an acceptable standard of care. People remain as proud to be Cuban as US citizens are proud to be American. In that connection, what follows here is a set of attempts to renew from both sides our knowledge of an older Atlantic world and the history of a complex relationship, even as we attempt in a century just begun to envision a new one of which we might be the mutual inhabitants and beneficiaries.

1

ROMANCING *CECILIA VALDÉS*

Last spring, on the first day of a return visit to Cuba, I walked the streets of my Havana of happy memory, spending a large part of the time in quest of the subject of a study I had begun two years earlier. Her name was Cecilia Valdés. She was the fictional heroine, I had discovered at the time, of a famous book that bore her name: a book indeed regarded by many Hispanic and Latin American readers as the national novel of Cuba. Further, her presence still seemed to be felt and manifested at many of the Havana locations described in the book. Accordingly, down by the docks, I spent a quiet moment at la Iglesia de Paula, near where she was born. Later, I stood on the summit of la Loma del Ángel, on the steps of the cathedral where her story allegedly ends, gazing out on her Havana. The year was 2012. It was the two hundredth anniversary of her birth, at least in the novel. It was also that of her creator, the exile Cuban novelist Cirilo Villaverde. By now I knew enough of both her and Villaverde, I thought, to understand that for Cuba she truly was in many ways still there, and so was her story.

Though many North American and Anglo-European readers have never heard of the text, critics versed in the history of Hispanic literature take it as commonplace to regard Cirilo Villaverde's 1882 fictional epic *Cecilia Valdés; o, la Loma del Ángel* (*Cecilia Valdés; or, the Angel Hill*) as the greatest Cuban novel of the nineteenth century and perhaps a contender for the nineteenth-century Latin American title as a whole. Equally well known to musicologists and other students of twentieth-century Cuban culture is the 1932 *zarzuela*—or, popular lyric-dramatic opera—of the same name, with a score by Gonzalo Roig and the libretto by Agustin Rodriguez and José Sánchez Avila and now regarded, along with comparable productions by Ernesto Lecuona and Eliseo Grenet, as an enduring classic of the movement in music and the arts called at the time Afrocubanismo. Produced at the centenary, *Cecilia*, an opulent 1982 epic film re-creation of the novel by the renowned director Humberto Solas, is now likewise cited frequently as one of the most ambitious historical examples of the post-revolutionary national Cuban cinema. These have been more recently followed by a provocative play in 1998, *Parece Blanca* (*She Looks White*) by the exile-writer Abelardo Estorino, and produced by the New York theater group, Reportorio Español, and a 2002 ballet, written for the Ballet Hispanico NYC by the dancer Pedro Ruiz, with music from famous Cuban zarzuela composers including Gonzalvo Roig and Ernesto Lecuona, as well as Leo Brouwer and Jose Maria Vietier. Among academic and scholarly readerships, mainly in Spanish, the work in its various forms has produced a large and sophisticated critical literature. And, as will be seen, two late twentieth-century expatriate Cuban writers—the first, the well-known gay novelist Reinaldo Arenas, and the second, the equally celebrated science fiction author Daina Chaivano—have made the Villaverde text the basis of new and significant literary experiments for our own time.

Such is the cultural history of what itself began as a young author's relatively modest 1839 attempt at periodical-length popular historical fiction, a melodramatic tale of forbidden love dated 1812–32, though arising out of events of the previous century and thus overtly inscribing conflicts of gender, race, class, and revolutionary nationality rooted in a shadowed colonial past. To this may be further added an extended history of composition and publication, with the 1839 story followed by a considerably longer 1842 novella, and then a full four decades later—nearly all of which the author had spent as a revolutionary expatriate in the United States—by a compendiously rewritten and enlarged 1882 New York edition nearly twice the length of its predecessor. As to overall visions of history, many assessments of the Villaverde text focus on the novel's mythic depiction of its titular character as the archetype of the tragic *mulata* and her ill-omened romance with a young, white, upper-class seducer (secretly, in fact, her half brother), eventuating in the pregnancy, illegitimate motherhood, and imprisonment of the heroine, and climaxing with the murder of the white lover by a vengeful *mulato* rival. Others emphasize the novel's depictions of the cruelty and violence of Afro-Cuban slavery, its tortures, punishments, and family separations, the arbitrary rules of race, labor, law, and caste. In many respects, all such observations, though depending on which version of the novel is being addressed, are more or less true. At the same time, the main romantic and political themes so described remain subordinated to a larger purpose, which might be best described as an attempt on the author-narrator's part to write a great, panoramic, family romance of the imagined Cuban nation—in its first half capturing life in Havana from the Bohemian artists' balls with their mixing of classes and races to the great glittering mansions, trading houses, and government centers of the colonial economic and political elites; and in the second extending the action into the surrounding exotic landscapes of mountain and tropical forest for dramatic scenes of life in the slavery hell of the vast sugar and coffee plantations of the interior. Meanwhile, a corresponding measure of the novel's reputation continues to lie not only in the enduring cultural centrality of the literary text to the Cuban and Latin American traditions of major fictional narrative but also in the degree to which the text has continued to write itself into new forms of art. To undertake the romancing of Cecilia Valdés through a study of Villaverde's composition of the text and its eventual life beyond is thus to launch into a history of authorship that is also an account, in the fullest sense, of the authorship of History, with the struggle of the novel's dislocated and dispossessed characters in particular against myriad categories of oppression—sexual, racial, social, economic, and political—serving as figures of evolving revolutionary consciousness and class struggle. In the passage from popular fictional narrative into national myth, *Cecilia Valdés* remains, according to one commentator—"as *Quijote* is for the Spanish, *Hamlet* for the English, or *Faust* for the German literatures." Accordingly, to trace out the layerings and unfoldings of the work's complex textual evolution is to find a true archaeology of the modern Cuban imagination.

In the beginning was a somewhat negligible short story, albeit already carrying the name of its legendary central character—published as an 1839 popular magazine melodrama in two installments of the sort fashionable at the time. Comprising materials from early chapters of the eventual novel, it purports to be the story of a beautiful young mulata the narrator has known during the early decades of the century who, having roamed the streets as a charming waif, is eventually seduced by a dissolute young white man, Leonardo Gamboa, the son of a rich merchant. At the end, the heroine simply vanishes, fulfilling presumably both her moral and social destiny. Extensive rewriting later in the same year, on the other hand, showed that the character and her story had taken a kind of strange imaginative possession of the author. The titular mulata had now become the heroine of a more than two-hundred-page novel of society; a subtitle—*la Loma del Ángel*—now rooted the text in a dense, vibrant, urban cultural geography and history. Accordingly, beyond the conventional role assigned the tragic mixed-race woman in the popular literature of the time—Anglo-European, North American, Latin American—the heroine had been endowed with a new mythic function. She had begun her movement toward possession of the Cuban imaginary. In the words of Rodrigo Lazo, "the mulata Cecilia Valdés, described as a 'little bronze virgin' who bears 'perhaps the most beautiful woman's face that existed at that time in Havana,' is a symbol of Cuban womanhood and, more generally, Cuban racial and cultural hybridity"—though here, in keeping with her earlier shadowy fate, she is still quickly revealed to be captive in an unbending, unforgiving system of race and caste—*peninsulare/gallego, criollo, mestizo, mulato, negro, esclavo*—and every gradation in between. To be specific, in the new novel version, Cecilia is given a complete back-story of early nineteenth-century colonial race, gender, and class relations as the exquisitely beautiful daughter of the mixed-race mistress of a ruthlessly ambitious Spanish immigrant merchant and landowner, with her mother, made insane by her suffering and abandonment, consigned secretly to a madhouse of the Hospital de Paula. As an infant, the child has been placed at the Convent of the Innocent, and assigned the last name Valdés—as with the famous Cuban mulato romantic poet of the era, Plácido, it is carefully noted, the common patronymic of the illegitimate. Later, the secret of her birth carefully guarded, she is remitted to the guardianship of her grandmother. She is, in fact, as we eventually learn, the illegitimate daughter of a rich, upper-class, but largely self-made immigrant gallego named Don Candido Gamboa, with his social position further cemented by his marriage to Doña Rosa, a *criolla* heiress of elite social standing. Meanwhile, the heroine grows from a mischievous street urchin into voluptuous early womanhood, with information about her parentage, as well as that about her continuing domestic upkeep, carefully maintained by the patriarch of the house of Gamboa. This all changes, through a variety of somehow fated coincidences, with the opening of her ill-fortuned and ultimately deadly romance with the handsome and gallant, but equally spoiled and frivolous, Leonardo Gamboa, son of her mother's seducer—not to mention, of course, secretly her half brother. Here, to put it mildly, in what turns out to be the remainder of the 1842 version, the plot has decidedly thickened. Meanwhile Leonardo acquires a lower-class rival, the mulato tailor and musician Pimienta, brother of Cecilia's best friend Nemesia. Through such unfoldings of a complicated tale of romance, we undertake a long and vivid journey with the main characters through the streets, businesses, households, customs, festivals, entertainments, glittering public spectacles, and shadowed private intrigues of colonial Havana. Then, rather abruptly, this version ends, as it has begun, with a mixed-race ball attended by various classes, bringing together the main characters and hinting at new plot strands in presentiment of dark fates and outcomes.

What of the well-known melodramatic denouement—Cecilia's impregnation by Leonardo, with the latter meanwhile securing his own proper, upper-class, dynastic union with the rich criolla heiress Isabel Ilincheta? The heroine's legal detainment by her father to keep her out of her half brother's clutches? The murder of the white lover on his wedding day on the cathedral steps of la Loma del Ángel by the vengeful Pimienta? The conviction and imprisonment of Cecilia, now the mother of an infant daughter, as an accessory? All this, it turns out, would have to wait for forty years and hundreds of new pages—essentially a second volume—composed by the author after decades of expatriation as part of an 1882 New York revised edition, probably begun in 1879 but not published in Cuba until 1903.

Here, as can be quickly seen by any reader, was not just a second volume but basically a second novel—and, the recognizable outgrowth of Villaverde's exile years as a revolutionary nationalist: most notably as an active supporter of various filibustero and annexationist schemes, with close involvement in those of Narciso López; and also as a long-term political and journalistic associate of José Martí. But now even these passions were trumped, it became clear, by those of the abolitionist crusader. When Villaverde came to write again, in what amounts to the second half of his tale about the little bronze virgin, *Cecilia Valdés* became one of the world's great antislavery novels. Elements of the antislavery plot, to be sure, can be found woven into the original story. At the beginning, there are the shadowy actions of Gamboa, after effecting the placement of his illegitimate daughter in a foundling establishment and the child's mother in a madhouse, insane and helpless when the infant has been torn from her, to insure the basics of infant nutritional survival: through his connivance with a physician friend, Monte de Oca, she is entrusted to a Gamboa family slave wet nurse, Maria de Regla. The latter, with Doña Rosa Gamboa weak after childbirth, is simultaneously required to suckle the infant Gamboa daughter, Adela—throughout the novel in her own relationship with her brother Leonardo, a kind of strange, incestuous, cross-racial double for Cecilia. Meanwhile, the slave-mother Maria has given birth to an infant daughter of her own. Eventually discovered in an attempt to keep her own weakening child alive while nourishing her Gamboa charge, she is given summary banishment to the nightmare world of the family slave plantation. At the same time, in the same domestic slavery sphere we see the spoiled, hot-blooded Leonardo administer regular beatings to Aponte, the family coachman. We learn of the mad street wanderer Dolores Santa Cruz, a slave woman industriously rising to the status of merchant and slave owner only to be stripped of her properties and her sanity by the colonial courts. More generally, we come to see slavery itself as central to the Gamboa fortunes, the material apparatus supporting the corrupt splendor. Gamboa, as it turns out, is a major investor in the African slave trade, with a ship in the harbor threatened with confiscation under terms of the English blockade and embargo. Utterly heedless of its human stowage, he undertakes cynical strategems to circumvent the law down to the proverbial letter. He smuggles aboard bundles of field uniforms to establish a pretense that the African slaves have in fact originated from a New World market, hence circumventing the technicality of the embargo treaty—for which he nonetheless excoriates his royal government for signing. "Bundles," he calls the ruse, discussing it with his hard-nosed wife. (The Spanish term, "bultos," with its criminal evasiveness, translates closely.) Slavery, we find, is at the very foundations of the House of Gamboa.

With the further, full-blown expansion of the 1882 text into a panoramic drama of evil encompassing the slave regions outside Havana, during long stretches the titular heroine, for all her eventual glamour and pathos, becomes a glorified version of what Henry James would have called a *ficelle*—her life and sad adventures the slender thread upon which much of the heavy political weight of the novel is suspended. Outside the city, the novel fills with depictions of master-class and slave-class life on the countryside plantations, very like those narratives by European, English, and US northern-state travelers of comparable antislavery sentiments, frequently moving for major stretches of their narratives into the countryside outside Havana for a visit to some slavery hell in opulent plantations immediately east or west. Here the particular plot stratagem providing transportation, while also linking the love theme of the first half of the text with that of the second, is the new romance of Leonardo with the rich, aristocratic Isabel Ilincheta, daughter of a wealthy businessman and landowner with a plantation neighboring that of the Gamboa holdings in Pinar del Rio. At the dynastic level of colonial elites, the match, of course, involves a consolidation of lands and major slave enterprises, not to mention, for the elder Gamboa, both general upward class movement for the family and particular distraction for the son and heir from the incestuous love of his illegitimate sibling. Beginning at La Luz, the refined coffee plantation of Don Tomas Ilincheta, and moving for Christmas festivities to the Gamboa sugar property, La Tinaja, where the Ilincheta sisters, Isabel and Rosa, are to be guests of Leonardo and his friend Diego Meneses, the novel accordingly moves into its own extended season in hell, with scenes of the elegance, grace, and leisure of the plantation elites repeatedly punctuated with harrowing vignettes of slave oppression, torture, cruelty, and brutality.

From the outset, we feel the dark energy of slave resistance—as noted by interpreters, perhaps foreboded by Villaverde's insistence at the beginning of the novel itself on 1812, in its reference to the widespread Aponte slave insurrection, as the year of the heroine's birth—brooding underneath the scenes of country retreat. So, in a signature moment at the very entrance to La Luz, Leonardo inflicts a beating on a tardy gatekeeper, justifying his severity to his guests with recitations about the old retainer's history as a sly runaway. Accordingly, the first evening's festivities are filled with talk about a rash of new Gamboa escapees, seven Africans including a woman. Most of the latter are quickly recaptured. One, consigned to torture in the stocks, has been severely bitten all over his body by dogs. The others, including the woman, are subjected to graphic floggings. Soon news comes that the slave in the stocks, Pedro, has managed to take his own life. On a horseback outing, the young people discover his companion in escape, Pablo, who has hanged himself and is being devoured by vultures. Back at the manor, the faithful nurse Maria de Regla compounds the narrative of suffering by reciting to her young former charges the story of her mistreatments by the mistress and of her subsequent sexual abuse amid a welter of lawless plantation male lusts. The Gamboa daughters plead mercy on her behalf. Doña Rosa allows her return to the city household but remains cruelly implacable in her racist convictions of the woman's perfidy.

In the novel's brief final section, the action moves back to Havana. There are complicated, hasty attempts to tie up various strands of plot. One, opened up at the conclusion of the first volume, has involved the menacing social behavior, after Maria de Regla's banishment, by the cook Dionisio, Maria's vengeful husband, who has been allegedly, or so the family is told early in the new volume during their country holiday, killed in a desperate robbery and escape attempt. In a startling interpolation, we are told that Dionisio's supposedly fatal knife wound has been at the hands of Pimienta. But we also discover that his death is a ruse and that he remains at large under an assumed identity. Meanwhile, during Leonardo's absence, Cecilia keeps company mainly with Nemesia and Pimienta. Her grandmother shows signs of rapid decline. Seeking medical help, the heroine attempts to contact the old convent physician Don Tomás Montes de Oca. She is recognized by the physician's wife, who recounts the details of her infant nurture by the black wet nurse Maria de Regla. The doctor consents to treat the grandmother, visiting her repeatedly until no hope is left. Pimienta and Nemesia, who have faithfully helped keep watch, assist the stricken Cecilia in the final rites and religious burial of her lifelong protector. Events then rush toward their conclusion. The returned Maria de Regla seeks to reunite with her husband Dionisio after their twelve-year separation. The latter is captured and jailed after his high-profile killing of a notorious black police captain, in the employ of the Spanish, commissioned by Doña Rosa to apprehend Dionisio. Details of their separation emerge in the story so as to inform the reunited young lovers, Leonardo from Dionisio, and Cecilia from Maria de Regla, about Cecilia's paternity and the ceaseless efforts by Gamboa to conceal it from his wife and son. Gamboa, knowing that his stratagems are at an end, persuades a magistrate to have Cecilia imprisoned in the Women's House of Correction. Leonardo, at length achieving her release, sets the two of them up, with his mother's connivance, in a happy domestic arrangement on the Calle de Damas. Leonardo finishes his legal studies. Cecilia gives birth to a baby girl. Meanwhile, however, plans are finalized for the formal union of the houses of Gamboa and Ilincheta. Cecilia, desperate and hopeless, summons Pimienta to exact murderous justice. She means for him to kill Isabel. On the day of the wedding, the couple emerges from the cathedral on the hill of the angel. Pimienta rushes forth and stabs Leonardo fatally through the heart, escaping unidentified into the crowd. Cecilia is sentenced as an accomplice to one year's confinement in the Convent de Paula, where she is reunited with her mother. Isabel Ilincheta renounces her wealth and takes vows as a Carmelite nun. Dionisio awaits trial for five years. Sentenced to ten years hard labor, he is sent by "the renowned Don Manuel Tacón" to the penal colony of Havana, where he is set to work paving streets.

To the last sentence, then, as throughout the novel, close dramatic developments involving the central figures mix in *Cecilia Valdés* with extended passages of exposition on issues of law and colonial politics, frequently involving lengthy discussions of social mores, racial attitudes, economic and class relationship; complex unfoldings in plot, character, setting, and theme likewise allow for huge chunks of narration and dialogue devoted to dress, dialect, architecture, household decoration, food and drink, literature and art. A teeming cast of fictional characters mixes apace with discussion of countless "real" historical figures, including the romantic slave rebel Plácido, the ill-fated, thrice-failed annexationist adventurer Narciso López, the patriot Felix Varela, and the captain general Dionisio Vives. As with the titular fictional figure and the complex constellation of characters of myriad race, gender, and socioeconomic status with which she is surrounded, so the latter play their appointed roles in history. In its very entitling, *Cecilia Valdés; o, la Loma del Ángel*, becomes a textual metonymy for a remembered and imagined world. And that world, even down to the identicality of initials and birthdate, is both the world of Cecilia Valdés and the world of Cirilo Villaverde. So, from his rewritings of the earliest chapters of nearly forty years earlier to his frantic summing up of his doubled romance/slavery plot, the yearning expatriate himself, writing the end of his mythic narrative and nearing the end of his own drama of literary and political nationality, is neatly characterized by Rodrigo Lazo. Villaverde, he says, conditioned by his long absence from his beloved homeland and decades of work in a revolutionary exile publishing culture, in the very language of Cuban place and emphasis on social and historical minutiae of description, "reterritorializes his memory and the text itself." As Lazo neatly puts it, "If I can't have Cuba in and of itself, he seems to say, I will have it as a book."

Thematically, as has been shown by Lazo, given the book's long and complicated history of composition, there were certainly consequences to Villaverde's equally long and complicated expatriate experience in what seem to be the novel's frequently inconsistent and/or shifting politics. Partly one may attribute this to seemingly overlong, after-the-fact political excurses on the laws of society at a given time and place, constructed from anecdotal memory, and blurring the status of relation between the narrator and his tale. But surely such perceived inconsistencies must equally have been a result of Villaverde's experiences and journalistic engagement with political topics over a long period of decades giving him occasion to change his own opinions. As a pre–Civil War annexationist, for example, he seems to have been largely in league with US southern proslavers, as demonstrated by his support for the quixotic filibustering of the anti-Spanish but proslavery Narciso López. (Narciso was also the baptismal name of Villaverde's son.) As a post–Civil War reform journalist, on the other hand, he was decidedly a Martí-style revolutionary patriot. And, as shown in the long final section of the novel, by 1882 he was nothing if not a fervent abolitionist. Yet particularly in the juxtaposition of plantation scenes of the second half with the glittering urban world of manners so lovingly rendered in the first, there is frequently a jar between the later narrator's displays of antislavery passion and a long series of earlier, rather technical, disquisitions on the intricacies of traditional codes of race and class. Here, frequently, the conflicted narrator can simultaneously adore Cecilia yet attribute much of her downfall to personal faults associated with her mulata heritage. Indeed, on any number of occasions he criticizes her, along with other black and racially mixed characters, for aspirations they should not really expect to be met in a white world. While the narrator of the Havana sections deplores racism, he still accepts in some degree the propriety and necessity of strict organizations of racial hierarchy and social separation.

Though it does not acquit the text of such ideological discontinuities, part of the problem, one may now perhaps see in retrospect, was Villaverde's own dexterity as a literary novelist—working, as his novel expanded over the years, across a wide variety of popular forms and expertly assimilating at crucial points what he recognized as their various political potentialities into his larger fictive designs. In section one, from the sentimental novel so beloved of nineteenth-century readers he fashioned a complex seduction plot and then wedded it to the dark psychosexual mysteries of popular gothic sensationalism. He then set the family romance so devised against the backdrop of that greatest of all achievements of nineteenth-century social realism, the novel of the city—in the process bringing the great world of Havana itself into the literary orbit of Dickens's London, Dostoevsky's St. Petersburg, Hugo's Paris. One writer has justly characterized the novel in this respect as a Cuban *Les Miserables* or *Oliver Twist*; as much to the point might be *Vanity Fair*. Or, in the fall of the House of Gamboa, the English novel of the period it perhaps most resembles—with the figure of August Melmotte, the corrupt, shadowy financier, trying to buy nobility and influence—is Trollope's *The Way We Live Now*.

As to the novelistic figure of the tragic mulata embodied in the titular heroine, Villaverde could draw on a wide variety of literary models, North American, Anglo-European, and Latin American. Given his long exile in the United States, both pre– and post–Civil War, particularly in the second section he would seem to have drawn most heavily on popular American abolitionist narrative. Most notable among texts in the genre would have been two: William Wells Brown's *Clotel; or, The President's Daughter*—a roman à clef of the Thomas Jefferson relationship with his mixed-race slave mistress, Sally Hemings; and Harriet Jacobs's *Incidents in the Life of a Slave Girl*—a narrative of forced concubinage and gothic sequestration.

Here, in the figure of the heroine, particularly as the first half of the text expands into the second, set upon the horrors of the plantation landscape, we are brought to the closest analogue. And that is the panoramic vision of the familial economics of slavery recurrently imaged in the role of the mixed-race woman in Harriet Beecher Stowe's *Uncle Tom's Cabin*. In the familiar doubled plot, Stowe sends the beautiful Eliza, with her mulato/mulata family, northward on the underground railway to Canada—eventually to be reunited with her own lost slave courtesan mother discovered, at the novel's very end, far to the south; meanwhile, wrenching her titular Black Christ from his wife and family, she sends Tom down the river, with a brief stop in the glittering purgatory of New Orleans, to his hellish death on the Red River plantation of Simon Legree. Here too, the city, with its complex urban system of race and slave relationship, is depicted in much of the richness and gaiety of Havana, a queer mix of urbanity and brutality. The plantation system, meanwhile, extends from the relative mildness of the border-state Shelby regime with which Stowe's novel begins—imaged in that of the Ilincheta coffee estate—to the hideous tortures and cruelty of the Deep South Legree cotton enterprise—a parallel to the Gamboa sugar plantation. For Stowe, no matter where it exists, in her gothic plot of miscegenation, doubling, and incest, slavery is a sin against God. For her slave characters, the wages of sin are rather ambiguously resolved: there is either recolonization to Africa or a martyr's death. Villaverde, the exile patriot, facing an even more intensely involuted plot, within the depiction of a society with its even more complex categories of race, gender, and labor, may again be excused a more troubled view of the institution, even as nearly two decades after American emancipation he burned to have slavery abolished as the great blot upon his homeland. The legalistic ending of the novel, accordingly, may be seen as quite in keeping both with Villaverde's antislavery politics and with the literary politics of his various assimilations of genre.

Thus, like its author, the readers and interpreters of *Cecilia Valdés* have continued to struggle with the novel in their own long and equally complex tradition of cultural response and revision. In the artistic realm, especially, the passage from book to zarzuela to movie and beyond continues to fuel new imaginative inscriptions and reinscriptions of national identity by succeeding Cuban generations even to the present—with both the text and its heroine remaining themselves endlessly creative and protean. The Lecuona/Roig zarzuela elects to truncate the text back into the first and second legendary, but ill-starred, love sections, much in the vein of European operatic tradition, with the concluding recognition scene, in a convent, reuniting mother and daughter. To be sure, in casting the heroine as *mestiza*, rather than mulata, it now seems notably retrograde in its revised racialization; but throughout, one also senses the matter of race as culturally reinscribed in the proud original celebration of the great native musical tradition of Afrocubanismo. As Susan Thomas has written, the result is a character who, much like her mulata original, "fetishizes herself first as a voice," then as a rattle and a bell, and "then identifies herself as a symbol of the Cuban spirit" (62). So, in the postrevolution reinscription and reextension of the text by the director Humberto Solas into historical film, the alluring heroine becomes a witch, attracting and entrapping the colonialist white male by Santeria. Yet again, by the director's own account, the objective was in fact to revisit the controversial and socially charged focus of the original on "the racial and cultural syncretism of the Cuban nation." In sum, the novel remains a story that grows only more complex and problematic in its retellings. Yet always there remains the critical insistence, as phrased by César Leante, that "Cecilia Valdés is the Cuban nation, because Villaverde's protagonist symbolizes, in her flesh and her spirit, the racial and cultural combination that determines the Cuban being."

Of Villaverde's own endless writings and rewritings, the novel ends where it begins, literally, in the completion of the cultural and literary cartography of its title. *Cecilia Valdés; o, la Loma del Ángel.* It climaxes on the summit, the crown of the hill of the Angel, the highest elevation of Havana. It is still there to be found, a distinct elevation, crowned by the legendary church of the same name, the site of baptism, among its other honors, for Felix Varela and Jose Martí. It was for years believed to be the final resting place of Christopher Columbus; it is still known to be the site of the steps where Pimienta stabs Leonardo Gamboa to death. As to Columbus, the crypt in the nave, once containing the purported bones, is now empty, with the scanty remains removed and returned to Spain, itself the ghostly seat of vanished colonial power. The steps, on which were committed the imaginary murder of the white aristocrat by the vengeful mulato, with the assassin vanishing into the anonymity of the crowd, remain as a violent figure of revolution. In all these respects, historical and literary, la Loma del Ángel thus remains all there even this year on the two hundredth anniversary of the heroine's birth. From there, Havana seems to re-create itself in the way it was two hundred years ago, in the especially complicated period 1812–31 or 1832. It remains the place where Cecilia spent her life as a character, with her fictive precinct written into history. It is also, however, as new as today. The locale in question, then as now, offers two ways of getting in or out. At the intersection of five streets, just behind the palace of the archbishop, one enters. One ascends the steps, uses the main entrance, follows the main aisle, makes the long approach to the altar. Behind lies the empty crypt of Christopher Columbus. One departs by the other door, behind the altar, to the street on which sits the old Governor's Palace. If one continues across the street, one may now walk directly into the Museo de La Revolución.

Throughout Havana, in Leante's translated phrase, "the Cuban being" as a place and a history is now imaged, under the direction of Dr. Eusebio Leal and the project of the living city, in such historical restorations of the national imaginary. University students, clubs, reading groups, undertake Cecilia Valdés's pilgrimages. Here too, the text remains unique among comparable legendary novels of their nations in the quite physical aspect of living history—in that nearly every location specified in the novel—market, shop, café, mansion, house, convent, cathedral, street, byway, frequently down to street address block (as is the custom, for instance, "between Aguacante and Mercaderes") and house or building number—can still be identified. Similarly one feels the entrenching of the social and material in lengthy historical inclusions—recitations of political episode, anecdote, event; intimate excurses on details of architecture, dress, art, entertainments, food, customs, amusements, holidays, celebrations, theaters, balls, festivals, manners, forms of address. Intermingled with fictional characters are actual historical personages and legendary individuals. Were one to address issues of language and translation—a matter far beyond the scope of this essay—one would hear myriad discourses and dialects, ranging from the classical Spanish of nineteenth-century elites to illiterates speaking in over-correction. In such voices of gender, race, and class, one would encounter the true polyphony of historical discourses: peninsulare, gallego, criollo, mestizo, mulato, negro; or, in the even more various vernacular: *blanco, rubio, negro azul, prieto, moreno, trigueño, jabao,* and *blanconaso*. Amidst the polyphony, one recovers a geography, a society, an art, an architecture, the whole teeming life of a culture.

The ever-unfolding text is the one entitled *Cecilia Valdés; o, la Loma del Ángel*. As such, even down to the title, it is at once the account of its own origin and the site of its return. It is history with a power far beyond bourgeois entertainment or postrevolutionary nostalgia, as with Georgy Lukács' assertions of the great works of nineteenth-century realism, the great account of world-historical class struggle. So the discourses of history and literature in Villaverde continue to rewrite the terms of art and ideology. And above it all, the Hill of the Angel still stands guard over Villaverde's great world, then and now. Can the titular angel be any other than Walter Benjamin's Angel of History? "His face is turned toward the past. Where we perceive a chain of events, he sees one single catastrophe that keeps piling ruin upon ruin and hurls it in front of his feet. The angel would like to stay, awaken the dead, and make whole what has been smashed. But a storm is blowing from Paradise; it has got caught in his wings with such violence that the angel can no longer close them. The storm irresistibly propels him into the future to which his back is turned, while the pile of debris before him grows skyward. This storm is what we call progress." Just so. Benjamin was writing about twentieth-century European fascism. Before that was the colonial enterprise, its genocidal harbinger and dread prediction, the tragedy of slavery, imperialism, and race. A short story, a novel, a national opera, an epic movie, moving now into the discourses of its newest formal and cultural evolutions, *Cecilia Valdés; o, la Loma del Ángel* continues to rewrite itself as a text of the great human struggle for liberation.

2

UN MILITAR ESPAÑOL DE ORIGEN VENEZOLANO

Among the most visited and quietly beautiful historical sites near el Castillo de San Salvador de la Punta de Havana—itself sitting serenely across the mouth of the harbor from the Castillo de Los Tres Reyes del Morro, the famous "Morro Castle"—is a small shrine marking the site of the 1871 executions of eight martyred Cuban university students accused and summarily convicted by the Spanish authorities of revolutionary insurrection. Their alleged crime seems to have been the defacing of a statue of a colonial worth. The proof of involvement even in an escapade so trumped up was itself largely nonexistent. Three years into the 1868–78 First War of Cuban Independence, the murders became an abstract or epitome of Spanish tyranny. Today marked by a small, graceful Greek temple and surrounding garden, and known as the Monumento de Estudiantes de Medicina, the place of execution itself stands as one of the most important sites in the city commemorating the nation's long struggle for revolutionary liberty. Nearby, and much less visited, is the site of another execution twenty years before. Here too, the executioners were the Spanish. Here too, the charge was revolutionary insurgency. In this case, the victim was not a Cuban, however, but a Venezuelan, one of the strangest figures in nineteenth-century Latin American, Spanish, American, and, finally, Cuban revolutionary history. To be specific, the prisoner to be officially dispatched—before a crowd, it is traditionally suggested, of nearly twenty thousand onlookers—was a three-time anti-Spanish filibustero and would be insurrectionist named Narciso López. A former field marshal of Spain, then a colonial official of the Royal government in Cuba, and finally a celebrated revolutionary exile and military adventurer engaged by US annexationist interests comprising a who's who of US mid-nineteenth-century politics, after three failed expeditions, he was summarily garroted on the spot in January 1851. That is, he was strapped to a chair, with metal bands around his wrists and ankles, and with his head confined in a metal cage and his neck tightly bound in a pressure apparatus. When a screw was turned—in López's intentionally humiliating case, by a slave executioner—the windpipe was broken and suffocation ensued.

As may be inferred even from the brief outline given above, the life of López seems itself sufficiently complex and involuted in its relations of power, nationality, and identity to be the stuff of a postmodern fable of Latin American political history. A slight but allegedly handsome figure with notably passionate dark eyes, even down to the reflexive symbolism of his baptismal name, Narciso López seemed driven from the outset to enact an intransigently self-willed concept of heroic destiny. Born to a Venezuelan landowner in 1797, the young López grew up in the midst of insurrectionary disorder and destruction, forced to move with his family from their war-ravaged plantation first to Caracas and later to Valencia, a revolutionary stronghold. There López found himself among the antiroyalist defenders, after Bolivar, suffering a heavy 1814 defeat in a battle called La Puerta, nonetheless called upon the townspeople of Valencia to maintain their resistance, promising to move to the rescue of the besieged garrison and renew the war from there. Shortly, the Liberator instead chose to retreat with his army into the neighboring sanctuary of New Grenada. In Valencia, the resistance lasted three weeks. When the Spanish arrived, they massacred nearly a hundred prominent citizens, including López's father. At that point, for reasons that remain unclear—having "no love," as one biographer puts it, "for the Spanish or for Bolivar"—the young colonial resistance fighter, celebrated for his bravery and leadership during the siege, chose to enlist in the royalist army, rising by 1823 to the rank of colonel. Of course, 1823 also turned out to be the year of Bolivarian rebel victory and occasioned López's evacuation to Spain, albeit with a brief first stop in Cuba, where he married the daughter of a wealthy noble and is said to have gained a lifelong interest in matters Cuban.

In a new Spanish career in the army and in government, López managed to navigate the early tumults of a series of military and political upheavals and battles over royal succession, known to history as the "Carlist Wars," serving as an aide-de-camp to the prominent general Jerónimo Valdés, ably commanding a cavalry section of three thousand men, and eventually being appointed governor of Madrid. In the process securing his place as a loyal protégé of Valdés, after the appointment of the latter as captain general of Cuba, López eventually migrated back to the island, where he managed to secure a series of high appointments, including the governorship of the strategically crucial Trinidad. With the 1843 replacement of Valdés by Leopoldo O'Donnell, however, López lost all authority, retaining only the empty rank of Spanish general. A series of economic ventures followed, all failures, with matters exacerbated by heavy gambling. In bitterness over his losses and resentment of his dismissals from power, López, in a new exercise of the talents for political intriguing discovered in Spain, turned to subversive activity against the colonial government. In this, his own motives were conflicted. While he had become committed to the cause of Cuban revolutionary independence, he also remained proslavery. Pursuing various avenues of insurrection, he secretly consulted the American consul at Havana, one Robert Campbell, himself an avid US annexationist, who explained that, with the Polk administration at present similarly conflicted over the slavery issue due to the fallout over the Mexican War, the current government was obliged to take a public position of amity with Spain. López, meanwhile, decided in the main that any credible anti-Spanish insurrection likely to succeed—proslavery or abolitionist—would almost surely gain US support.

Accordingly, in that great year of international revolution, 1848, López, by now in touch with the cabal of rich, prominent, proindependence Havana figures known as el Club de la Habana, as well as the novelist Cirilo Villaverde—himself soon to become a revolutionary exile—threw his full efforts into the fomenting of a local insurgency, centered on Cienfuegos, planned for mid-June. His preparation was interrupted by appeals from el Club de la Habana to delay such action so as to coordinate it with a simultaneous US-led invasion they also intended to sponsor under the leadership of a US Mexican War general named William L. Worth. The design of a coordinated attack never materialized. Meanwhile, betrayed by a local youth, the revolution on Cuban soil—in a pattern that, until nearly the end, would become the story of López's life—collapsed before it began. Fleeing to Matanzas, López barely managed to take ship, aboard a US vessel bound for Providence, Rhode Island. In Cuba, he was sentenced to death in absentia.

In short order, there followed the sequence of filibustering adventures that now comprise what might be considered the López legend. If they hadn't resulted in numerous deaths, including ultimately the central figure's cruel execution by garrote, the rest might read like a manic nonfiction novel, a comedy of politics constantly bordering on the surreal.

The first, though the most ludicrously abortive, probably remains the most famous, implicating, as it did, a startling number of American personages from both north and south. Almost immediately upon his arrival in the United States, López seems to have formed a friendship with John O'Sullivan, journalist-editor of Manifest Destiny fame, who had been conducting his own annexation negotiations with el Club de la Habana planters and industrialists regarding possible US government purchase of the island for one hundred million dollars. Under a not altogether enthusiastic Pres. James K. Polk, this scheme went forward sufficiently for then Secretary of State James Buchanan to make an actual offer to Spanish minister of foreign affairs Pedro Pidal. With a quick Spanish rebuff on the record, a new Whig administration under Zachary Taylor in 1849 set its face against any such further dealing. López, meanwhile, in touch with the revolutionary Cuban émigré community, now including the recently arrived Cirilo Villaverde, had been busily going forward with a formal military plan of revolutionary invasion—called in those days, as such schemes would continue to be until the Spanish-American War fifty years later, a filibustering expedition. The chief locations of recruitment and preparation were New York and New Orleans. In competition for financial support, López jostled unhappily with rival Cuban factions. He did better with an inventive scheme, to be repeated several times over the next years, of selling bonds to US financial speculators on the credit of the new revolutionary Cuban government to be established, presumably by himself. (Indefatigably, even as his first enterprise was going down the drain, he came out openly soliciting funding through widely published appeals for what amounted to his own political action committee, a group grandly entitled the Junta Promovedora de los Intereses Politicos de Cuba.) Meanwhile López busied himself with seeking out possible military mission commanders. The recent Mexican War, if causing a variety of inconvenient kinks in the relationship with the royal government of Spain, at least supplied a healthy talent roster of US field officer candidates. Chief among these was the now largely forgotten William L. Worth, already solicited by el Club de la Habana for the failed 1848 expedition. His appeal seems also to have involved a desperation for employment born of personal improvidence. He was a man who needed money. At some point, he wound up being ordered by President Polk, with an eye to larger international relations, to dissociate himself from any such troublesome anti-Spanish conspiracy. He shortly died of cholera. After Worth proved unavailable, a second likely figure, also a military hero of the war, turned out to be US senator Jefferson Davis. He was offered a hundred thousand dollars and a fine coffee plantation. When Davis demurred, he in turn suggested an accomplished young protégé, Robert E. Lee, who wisely said no as well. Apace, attempting to stir enthusiasm among southern proslavery enthusiasts, López had been courting John C. Calhoun. With the money coming in, the expedition was organized to launch itself with concurrent departures of expeditionary units from New York and New Orleans. Unfortunately, the planning was also carefully monitored by exercised officials of the Zachary Taylor administration. Through a series of government raids and confiscations in New York harbor and at Round Island, off the coast of Mississippi, the enterprise never got beyond US shores.

For López's second invasion—sometimes, for its objective, called the Cárdenas expedition; and sometimes, for its flagship, as well as its vehicle of ignominious retreat, called the *Creole* adventure—the first of two to actually reach the island, the general sought the support of a figure again little remembered now except to historians, Senator John Quitman of Mississippi, who was at the time a major advocate and promoter of Latin American adventurism. Also of great influence among southern proslavery annexationists was another supporter-recruit, editor of the *New Orleans Delta* and former US senator John Henderson. Again, widely advertised and promoted bond sales proved ready money. Purchases included real invasion-worthy ships; recruits included 435 real soldiers, mainly from Louisiana and Mississippi but also arriving from Kentucky and the Ohio River valley. Recorded as well, presumably new arrivals from the 1848 European revolutionary barricades, were some Germans and Hungarians. Of Cubans, there seem to have been but as few as nine or as many as fifteen. In late April and early May 1850, three serious vessels, the bark *Georgianna*, the brig *Susan Loud*, and the steamer *Creole*, left New Orleans with 225, 150, and 130 filibusteros respectively. On May 19, a massed landing force came ashore at Cárdenas, some one hundred miles east of Havana. The city was briefly held. Nowhere to be found was any sign of a concurrent popular uprising the adventurers had been encouraged to anticipate. With reports of advancing Spanish reinforcements, López ordered a rapid reembarkation and departure from Cuban shores. By May 21, the swiftly flying *Creole* was back in Key West, Florida, and the expedition disbanded.

Arriving shortly afterward in Savannah, Georgia, López was arrested by US authorities. After being released, he was traveling to New Orleans, where he was cheered as a national celebrity, when he was rearrested and charged with violation of the US Neutrality Act of 1818. López was eventually freed from indictment. Meanwhile, as a new president, Millard Fillmore saw fit to set his own international relations policy by issuing a national proclamation of antifilibustering policy. Undeterred, López was already planning a new expedition. Centers of recruitment were established along the Atlantic from New York to Savannah and also, as before, along the Louisiana and Mississippi regions of the Gulf. This time one military wing would be commanded by a bold, competent US-Mexican War veteran, William L. Crittenden, nephew of the influential US senator from Kentucky, John J. Crittenden. The other, of course, would be led by the old Venezuelan-Spanish-Cuban warrior himself. In late July, again buoyed by encouraging, but again sadly untrue, rumors of widespread popular insurrections throughout Cuba waiting to ignite upon US arrival, this final expedition made haste out of New Orleans, in defiance, it turned out, of both official US policy and its own military prospects for success. The objective this time was Bahia Honda, a sheltered landing spot some forty miles west of Havana. The greeting this time turned out to be a major, coordinated colonial Spanish Army response. Crittenden and fifty members of his regiment, captured at the village of Tabla de Agua, were taken to Havana and executed en masse by firing squad. (The US officer's final words, it is alleged, when told to kneel before his executioners, were: "An American kneels only to his God, and always faces his enemy.") López, surrendering after a general rout of his forces at Las Pozas, was likewise taken to Havana, where he was—apparently to his great disappointment, having expected a soldier's death by firing squad—summarily garroted. The Spanish authorities, it would seem, were simply tired of his vainglorious military-adventurer nonsense.

Of the invasion party, 160 prisoners were transported to Spain, where, after diplomatic appeals, they were eventually released. Regarding the incident at large, the US government felt obliged to offer a manifestly hollow anti-Spanish protest in support of those executed and otherwise maltreated in the cause of world freedom. In New Orleans, where López had been a popular celebrity, a mob duly attacked the offices of the Spanish Consul. But mainly López in the short and long run joined a list, itself now something of a historical curiosity, of notable American filibusteros in Latin America, extending from the early nineteenth-century adventurism of William S. Smith in López's own Venezuela to that of the eventually notorious William Walker in Mexico and Nicaragua. (If stretched to literature, it might include the shipwrecked comitatus of Stephen Crane's story "The Open Boat," itself based on Crane's experience in the abortive gun-running voyage of the S.S. *Commodore*.) In most accounts of the political language of the era, it is said that, if nothing else, López brought the term "filibuster"—derived from the original Dutch *frijbuiterie*, which translates as "freebootery, buccaneering, piracy"—into US popular currency, where it would remain well into the final war of Cuban Independence. In keeping with such usage, to this day the latter also remains, called by Cubans, it should be noted, the Intervención.

Curiously, the one thing for which López was not at all remembered at the time, would eventually make him a part of Cuban history forever. It was a banner his forces carried at Cárdenas, modeled, it was said, on some combination of Texas and US national designs, but translated into terms of Cuban struggle: three blue stripes, symbolizing the threefold division of the country into occidental, central, and oriental sections during the independence campaigns; two white stripes for the purity of the Cuban cause; a red triangle, itself of Masonic symbolism (of importance to el Club de la Habana) for the blood of freedom fighters; and a white star for independence. Eventually embraced by the general independence movement during the nineteenth century, and enduring through the upheavals of the twentieth century, including the Communist revolution, the design remains to this day that of the Cuban national flag.

Quixotic would be the operative term, had López not been so wildly ungoverned an adventurer-opportunist who caused so much bloodshed in so many places to so little end. A man of immense physical courage; imposing in visage, stature, and bearing; yet also impulsive, impatient, heedless; he seems throughout his life to have remained curiously bewildered about his own motives and ambitions. This remained the case even down to his final speech. In some places his last words are reported thus:

"My death will not change the destiny of Cuba!" The truer account, characteristically heroic but abortive, seems to have involved, on the scaffold, a long, prepared, formal oration that he hoped to give in its entirety. "Countrymen," he began with notable calmness, "I most solemnly, in this last awful moment of my life, ask your pardon for any injury I have caused you. It was not my wish to injure anyone, my object was your freedom and happiness." At this point, an officer in the execution party is said to have told him to cut it short. In response, he abruptly concluded, "My intention was good, and my hope is in God."

Thus went the politically confused last words of a military adventurer in service of US annexationists on behalf of the people of Cuba—whom even to the end he hadn't quite figured out, except as fellow participants in some strange revolutionary dream of combat and conquest in which he would be the liberator. In the Cuban history schoolbooks to this day, he rates but brief discussion as typical of the annexationist phenomenon. "*Un militar español de origen Venezolano,*" he is called. Of which new people or new revolutionary land he would become the national hero, he remained to the moment of his death not quite sure.

3

MAMBISES IN WHITEFACE

Whether in war, politics, trade, or popular-culture history, the United States has always required an image of Cuba constructed in terms of its own ideological presuppositions. This has been emphatically true of the racial imagination, from the days of the pre–Civil War annexationists through the current half century of the Communist era. Nowhere was this more apparent than when it mattered the most historically, in the crucial moment of US-Cuban military collaboration concluding the 1895–98 Cuban War of Independence. In popular culture representations, including photography, illustration, and journalistic report, it was a political moment that would require a distinct "whitening" of the war both in racially inflected images of US military liberators on one hand and of their Cuban revolutionary counterparts on the other. In wartime images of American forces, much downplayed would be the significant combat roles of major African American units; with regard to their Cuban counterparts, even more pronounced would be the attempt to create for US consumption racially sanitized depictions of a revolutionary army with highly visible black and mulato leaders and a soldiery in many units heavily and proudly Afro-Cuban.

In fact, as far back as the first stirrings of an active Cuban revolutionary independence movement against Spain in the mid-nineteenth century, response in the United States was dictated by a distinct racial subtext. From the highest levels of government to the arena of popular myth lay a fear, pervasive among supporters and opponents alike, that the Cuban Revolution—reimaging Toussaint L'Ouverture's Haitian overthrow of colonial mastery a century earlier, but *now* in a place ninety miles off the southern tip of Jim Crow America—would be in large measure racially "black." This was an island, after all, so entrenched in its own institutional history of a white minority's enslaving of a vast population of African chattel and their descendants that pre–Civil War southerners had been tempted to several schemes of annexation—most famously those led by the Venezuelan filibustero Narciso López, finally garroted in Havana after a third ill-fated try. As to post–Civil War and postemancipation attempts by US leaders to manipulate official perceptions *of* and policy *toward* the revolutionary patriots, negotiating a racial politics of whiteness versus blackness seems to have been from the outset a primary consideration, with whiteness always figured most visibly in the featured role. In this regard, one influential American fresh from the scene felt impelled to assure the American secretary of state that this was "no nigger rabble." These were the words of Paul Brooks, the American owner of a large sugar plantation near Guantanamo in Oriente Province, Cuba, during an 1895 call on Richard Olney, Grover Cleveland's new appointee, at Olney's office in Washington, D.C. Brooks, perhaps nervously recalling an earlier anti-Spanish uprising of 1868–78, begun by the patriot Carlos Manuel de Céspedes by freeing his slaves and exhorting them to join him in revolution, was attempting to give an insider's assessment of the new Cuban military independence movement making its latest renewal of the decades-old war with a recent invasion into western Cuba. At the same time, these were the same bands of rebels Olney had also heard described by Spanish minister to the United States Enrique Dupuy de Lôme as belonging to the lowest social orders. "A rebel victory," Lôme warned Olney, "would devastate the island; independence would presage only anarchy." But there was more than that. It would also be black anarchy. "If this were so," Olney offered in return, "all right-thinking Americans should pray for Spanish success."

Popular culture representations of US-Cuban relations of the era—as Louis Pérez has shown, working their way through prewar, wartime, and postwar evolutions—likewise pandered to such racial anxieties, working for a variety of reasons to disguise what might seem to Americans the disquieting racial demographics of a movement that, in fact, from the outset, was never less than 30 percent Afro-Cuban and by the time of direct US military involvement was 60 percent—with the latter figure, by no surprise, corresponding exactly to the late nineteenth-century racial demographics of the island itself. (As will be seen, in some individual units, according to Cuban sources, the percentage may indeed have run as high as 85.) This was done mainly by focusing on mediagenic leadership figures in the traditional Western (read Anglo-European and Euro-American) revolutionary patriot-statesman mold—a Kosciuszko, a Garibaldi, a Higgins, a Bolivar. Early response in the United States was shaped by popular glorification of the distinctly Hispano-Cuban expatriate leader José Martí, a poet, essayist, journalist, and revolutionary philosopher—though much downplayed, of course, were the latter's alarmingly progressive views of a genuinely postracial revolutionary society. After Martí's early death in an 1895 skirmish, shortly following his arrival back on the island, guerrilla leadership was shared by two inspirational military figures, Máximo Gómez and Antonio Maceo, one Hispanic and one mulato, of relatively equal heroic stature, but with the latter's role, after his early death in battle, quickly romanticized offstage as "the Bronze Titan" ("el Titan de Bronce"). In the role of general commanding the insurgent forces, Gómez then became the main face of the revolution, fighting on until eventually joined and supplanted, in the American area of operations on the western part of the island particularly, by the aristocratic criollo Calixto García. Meanwhile, as to cultural image, the Spanish had the bad judgment to replace a relatively humane military proconsul, Arsenio Martinez Campos, with the despicable Valeriano Weyler, remembered mainly to history as inventor of the *reconcentrado* [concentration camp/pacification] policy—and conveniently half-German.

Once the United States officially entered the war, the national publicity spotlight shifted in turn almost immediately and entirely away from the Cuban rebels to focus on fighting young American heroes giving their all for the cause: the selfless young US Army lieutenant Andrew S. Rowan carrying the famous message to García; the martyred bluejackets of the navy going to their deaths in the treacherous sinking of the USS *Maine*; a combined force of cowboys and New York socialites riding and shooting their way to the top of San Juan Hill. (On the topic of race, one might also note the perverse spotlighting at the upper levels of command of celebrated ex-Confederates, including Fitzhugh Lee, son of the great Gen. Robert E. Lee, and of a grizzled old cavalry retread, Fighting Joe Wheeler. In one engagement, with the Spaniards rapidly retreating from their positions, the latter was said to have exclaimed, "After them, boys! We've got the Yankees on the run!") Indeed, by the time the US expeditionary forces arrived for their three-month 1898 campaign, they completely monopolized the spotlight; and they never gave it up. The war made a number of Americans famous—Teddy Roosevelt, William Randolph Hearst, Richard Harding Davis—and enshrined a host of popular American expressions—"filibuster," "jingoism," "yellow journalism," the "Rough Riders," the "Splendid Little

War." It became the war of the celebrity journalist. It was one of the last wars of the great illustrators and the first war of the great photographers. It was actually the first movie/newsreel war. And once it went American, it was blazoned as all-American fighting by all-American boys.

Actually, regarding the racial makeup of the American forces themselves, as is now well known, in the Cuban and Puerto Rican theater that is our particular concern, it hadn't been that at all, with a full two-thirds of fighting troops drawn from what were euphemistically termed "colored" ranks. Four major units especially, all heavily engaged in combat, the Twenty-Fourth and Twenty-Fifth Infantry Regiments and the Ninth and Tenth Cavalry, had been black, although officered by whites, with the latter of these formations actually credited in saving the legendary Rough Riders from extermination under heavy fire at San Juan Hill. That story has been told. The one that has not concerns the corresponding and equally cynical sanitizations and manipulations of images of race in representations of the Americans' Cuban revolutionary brothers-in-arms. For these too, when they were allowed at all, had to be as safely expunged for US audiences of emphasis on nonwhite participations and contributions as those designed to minimize the role of the Buffalo Soldiers. Indeed, if anything, the matter of race here seemed even more pressing. If not all-American—the fact being that Cuban already meant Caribbean, and Caribbean in turn meant criollo, mestizo, mulato and the like—the prototypical Cuban revolutionary patriot, like his leaders, had better be formulated for domestic consumption by Americans in support of their troops as racially of a predominantly European or at least Euro-Caribbean strain. The last thing after all, the assumption seemed to be, postreconstruction Americans North and South wanted to see was yet another insurgent population of postslavery descendants of New World Africans. Or, as phrased by Hearst illustrator Frederic Remington, for all the worth of an exciting Cuban War, there was also the dismal prospect of Americans getting "killed to free a lot of damn n——s who are better off under the yoke."

Accordingly, from start to finish in this final military stage of the Cuban independence struggle, beginning with the local insurgency phase of the 1880s and extending into the "American" phase of the late 1890s, US representations of rank-and-file Cuban revolutionaries actually do reveal a remarkable consistency of what might be called ratio of whiteness to blackness. Revolutionary soldiers striking military poses with at least rudimentary uniforms and weaponry tend to be European looking. On occasion, certain figures in support roles may be Afro-Caribbean in feature. When white and black figures are intermingled, anyone in a leadership position is invariably white-Hispanic (in the local terminology, peninsulare or gallego), criollo, or, at the very most mestizo. Visible more than a hundred years later on the Internet archive, official military-release propaganda photos in these respects disdain all subtlety. One, entitled "Cuban Soldiers Killed by the Spanish," shows clearly six markedly European-looking Hispanic males lying side by side in a common grave; another, "Cuban Allies of the U.S.," shows four paramilitary stalwarts in various styles of uniform. They are all completely European in feature.

Rendered into contemporary print, of parallel outline in racial representations of Cuban soldiery is the extensive visual record of the conflict contained in a folio-sized, quasi-official commemorative volume of 1898, designed for the parlor or library table, and grandly entitled *Photographic History of the Spanish-American War: A Pictorial and Descriptive Record of Events on Land and Sea with Portraits and Biographies of Leaders on Both Sides*. Three hundred thirty-five plates are listed, the large majority dealing with the Caribbean rather than the Pacific theater of war. Of these, precisely two are devoted to the representation of groups of Cuban Revolutionary volunteers in the role of auxiliary troops. One is of a unit of thirty or so infantry soldiers, in various states of uniform. Most are distinctly Hispanic in appearance; some may be said to be mestizo; in the rear rank may be seen what appear to be just two mulatos, or at least of African feature. The other is entitled "Cuban Scouts." Here, two irregulars are pictured firing their rifles from a kneeling position; barefoot, tattered, ragtag as they may be, even these, however, are markedly Euro-Cuban.

As to wartime representations of Cuban civilians coming into contact with their North American liberators, where there are scenes of "official" crowd gatherings—dockside greetings and farewell parades, victory celebrations, treaty signings, and the like, the populations appear to be well dressed and mainly Caucasian, in many cases quite cosmopolitan and European looking. Boulevardiers pose before storefronts and offices on busy commercial arteries. Señoritas wave from balconies. In contrast, Cuban peasants and refugees, slum dwellers and/or victims of the reconcentrado program, are almost always black and helpless looking, arrayed against squalid scenes of backwardness and poverty. A notable exception here, it might be observed, is the first plate in the parlor/coffee table volume described above. Entitled "Why We Fought," it is a stark photoengraving, quite graphic in detail, of three suffering, emaciated, skeletal victims of the reconcentrado system. Here, they are all carefully given dark complexions, but with distinctly sharp, even finely etched Euro-Caribbean features.

Newsreels, pioneering experiments in the form, reveal a similar mix. The occasional view is given of a racially miscellaneous Cuban auxiliary soldiery boarding ships from US soil. A scene of arrival in Cuba offers a similarly mixed greeting party. Both films, by virtue of rudimentary technology, have a distinct lack of definition. Facial features and colors of skin and hair remain fairly indistinguishable. A queer handful of films, styled as reenactment newsreels, make race more pronounced. Two in retrospect seem especially notable. One, entitled "Execution of Prisoners," stages the activities of a Spanish firing squad, who march in with their victims, captured rebels, both white and black. They march them up to the wall of a house and rapidly shoot them down. The second is entitled "Spanish Ambush." Here, a revolutionary guerrilla sniper fires from the upper window of a house at a party of Spanish people. It is, rather ludicrously, the same house against the wall of which the execution in the other film is staged. One imagines that the same cast of reenactors is being used. In this case, the sniper is dragged out, beaten, and summarily executed. His racial identity here seems importantly visible. A simple peasant, guerilla franc-tireur, operating on his own, he is solitary, helpless, and black.

In pronounced and abundant contrast to such American representations of the conflict, a rich archive of wartime Cuban photography, illustration, and popular art of the era, readily available to visitors, provides a markedly different overall racial picture. There, if anything, accounts of the military dimension of the entire late nineteenth-century independence struggle frequently highlight the heavily mixed-race character of the independence struggle and the heroism of a distinct group of fighters of color known as the Mambises. (The term itself, in fact, remains part of the historical vocabulary of most reasonably educated Cubans.) Indeed, an entire freestanding 1998 paperback volume on mixed-race revolutionaries—*La Comida in el Monte: Cimarrones, Mambises, and Rebeldes*—is not difficult to find in bookstores. As with most sources, the political line of the text may be that of the current government, but the relevant illustrations themselves remain distinguished by their historical ubiquity and abundance. Mambise cavalry are totally black. Two Mambise infantrymen, oddly mirroring the American "Cuban Scouts" described above, even down to the side-by-side kneeling positions in which they take aim with their rifles, are as deeply black as their counterparts in the US illustration are visibly white. Related representations draw attention to composite criollo, mestizo, mulato, and negro/esclavo mix of fighting units by way of emphasizing the racial brotherhood of fighters in the struggle for revolution. By a curious historical sidelight, these images, with a text in consonance with the argument ventured here, may also be seen by US viewers at a website maintained by an exile Cuban, Orestes Matacena. A second, related text, published in a 2000 Cuban edition by the University of Texas historian Aline Helg—*Los Que Nos Corresponde: La Lucha de los Negros y Mulatos por la Igualidad en Cuba 1886-1912*—strongly corroborates, on the basis of contemporary photography and illustration, the widespread imaging of multiracial effort in the independence forces.

A similar emphasis on racial diversity in the independence soldiery is documented with copious photographic and illustrational evidence in readily available popular histories of a more general nature. An anonymously authored textbook, *Historia de Cuba*, features a wartime sketch of Maceo as its cover illustration. The combat chapters devoted to the 1895-98 war accordingly feature his heroic leadership with significant pictorial representation of the Mambise contribution. A 2000 government school text with the same title by Prof. José Canton Navarro features in its sections on the war the leadership of Maceo and illustrates the famous Mambise "*carga al machete*," the heroic charge of African irregulars attacking on foot with their lethal machetes and slaying heavily armed and uniformed Spaniards hand to hand. The 1995 *Heroes de la Independencia de Cuba* by Paul Rodriguez and the 1994 *Dias de la Guerra Chronologica* by Raúl Izquierdo Canosa both approach the 1895 war with a focus on major revolutionary political figures and commanders. Both give copious attention to the leadership of high-ranking black officials, nearly all of them pictured, including Antonio Maceo and his brother Jose, as well as other mixed-race or black commanders such as Sanchez, Valdiva, Tejera, Molina, and Bandera. Of the twenty-seven major generals shown in portraits by Canosa, seven are mulato or negro.

For conclusive evidence on the point, a text, which surely seems as definitive as any to be imagined concerning wartime representations of Cuban revolutionary fighters of the 1895–98 war, is that assembled by Marta Casals Reyes and Jorge García Hernández, entitled *Catálogo de Fotos de la Guerra de Independencia de 1895* and taken from the records of the oficial Fototeca del Archivo Nacional de Cuba. Here the record of contemporary photography and photo-illustration is compiled, cataloged, and described, with a rich selection of images. And here, across a wide array of archival war photographs, the mixed-race military effort continues to reveal itself in image after image. Sometimes the combatants are nearly all dark skinned, discernibly mulato or negro. Sometimes they preponderate toward gallego/peninsulare, criollo, and mestizo. In most instances they seem simply to comprise groupings of who they actually were at the time, black, brown, white, in their camps, assembling to go into battle, or being memorialized in its aftermath. In picture after picture, they all become at one while existing in their larger, common, multiracial identity, with the sole legend at the bottom of many of the photographs, simply reading: "Jefes, oficiales, y soldados del Ejercíto Liberatador."

A similar proliferation of multiracialism pervades the larger cultural symbologies of history and art familiar to most Cubans. In Havana's Palacio de los Capitanes Generales, for instance, one large chamber features extensive displays of military artifacts and memorabilia, centered on the heroic leadership of three major figures: Máximo Gómez, Antonio Maceo, and Calixto García. The room is dominated by the wall-sized combat painting by the great early twentieth-century Cuban artist, Armando G. Menocal, *The Death of Maceo*. The latter is further augmented by major works among the fifteen or so Menocals displayed in the Museo Nacional de las Bellas Artes (Cuban Section). One, entitled *Máximo Gómez en Campaña*, features the general with a command and staff group of nine figures, including one black and two mulatos. Another is the artist's rendering of a furious *carga al machete*, with twenty dark Mambi fighters charging past a fallen white commander with stern bravery. Another lift from wartime photography is a depiction of "Caballaría Mambisa" (Mambise cavalry). Of fifteen Afro-Cuban figures, three mulato/negro riders have complete, personalized facial features; the rest carry African faces hauntingly in shadow.

As to historical genealogies of Cuban independence struggle, in a walk along the Havana Malecón in 2010, images of Che Guevara, Fidel Castro, and Camilo Cienfuegos fade into the wall while great heroic statues continue to honor a triad of nineteenth-century revolutionary predecessors. At one extreme of the long seawall walk is Calixto García. At the other is Máximo Gómez. In the middle, dominating a park for the children of Havana, is Antonio Maceo. Decorative panels on the side of the pedestal supporting the huge equestrian statue in bronze depict Maceo's humble birth, his black father, and his revered mother, Mariana Grajales Coello, herself a national heroine. The other, with many of the figures represented given African features, emphasizes his liberation of the enslaved. A multitude of figures of statuary attend Maceo on the ascendant pedestal. They are Cubans of all visible races, together. Of the three statues, it is significant that the revolution left them standing, as they did not many others. One can only infer that they were part of Cuban memory that no one ever thought to deny.

Of such denial on the part of US historical memory, from the start, not surprisingly, the markedly contrasted "whitening" tendencies of racial selection and valuation in US representations of the war and its aftermath seemed to prevail not just in photography and illustration but also in major written accounts. A report from the front by the celebrity correspondent Richard Harding Davis, for instance, quickly gets through a description of a Cuban patriot contingent included in an American landing force with no references to race. Shortly, however, a spotlight paragraph about a personal visit to García specifies a gathering of his supporters and a larger crowd of welcome as comprising "Cubans and negroes"—as if, somehow, these were categories that needed to be separated. García himself, in contrast, is pointedly described as "a handsome man, with a white mustache and goatee," who "looks like Caprivi, the German Chancellor."

And then there was his celebrity-politician counterpart, Teddy Roosevelt, who, though fancying himself, when not playing soldier, something of a gentleman historian-journalist, seemed never one to keep his political opinions a secret—even if perhaps too glaringly close to betraying the secret official line. "The Cuban soldiers were almost all blacks and mulatos," he observed, "and were clothed in rags and armed with every kind of old rifle. They were utterly unable to make a serious fight, or to stand against even a very inferior number of Spanish troops, but we hope they might be of some use as scouts and skirmishers. For various reasons this proved not to be the case, and so far as the Santiago Campaign was concerned, we should have been better off if there had not been a single Cuban in the army. They accomplished literally nothing, while they were a source of trouble and embarrassment, and consumed much provisions."

More humane and circumspect, if as conventionally racist, was their star literary counterpart, Stephen Crane, who wrote of the Cuban revolutionaries he saw: "They were a hard-bitten, undersized lot, most of them negroes, and with the stoop and gait of men who had at one time labored at the soil. They were, in short, peasants—hardy, tireless, uncomplaining peasants—and they viewed in utter calm these early morning preparations for battle." The word "negro" is determining. They are terrible at close-order drill. They are stolid with their wounds: "And—look—there fell a Cuban, a great hulking negro, shot just beneath the heart, the blood staining his soiled shirt. He seemed in no pain; it seemed as if he were senseless before he fell. He made no outcry; he simply toppled over, while a comrade made a semi-futile grab at him. Instantly, one Cuban loaded the body upon the back of another and then took up the dying man's feet. The procession that moved off resembled a grotesque wheelbarrow. No one heeded it much. A marine remarked: 'Well, there goes one of the Cubans.'" They are terrible shots: "The Cubans, who cannot hit even the wide, wide world." To Crane's credit, this undertone of race could prompt an explicit commentary. "Cubans Held in Contempt," he would headline one item. "To put it shortly," he admitted, "both officers and privates have the most lively contempt for the Cubans. They despise them. They came down here expecting to fight side by side with an ally, but this ally has done little but stay in the rear and eat army rations, manifesting an indifference to the cause of Cuban liberty which could not be exceeded by one who had never heard of it."

Cowardice, ineptitude, indiscipline, laziness, beggarliness: as coded terms of racial contempt for a nonwhite, non-Western, non-Anglo-European ally, these could have been written in Saigon seventy years later. The difference here would have been the unspoken word: "nigger," as opposed to, seventy-five years later, "gook." If one knows where to look there certainly seems to have been a good deal of it going around in the army at the time. "The valiant Cuban!" recalled one sadly representative American lieutenant. "He strikes you first by his color. It ranges from chocolate yellow through all the shades to deepest black with kinky hair." Matched with this, he went on, is "the furtive look of the thief" and bodily infestation "with things that crawl and creep, often visibly, over this half-naked body, and he is accustomed to it that he does not even scratch." Today, perhaps, in Baghdad and Kabul, where the operating expressions would be "raghead" or "haji," the attitude remains essentially the same.

The foregoing analogies, on the other hand, pertaining to recent American involvement in notoriously undecided or even lost insurgent struggles, should not be allowed to blind the reader to the actually relatively strong Cuban revolutionary position in 1898 against their Spanish overlords on the eve of official American commitment. Unlike the South Vietnamese, or the later provisional governments in Iraq and Afghanistan, the Cubans were really well on the way to winning the war before the Americans arrived. In fact, there were no real attempts at coordination with revolutionary forces, no matter what their racial makeup. Any such official yoking, after all, would have required some eventual diplomatic recognition of revolutionary elements. As complete was Americans' disdainful inattention to voices of any who considered themselves as fighting for racial as well as conventional political liberty. Thus went unheard, for instance, the Afro-Cuban Esteban Montejo, who fought the war, he said, because "it wasn't fair that so many jobs and so many privileges happened to fall into the hands of the Spaniards alone. It wasn't fair that for women to work they had to be daughters of Spaniards. None of that was fair. You never saw a black lawyer because they said that blacks were only good for the forest. You never saw a black teacher. It was all for the white Spaniards. Even the white *criollos* were pushed aside. I seen that myself. A night watchman, whose only job was to walk around, call out the hour, and put out the candle, had to be a Spaniard. And everything was like that. There was no freedom. That's why a war was necessary." But if he expected things to change under the auspices of la Intervención, he goes on, he was quickly disabused of such hope. "The Americans didn't like the negroes much," he says. "They used to shout 'Nigger, nigger,' and burst out laughing. If you joined in the joke they went on trying to annoy you, but if you took no notice they left you alone. They never tried to interfere with me; I couldn't stomach them, and that's a fact. I never joked with them, I gave them the slip whenever I could. After the war ended the arguments began about whether the negroes had fought or not. I know that ninety-five percent of the blacks fought in the war, but they started saying only seventy-five per cent. Well, no one got up and told them they were lying, and the result was the negroes found themselves in the streets—men brave as lions, out in the streets. It was unjust, but that's what happened."

A revolution in the name of human fairness: what, according to American propaganda, could be more American? But only if it turned out to be cleansed of any associations with a "nigger rabble." (Nor did postwar policies prove to be any exception, with blacks systematically excluded from government and administrative posts. More than a half century later, 95 percent of exiles during the 1959 revolution turned out to be white—beneficiaries of new client regimes presiding over a population never less than 60 percent black.)

What did this all mean to Americans at the time? To black Americans, ironically, much more deeply in the know about racial configurations of the conflict than their white counterparts, through alternative sources of information—not the least a network of African American newspapers—war news meant a lot. What seems unquestionably a choice at highest policy levels, the sending of significant elements of black troops to fight a black war, may have been a cynical maneuver well disguised at the level of general public reporting. The black troops and/or black Americans seem to have understood this. But they still took great interest and even pride in the war's dimension as a "Negro" struggle. Most black Americans supported the war. Black newspapers heralded the accomplishment of black units. In the white press, occasional identification of units as "colored," with notable contributions and braveries credited as proving them worthy of their white counterparts, became featured items. Even in condescension mixed with happy-go-lucky caricature, readers fed on scraps from the newspaper table of the estimable Richard Harding Davis: "The negro soldiers established themselves as fighting men that morning," he concluded after one action, "and the chuckles they gave as they shoved the cartridges into their belts showed that, though they did not have food or water, so long as they had ammunition they were content." "Cuba" itself, considered in some totality of the cause of freedom, was embraced as a "colored" country, and the fallen Maceo, deemed the African father of *Cuba Libre*, became a martyr to black Americans. Accordingly, the cause could also make an occasion for black protest. "Talk about fighting and freeing poor Cuba and of Spain's brutality; of Cuba's murdered thousands, and starving reconcentradoes," wrote one black chaplain/editorialist back to a Cleveland newspaper. "Is America any better than Spain? Has she not subjects in her very midst who are murdered daily without a trial of judge or jury? Has she not subjects in her borders whose children are half-fed and half-clothed, because their father's skin is black?"

To white Americans, Cuba became a case of the new national business of imperialist muscle flexing as usual—picking up the white man's burden by cleaning up dirty little wars and then installing white men's surrogates. As in the Philippines, where Hispano-Filipino elites were established as a permanent ruling class above the masses of native peoples, in Cuba, Euro-Caribbeans were installed over descendants of African slaves. And so it would remain well into the new century and beyond.

Cuba Libre. That had been the revolutionary rallying cry from the beginning. It had been a cry of all Cubans, not least the most eager and brave coming from those least emancipated. This special role of Afro-Cubans was realized early on by the sainted Martí. "The black man has drawn his noble body to its full height and is becoming a solid column for his native liberties," he proclaimed. "Others fear him; I love him." Ultimately, the United States decided that the complexion of the face of the revolution should be otherwise. And they made it happen that way in photographs, movies, and words. The point is perhaps best illustrated by a popular propaganda poster of the era, itself with the title *Cuba Libre!* The focal figure is a beautiful, tortured, suffering woman, gowned in the Cuban revolutionary flag, confined to a dungeon but standing free of her chains, arms upraised, appealing for rescue from the brutal oppressor. A Caribbean *passionaria*, one might call her. She is the very figure of Liberty, albeit with a certain Latin exoticism to be sure: criolla; possibly mestiza; at the limits of racial fantasy, dusky tragic mulata. As to classical beauty and outline of face and feature, nonetheless, she could not be more white. In a war that was very much about race, the order of the day remained erasure.

4

THE GHOST OF WALKER EVANS

In the early 1930s, at the height of the Great Depression, a young American named Walker Evans forsook his privileged education—a graduate of Phillips Exeter Academy, he had finished one year at venerable Williams College in Massachusetts—to go out and find a way of bearing cultural witness to History. As with so many others of his artistic generation in those turbulent political years, that seems for Evans to have been the great calling: to render into art the world's historical struggle between the powerful and the powerless, the haves and the have-nots, the exploiters and the exploited. Evans was a fast learner who quickly found his medium. This was made clear—after a year in Paris discovering he was not meant to be a writer and the rapidly successful development, upon his return to New York, of a new career in photographic art—in the radical images of life produced from the place he chose as the site of his first extended essay in photo-documentary. That place was Havana: up to the end of the nineteenth century, and the Spanish-American War (called by many Cubans then *and* now la Intervención), arguably the greatest, richest, and most storied city in the Western Hemisphere; and in 1933, the epicenter of Latin American dollar diplomacy in the hangover years after the gaudy North American investment spree known as "*la danza de los milliones*"—the dance of the millions—now sunk into a reign of poverty and oppression under the US-supported dictator, Gerardo Machado.

What follows is a study of Evans's remarkable but generally little-known Depression-era photographs of working-class Havana, where he first perfected the modernist technique he would later describe as "nonsubjectivity" and/or the positioning of the photographer as "objective purist." In this connection, I first examine the 1933 Havana photographs in their relation to those of the far more famous depictions later in the decade of Alabama sharecroppers in *Let Us Now Praise Famous Men*; the argument then moves to later objectivist experiments in New York and elsewhere, with the intention of showing how deeply the Cuban experience proved foundational to Evans's sophisticated understanding of the camera's unique role in exploring—and frequently challenging—modernist assumptions of relationship between art and ideology. I then conclude with a return to particular photographs from the Cuban collection to show how, in putting the human subject into the historical frame—a record of particular people, at a particular time and a particular place in history—Evans found a great art of contextualization and synthesis. In Cuba, that is, confronting the historical and political claims of a deeply ideological century, Evans the artist would simultaneously discover the means of honoring a career-long belief, at once deeply intuitive and technically hard-won, in the photographer's capacity to produce some great, enduring vision of the human.

In Cuba, Evans's specific assignment was to provide a photographic annex to a book-length exposé of US corporate domination of the island, under the protection of the latest politically and economically corrupt client regime, by a journalist named Carleton Beals, entitled *The Crime of Cuba* (*El Crimen de Cuba*). In published form, Evans's contribution ran to an impressive twenty-eight-page cycle of photos, a total of fifty-seven plates in all, with one or two in journalistic evidence of dictatorial torture and violence added from Cuban sources. As is still quite recognizable, most were shot in the gritty streets of what then and now would be considered the everyday Havana of the people. Not much is there of colonial Havana, the grand spaces and historical edifices, the Plaza de Armas, Plaza Vieja, Plaza de la Catedral, the Malecón with its grand harbor and ocean vistas, nor the great colonial monuments, the Palacio de los Capitanes Generales, the Catedral San Cristobal, the Greek Templete and its legendary Ceiba tree; the magnificent fortresses of el Morro, La Cabaña, La Fuerza, La Punta, guarding the great arc of the bay. Neither does one find much interest in the more recent showplace Havana, not the Capitolio, the Teatro Tacón, the elegant Paseo and Parque Central, the great modern hotels—the Telegrafo, Inglaterra, Sevilla, Plaza, Nacional, nor likewise in an evolving Vedado, extending in those days from the stately Universidad de la Habana along sweeping boulevards and avenues into the grand residences of the rich upper classes. Evans seemed to stay largely with the winding streets, down by the harbor terminal and main railroad station, in the shadow of the ruins of the old city wall, concentrating on what is still today the central market where people buy their daily food and drink, common articles of clothing, newspapers and magazines, a quick glass of uncut rum, a cup of café leche or cane juice. Now, as then, one follows the old street names: Bélgica, Sol, Luz, Compostela. One wedges into the crowd, carried along by the flow, or navigates patiently at crossing points in the stream, a great sea of people—white, black, mulato, mestizo—and every shape and shade of other possible human being imaginable: real people, going about the business of their lives.

One can only infer that Beals's book was not a big seller. (In August 1933, as it turned out, Machado hurriedly resigned and fled the island.) Even today it remains a little-known title and a used-bookstore rarity. The Evans photos likewise seemed consigned to obscurity. Still, on the basis of his photographic contribution, what Evans surely got out of it at the very least had to be a well-earned confidence in his own professional and aesthetic development. Distinctly ancillary at the time, though historically fascinating as a matter of both autobiography and art, seems to have been a friendship Evans struck up during the assignment with the famous American writer Ernest Hemingway, who happened to be living and writing down in the old city at the Hotel Ambos Mundos and needed a drinking companion who might enjoy basking in the glow of the older man's celebrity. Evans drank with him for three weeks, and trusted him to the degree that, fearful that his work might be confiscated by Machado's agents before he could get out of the country, he developed a selected set of negatives and left the prints with Hemingway. Not so ancillary was the photographic dividend when the plates showed up decades later. Deemed worthy in themselves of a special exhibition by the Metropolitan Museum of Art, and occasioning the reprint of the complete photos in a free-standing volume, they now confirm for us what the Beals collection had already promised. During the three weeks Walker Evans spent as a young photographer in Cuba, he had established the technical and artistic foundations of his documentary method.

If Evans was a gifted unknown in Havana, his next cycle of photographs would change all that. These, taken during 1936–37 in the Alabama Black Belt agricultural region, would focus on white sharecroppers under the Depression-era Roosevelt flagship assistance program known as the Works Progress Administration (WPA). Again, the documentary project was a collaborative one with a text. This time, the author was James Agee—in striking complementarity to Evans, a Phillips Andover graduate with a college degree from Harvard. The subjects were members of three sharecropper families, enshrined to history as Gudger, Woods, and Rickett, though actually named Burroughs, Fields, and Tingle. The setting was made up of the bleak, cropped-out, unforgiving fields, with their human contours demarcated in the barely habitable shacks and cabins, the dirt roads, and crossroads stores. The Agee narrative was mournful, poetic, elegiac. The Evans photos were memorable for the stark, unadorned, uncompromising black and whiteness of their composition, frequently rendered even more haunting by the penetrating gazes of the human subjects.

Initially Agee had begun the project on assignment from Henry Luce's *Fortune* magazine, with Evans on loan from the WPA. Even so, with such proletarian political content, it quickly proved something Luce, Inc., didn't want to handle. When it turned into a quasi-official public project, one might ask why the focus remained with white sharecroppers, when so many impoverished tenant farmers of the region, held perpetually in indentured servitude, were direct legatees of African slavery, with some estimates suggesting a 50-60 percent black sharecropper population. In this case, to pose the question in such terms is to supply the answer. For the project at hand, the Depression-era agonies of rural Americans must have seemed sufficient in themselves, without bringing in larger questions of racial hatred and oppression. At a closer range, white sharecroppers were also politically much more visible, officially organized into the Southern Tenant Farmers Union, founded in 1934. Further, one could cite the prevailing literary fashion of a host of '20s and '30s American exposé-style books devoted to the lives of poor whites, including Hubert Harrison Kroll's *Cabin in the Cotton*, Erskine Caldwell's *Tobacco Road*, and John Steinbeck's *The Grapes of Wrath*. Accordingly, on this account it would not be unfair to note *Let Us Now Praise Famous Men* as simply reflective of the literary and publication values of the times. On questions of art and cultural witness, it would further be accurate to claim that Evans almost certainly saw the portion of the American South he was committing to historical and ideological record as a world not all that different from the Cuba he had photographed a few years earlier—a place of deeply human hardship, want, suffering, and sadness, yet also presenting a face of human dignity and indomitability. To update the language to our own geopolitical vocabulary, the streets of Havana, Cuba, and the hardscrabble fields of Hale County, Alabama, were both for Evans what we would now call

"Third World" places. Further, anyone who has seen the Cuba photography of the '30s would be hard pressed to say that Walker Evans wasn't interested in photographing nonwhite subjects. To him they were all people. His photos were intended to show just that: their human subjects then and now strike us as individual people, each with a basic human worth and dignity. So declaimed the title of the Agee-Evans text, from the book of the Apocrypha known as *Ecclesiasticus*: *Let Us Now Praise Famous Men*. Lest anyone should miss the contemporary political point, the epigraph from Marx—"Workers of the world unite and fight. You have nothing to lose but your chains, and the world to win."—put the message of basic human worth more directly, though a note protested "neither these words nor the authors are the property of any political party, faith, or faction." Still, no one could dispute that the subject of the book, in the dimensions of both the verbal and the visual, was History.

Thus emerged in the 1930s two texts of social documentary, political and economic exposés—albeit in quite different modes to different ends—linked and remembered today on the basis of Evans's photographic contributions, their distinguishing feature the artist's use of the camera as the instrument of a singular, independent, modernist objectivism—dispassionate, realistic, even mechanical, yet in the same moment, "literate, authoritative, transcendent." "Nonsubjectivity" was the word Evans himself most habitually used. In the great age of new interpenetrations between art and ideology, Evans, like Flaubert, whom he frequently invoked, still believed it possible for the camera, at least, to profess no particular political position. "I think I incorporated Flaubert's method almost unconsciously," he said once in retrospect, "but anyway I used it in two ways. Both his realism or naturalism, and his objectivity of treatment. The nonappearance of the author. The nonsubjectivity. That is literally applicable to the way I want to use the camera and do." And so testify the great, classic Evans photographs of the '30s, the already mature records of an art celebrated throughout a long career and beyond as the signature achievement of an "objective purist": in the great world of History, the work of the practitioner of an art of "fastidious reserve" so rigorously maintained as to produce images "self-consciously iconographic, stubbornly refusing to present anything but themselves"; and concurrently in the human dimension, equally that of a committed but respectful documentarian exercising "a spare precision that emphasized the dignity of his subjects."

The wording here is that of the cerebral, carefully developed, self-discovered aesthetic vocabulary of the mature master photographer on style. The style itself was earned by a long journey toward a mature vision—that of the common humanity of people in the context of a frequently stark, impersonal, omnipresent twentieth-century world—that began in a kind of clangor of initially opposed perspectives and attitudes toward the modern photographic subject. From the early career, as one might expect of an apprentice modernist, there came New York photos of great period impressiveness, much in the modernist style of Stieglitz, Steichen, and others; and though Evans contended at the time and afterward that his approach was as much a reaction as an homage regarding such famous contemporaries, he had clearly adopted the impersonal, monolithic, architectural, and technological landscape of the city frequently to the exclusion of the human subject. There were skyscrapers, bridges, railroads, subway stations. His most famous early image was a quite self-consciously angled and abstract representation of the Brooklyn Bridge, adopted to accompany a text of the Hart Crane modernist epic, *The Bridge*. Appearing occasionally was the individual human portrait—the longshoreman; a harried, elderly, owlish female pedestrian; a couple at Coney Island; a dispersing crowd from the Lindbergh parade. In contrast, the Cuban collection evinced a new concentration on heavily human subjects set once more against a twentieth-century urban setting, but deeply integrated into the particular local, historical, economic, and political environment. In turn, this would be the American Deep South manner of the text that would come to be regarded as his masterwork, *Let Us Now Praise Famous Men*, with nearly complete assimilation of twinned concentrations on the gaunt, worn-out rural families and the bleak barrenness of the Depression-era sharecropper landscape.

Then, afterward, as if it was time for a new experiment in addressing the human subject on one hand and larger images of history on the other, there came an almost complete separation of view. In the famous New York subway photography of the early World War II–era, frequently practiced with a hidden camera, Evans produced a long, largely unbroken sequence of almost exclusively human individual vignettes. To be sure, always was the abstract, impersonal presence of techno-history, the anonymous backdrop of the train, the sense of dark, crowded, urban underground, the teeming perpetual nightside city. Then, in later life, came a return to signature New York urban scenes, office building, restaurant, street, and storefront. But newly within them as well was readily apparent a human emphasis on distinctive people with distinctive identities: two businessmen, four businessmen, two construction workers, four men with ties, men playing basketball, man reading a newspaper, man in the street, tour guide, man in a leather jacket, man with laundry, young man in jeans. A masterpiece of the set is surely *Cook Standing in Sidewalk Cellar Door* where the subject, a middle-aged, slightly overweight figure in stained whites literally ascends to street level out of an underground stairway or elevator. In these great urban scenes, the last of the well-known Evans collections, interspersed with individual human moments, a certain late-life peace seems to have been made between the idea of the individual subject and the world-historical spectacle of modern life.

For Evans, this was nothing if not an earned aesthetic, in attitude, selection, perspective, arrangement, and final presentation as the photographic text. And so, now, in the relatively little known early Havana photographs, it is now nearly impossible in retrospect not to see how and where the art was born. Though they were mentioned in one short paragraph in Evans's *New York Times* obituary—as opposed to the extended treatment given, for instance, to the decidedly more famous work of the same period, *Let Us Now Praise Famous Men*—it does not now seem too much to say that they comprise the crucial first step toward a modernist iconography whereby Evans learned to explore the full possibilities of the idea of the human individual against the rendering of the objective backdrops of twentieth-century political and economic history in its fullest sense.

A useful means of exploring the proposition exists, as it turns out, in an account of the actual process whereby the Evans Havana photos were taken and eventually assembled into a collection provided by the researcher Alfredo Jose Estrada, who has tracked down the particulars of something resembling a documentary record. It begins with Evans, given a two-week travel advance by the publishers of the Beals volume, beginning to shoot, as if by strangely apposite coincidence, on what was then Cuban Independence Day, 20 May. He started with crowds in the Parque Central, with its statue of José Martí, across from the Capitolio. As the shooting progressed, according to Estrada, Evans, having intentionally eschewed familiarity with the specifics of perspective or argument in the

Beals text, took pictures of all parties: beggars; dockworkers, coal shovelers; an insouciant, drowsing stevedore in a jaunty straw hat, a cigar hanging idly from his lips; a starving family, a mother and three daughters, in a residential doorway; a tastefully dressed mulata with handbag and jewelry, backgrounded by a second figure, male, in a suit, lounging against a nearby lamppost; a younger, quizzical-looking mulata teenage girl, demure in a white dress, propped against a trash can, holding in one hand a cigarette. Larger urban street scenes provided a sociopolitical complement: a framed portrait of a mule, a wagon, and two men, with the farm wagon parked on a curb against a distinctly urban backdrop, heaped with long stalks of raw sugarcane; a horizontal row of second-floor balconies, each filled with clusters of spectators to some event taking place in the street below; an elbow-to-elbow political crowd on the steps of the Capitolio, photographed from above, perhaps some of the 20 May 1933 Independence Day celebrants. Evans was careful to record the impedimentia of the everyday lives of the everyday people of the city, the fruit in the marketplace, the stalls offering the promise of quick happiness of lottery tickets, the cheap restaurants, the newsstands, the movie theaters. Totalitarian political atmospherics, as Estrada points out, were quietly supplied by pictures of Machado-era police, soldiers, and plainclothes thugs, frequently recognizable by their straw boaters and known as *abecedarios*.

Regarding the latter, Estrada proves newly insightful as regards origins of one of the most famous pictures in the collection, that of the arresting, iconographic, strangely definitive "Havana Citizen," as Evans mysteriously called him in the caption. A tall, thin, but hard and muscular man in his twenties or thirties, very black in complexion, exquisitely, dandily turned out in an immaculate white linen suit and straw boater; he is posed near a newsstand with a Coca-Cola sign, where magazine and newspaper display racks feature contemporary titles such as *Bohemia* and *Carteles*. One of most important details in the photo turns out to be a banner headline, *GRAN TRIUNFO DE CHOCOLATE*—the boxing victory of Kid Chocolate, Cuba's great bronze hope, over Louis Stevens on May 28 of that year in London. The "Citizen" may indeed be one of Machado's dapper enforcers; a small smile suggests that he is also a proud Cuban, savoring a moment of national victory.

Other famous inclusions, now regarded properly in their way as iconic, include a *guajiro* family emigrated to the teeming city. They are mestizo rather than mulato, and in their mixture of adults and children represent some extended arrangement. Photographed against the backdrop of a palatial urban dwelling, back-country agricultural people framed by tropical plantings that are clearly part of luxuriant, expensive urban landscaping, they are all busy eating pieces of fruit. A solitary black guajiro in another picture stands under a peeling wall on a back street in a poor area. Painted above him on the wall is a sign photographed with incomplete text, perhaps for some kind of restaurant or food stand. It reads "y Frituras aves y Huevos Helados." The black guarijo appears to be carrying all his possessions, a small satchel in one hand, a crude larger bag slung over his shoulder.

Of note throughout is that there are few representations in the collection, aside from crowd scenes, featuring anyone of demonstrably European racial origin, peninsulare, gallego or criollo. There is certainly no North American.

On the other hand, again in one of the most famous pictures, there is American cultural presence, namely an advertisement for Evans's new Havana friend, Ernest Hemingway. It is an outside street shot, showing a movie poster, in Spanish, for a movie version of *A Farewell to Arms*, starring Gary Cooper and Helen Hayes. Similarly, as Estrada points out in a telling insight, any number of Evans's shots accompanying the Beals text could have served eloquently as illustrations for Havana scenes in *To Have and Have Not*. This is also true of an extra image not of his own photographing that Evans chose to collect and include in his final selection. It is a gruesome head-and-shoulders shot of a young man lying on the ground whose throat has been cut. An accompanying sign reads, "El ABC dara esta muerte a todos los lenguilargos" (The ABC [*abecedarios*] will give this death to those who talk). The young man, identified as Manuel Ceperos, seems to have been one of Machado's inside informers, apparently killed in retaliation by the ABC.

Finally, if Evans himself had come to grief in Havana, there would still be the textual legacy of the priceless forty-six prints entrusted for safekeeping to Hemingway. Taken back to Key West, misplaced, and forgotten, they were appropriately rediscovered in 2002 in a storeroom of Sloppy Joe's. The next year, they formed the body of a separate exhibition at the Key West Customs House. There they reminded the world nearly three-quarters of a century later what the original Beals text had shown about Walker Evans's 1933 Havana photographs and the making of an art. Somehow like Hemingway himself, Evans had figured out that the modern artist should seek to reconcile the purity of the aesthetic image with the measured, enforced, economical objectivity of the journalist. Walker Evans had gone to Cuba in search of History. Once there, he had found what he was looking for, and a style to go with it.

5

IGNACIO PIÑEIRO, GEORGE GERSHWIN, AND THE SCHILLINGER SYSTEM

What follows is a fable about the transcultural alchemy of art. Its broad purview takes in the early twentieth-century musical cultures of Cuba, the United States, and Europe. Its array of styles includes Afro-Cuban *rumba/salsita*, American jazz/Tin Pan Alley, and European modernism/popular classicism. Its topical focus will be on a specific case of the twentieth-century musical imagination, a conjunction of history and art memorialized in a work of brilliant, original, syncretic, high-modernist genius, George Gershwin's *Cuban Overture*. Its historical particulars come down to us in the concentrated image of a time, a place, a cultural moment, it might be called, involving a set of strangely coinciding cultural vectors. The first to be considered here involves the emergence in the golden age of Cuban and American broadcast radio music and popular recording of a notable Cuban artistry, on the part of various songwriters and performers, arising out of the traditions of Spanish *son/canción* and African percussion—at the time, called rumba, and in this case centered on the work of the biggest such celebrity of the era, the pioneering Afro-Cuban entertainer Ignacio Piñeiro ; the second treats a high moment of personal artistic passage into an extraordinary period of creative orchestral genius by a famous American composer, songwriter, and pianist, George Gershwin, the son of Russian Jewish immigrants, best known at the time as a modernist exponent of jazz and the popular American song. The third concerns the appearance and sudden rise to widespread influence among American composers of the era of a European-educated Russian German musical theorist and teacher of formal orchestration, Joseph Schillinger—a codifier of elements of classical harmony, counterpoint, and orchestration claiming to have achieved a complete mathematical system. So, out of such a creative synergy, in keeping with the spirit of the literary and artistic experimentalism of the era, would emerge an achievement of eclectic modernist genius. At the heart of the achievement and the genius would be the power of Cuba and the Western musical imagination.

All of this, to be sure, is a large claim to make. In the eight decades since its premiere, George Gershwin's *Cuban Overture* has never managed to outlive its conventional reputation as a musical curiosity—a brief, intense, even scintillating, but second-line set piece in the composer's canon. Put beside a parallel production of the same great creative period, such as *An American in Paris*, for example, it has always seemed Gershwin's "American in Havana," so to speak, and a poor relation at that: a cut up from "The Peanut Vendor," a popular Cuban import/jazz band favorite of the period; a cut down from Ravel's *Bolero*, conventionally invoked as its closest twentieth-century classical analogue. Usually, in studies of Gershwin's life and music, it becomes the subject of a brief, amusing chapter on a February 1932 bachelor trip to Havana in the company of the publisher Bennett Cerf and the stockbroker Daniel H. Silberberg, with a few colorful Cuban anecdotes thrown in—nearly always including the one about the fourteen- or sixteen-piece rumba band hired by the composer's friend Henry Gitelson that showed up to serenade the composer outside his room at the Hotel Almendares at four in the morning. Most such accounts then wrap themselves up with a sketch of early performance history: the work's 16 August 1932 debut, under the title "Rumba," in an all-Gershwin outdoor concert at the now vanished Lewisohn Stadium on the City College of New York campus at 138th and 139th Streets on the upper west side, overlooking Harlem; its second playing, under the permanent title, at a 1 November benefit concert by two hundred unemployed musicians at the Metropolitan Opera House, as part of the second half of a program beginning with the Franck *Symphony in D minor*—where it was further squeezed in after the *Gershwin Concerto in F* and *An American in Paris* and before a concluding orchestral medley of Gershwin songs.

The rest of the artistic history of the composition as a matter of performance and recording may be predictably recounted. Though widely known, it is nearly always relegated to popular, rather than critical regard, as brief, jazzy, colorful, exotic—a kind of sui generis orchestral bagatelle. One brings to mind Tchaikovsky's *Cappriccios Espanol* and *Italien*, Chabrier's *España*, or, yes, Ravel's *Bolero*. The *Cuban Overture* is likewise always part of the Gershwin musical catalog but barely. In performance, it is good for a dazzling concert opener or a rousing finale, perhaps even short and exuberant enough for an encore. In recording, it occupies a ten-minute spot to take up the remaining space on a recording of more familiar pieces. In classical broadcasting, it is likewise a good way to begin or wrap up the hour—not unlike, yet again, *Bolero*. In an offering of Gershwin or some set of selections in the general domain of popular classical music, it is something thrown into the mix to diversify the usual contents, but probably not enough to warrant a new purchase.

My direct purpose here, as may already be suggested, is to rescue the *Cuban Overture* from the realm of anecdote as an important Gershwin composition in its own right; but in a larger sense, it is also to put the barely ten-minute work in its modernist contexts, to see it as the production of a synthesizing musical genius at a crucial moment of artistic inspiration. Here, in its full, dangerous, throbbing, percussive and brassy allure, is Cuba in the '30s, just at the end of the "Dance of the Millions," between Machado and Batista, after the Platt Amendment and before the Mob, a time, a place, and an atmospherics. Here too is Gershwin, New York Jazz Orchestra Gershwin, *Rhapsody in Blue* or *Concerto in F* Gershwin, as modern-orchestral-genius Gershwin as any of his compositions will ever again be. Here too is the work of transatlantic experimentalist-modernist Gershwin, tightly abstract, intellectual, and almost academic in its play of structure and counterpoint, carrying itself out of Cuban rumba and salsita, American jazz and Tin Pan Alley, into an orchestral classic in the great twentieth-century European tradition of Debussy and Strauss, Ravel and Stravinsky.

To attempt to put this musically, from the shimmering free fall of its opening measures, followed by a breakneck rush into the driving rhythms and melody of the main rumba theme, George Gershwin's *Cuban Overture* is all Gershwin at his height of synthesizing and assimilating genius. A scintillating plunge of high woodwinds and marimba echo drops the reader into a pulsing stew of Afro-Caribbean rhythms and music, with the main theme and rumba line, carried by staccato trumpet, and backed by a second-theme melody of smoothly echoing horns, immediately recognizable as that of the Piñeiro classic, *Échale Salsita*; rhythm is likewise supplied by sounds and patterns immediately recognizable as those of Afro-Cuban percussion instrumentation, maracas, claves (keys/Cuban sticks), bongo drums, guiros (scraped gourds). All this is in turn played against a swirling background of melodious strings. A bluesy slow movement, introduced by solo clarinet, and reminiscent of *Rhapsody in Blue*, *Concerto in F*, or *An American in Paris*, follows in a happily characteristic set of Gershwin jazz variations—a "three-part contrapuntal episode," the composer called it in the program notes—rising to a signature climax. The entire complex artifice is then wrapped up and reprised in a sudden return to the driving main theme, this time in full classical counterpoint and orchestration. Again, the program notes are technical and specific. "The finale is a development of the preceding material in a *stretto*-like manner... [with] a coda featuring the Cuban instruments of percussion."

One is tempted to say of the *Cuban Overture* that there is nothing like it in Gershwin. Or perhaps, given the Cuban inspiration, it would be as proper to say that it is like everything in Gershwin yet completely and utterly itself. The swirl and dazzle, the patterns, rhythms, harmonies, tonalities, major and minor keys, the interplay of fast and slow movements that produce a bursting cascade play of energy, color, and excitement literally sweeping one through the first movement; the slow, sad, soulful, but jazzy harmonies that carry one through the middle section, somehow bespeaking an unappeasable melancholy; the building to a new climax, followed by the sudden breaking forth into a new, concluding, exuberantly triumphal rumba that returns one to the baseline of the program music, now charging off to repeat a previous theme, to pick up a new one, to introduce another yet, and then somehow to return them in dazzling combination: it is modernist genius in the key of Ravel, yes; Respighi, perhaps; Stravinsky at the outside; Gershwin, to be sure.

But this is getting far ahead. In the bracketing Afro-Cuban and Western classical influences described above, one cannot overstate the crucial role of the first. And in the particular instance described, neither can one understate the pivotal role of a single key figure, the black Cuban composer, musician, and bandleader, Ignacio Piñeiro, known as the father of *son*, with the latter traditionally regarded as the medium whereby African music properly entered mainstream popular musical tradition on the island. As will be noted, Gershwin may have known Piñeiro's music either by hearing it in New York or in Havana. Most surely, he knew Piñeiro's most famous composition, *Échale Salsita*, which he could not have missed during his 1932 sojourn, coinciding with the height of its radio and recording popularity. *Échale Salsita*: in vernacular translation, it roughly means "stir in" or "pour on" "the heat." Duly, along with Gershwin's employment of the new African rhythm instruments he discovered in the *son* tradition, this specific Piñeiro composition would also provide the main melody line in the overture. In so making this appropriation, he would appropriate not just the Piñeiro musical legend but the rich Cuban musical history that lay behind it. Gershwin, as he had found jazz and blues in his own homeland, had come to touch on the spirit of Afrocubanismo.

The fortunes of contemporary encounter with particular Cuban musical history were also crucial to the moment. Indeed, Gershwin's stay at the Hotel Almendares and his visits to famous entertainment venues in and around Havana could hardly have come during a more exciting period of Cuban music, with representatives, including Piñeiro himself, in the late 1920s and '30s reaching New York, it might be noted, where Gershwin may already have known something of the *rumbero* style. In Havana he got to see it straight on: the process whereby Afro-Cuban forms from the east of the island with names such as *son* and rumba had begun to displace and inscribe themselves into more traditional forms of high culture such as *canción* and *danzón*. (*Son* meant, literally, "sound"; rumba was a dance with African rhythms and native percussion instruments.) In the popular spotlight, famous hot Cuban club and hotel bands such as the Palau Brothers Hollywood Orchestra played at the Almendares; the Castro Brothers Orchestra at Hotel Nacional; Moises Simons on the Plaza Roof. Also prominent on the island scene was Justo "Don" Azpiazú's Havana Casino orchestra, having already played New York at the Broadway Palace Theater and produced a best-seller recording destined to become a jazz classic, of *El Manicero*, (*The Peanut Vendor*). The latter was an example of *son pregón*—the music of the Cuban street seller. Gershwin found himself happily alive amid the indrenching and instilling musical atmospherics of it all, no doubt including that legendary hired band showing up at four in the morning for an impromptu concert outside the composer's hotel balcony.

He seemed to save his best enjoyment, however—indeed expressing such a preference—for small, pickup groups—including one called the Septeto Nacional, featuring Ignacio Piñeiro himself, which he heard at a private party hosted by J. P. McEvoy. In an earlier incarnation, the group had also made their mark in New York in 1927. Now enormously popular on Cuban radio, their music was so stirring and ubiquitous, by some accounts, as to have allegedly had a personal George Gershwin visit to the Havana Station CMCJ to seek out further information. In other elaborations of the Havana sojourn, he is further purported to have conferred directly with Piñeiro, exchanging musical ideas and jotting down themes from the group's most popular songs. As noted earlier, what he carried back with him surely, whether by musical inscription or memory, was the indelible impression specifically of the famous composition by Piñeiro, the *son pregón* entitled *Échale Salsita*. Within months, he would be making it the entire melody line of the *Cuban Overture*. Of equal importance, however, would be his appropriative writing of a whole new percussion line. To be specific, exotic-sounding maracas, bongos, claves, guiros—hardly the stock in trade of Anglo-European classical music theory or doctrine—would form for the urban, cosmopolitan, American Gershwin a native, original, indispensable language of composition: important enough, as will be seen, to be drawn on the title page of the original score and, at a first performance, physically displayed in front of the conducting podium. These would be the secret key to the integration of the Cuban elements into the synthesizing alchemy eventuating in the original brilliance of the *Cuban Overture*. They would also have crucial results for later composition. Before the *Cuban Overture*, the African influence in Gershwin had expressed itself in jazz, blues, ragtime. After the *Cuban Overture*, founded on the experience of *son*, rumba, salsita, the pipeline went directly to Africa. It is at least possible to suggest that had there been no two weeks in Cuba in 1932, one never would have seen *Porgy and Bess* in the form it actually came to take.

George Gershwin himself in 1932 embodied a story endlessly told and retold: one of those instances of an American artist, amid the multifarious cultural influences of what Walt Whitman called "a nation of nations," on whom nothing is lost. Begin with Gershwin the assimilated Russian Jewish Tin Pan Alley genius, with influences including the Yiddish theater, vaudeville, Broadway, the popular American songbook, jazz, ragtime, the blues. Add to that golden-age American musical theater, sheet music, radio, recording, and the movies, with musical theater credits including "George White's Scandals," "Lady Be Good," "Oh, Kay!," "Strike Up the Band," "Funny Face," "Girl Crazy," and "Of Thee I Sing." Add to that individual classics with titles like "Love Walked In," "I Got Rhythm," "The Man I Love," "Someone to Watch over Me," ad infinitum. Then one may additionally contemplate *Porgy and Bess*, the most famous opera ever written by an American, the large classically influenced orchestral pieces and concertos for solo instrument, in modernist extensions of the work of such contemporaries as Rachmaninoff, Prokofiev, Ravel, Debussy. Before the *Cuban Overture*, such work already included *Rhapsody in Blue* (1924), *Concerto in F* (1925), *An American in Paris* (1928); and the *Second Rhapsody* (1931). The *Cuban Overture* would be the last large orchestral performance piece he would write in this great first creative era. Only one further composition possibly compares: the brief "I Got Rhythm" variations of 1934.

George Gershwin was a young man in a hurry. He was also a young man living on borrowed time. His period of major creative contribution spanned roughly eighteen years. He died, of a brain tumor, before he was forty. As to formal theories and structures of classical composition, in the case of the *Cuban Rhapsody*, coming near the end of his great creative orchestral period, though before *Porgy and Bess*, one cannot overstate the importance of the overarching conceptual framework known at the time as the Schillinger system. Here the reference is to Gershwin's well-documented professional immersion after his return, followed by four years of regular instruction, as a composing student of Joseph Schillinger, augmenting his myriad acquisitions of style as a popular composer with a strict classicism, itself requiring that he learn the techniques of a completely mathematical system of composition, a plan of nearly pure modernist abstraction. Though quite technical, it might be best described as what we would now call algorithmic—a linked succession of steps, frequently involving repeated operations, for solving a complex scientific, mathematical, or engineering problem. In the simplest musicological terms, that is, the Schillinger system made possible computations, even down to formulas on graph paper achieved mathematically with a slide rule—which could be transferred to the musical page to express corresponding values in melodic and harmonic intervals. The inventor, Joseph Schillinger, a Russian immigrant and musical theorist and trained at the St. Petersburg Imperial Conservatory of Music, developed a method of composition based, he claimed, on purely mathematical principles. Called, on the basis of its abstract scientific precision, the Schillinger system, it also possessed among its other merits a compactness and eminent teachability. In this, it should be noted, Gershwin was joined by other composers and prominent mainstream musicians as diverse as Benny Goodman, Glen Miller, Tommy Dorsey, and Oscar Levant. Further, it should be added, the system was hardly the lockstep set of mathematical principles disparaged by the latter—"composition in six easy steps," the dyspeptic Levant called it—foreshadowing as it did the post–World War II avant garde American experimentation of figures such as John Cage and others attempting to reduce the arts generally to scientific principles.

For the particular artist-composer in question, George Gershwin, the creative picture was manifestly rather more complex, with Schillinger turning out to have been one of many mentors, albeit in the present case a pivotal one, in a history of musical education Gershwin took very seriously as an attempt to address intricate, abstract principles of composition and orchestration. Early teachers included Charles Hambitzer, who introduced him to classical music, and Edward Kilyeni, with whom he studied theme, harmony, counterpoint, and other basics in 1915–21. More ambitious international explorations on Gershwin's part as an aspiring technical composer and orchestrator have become part of celebrity legend. In Paris, inquiries were made to Maurice Ravel as a prospective mentor; in reply, Ravel allegedly suggested that it would be best for the young American just to continue writing first-rate Gershwin as opposed to second-rate Ravel. The Russian Alexander Glazounov was more peremptory, basically saying that Gershwin still did not know enough about music to begin to study orchestral composition. With Arnold Schoenberg in Hollywood (1932–36), along with tennis games, Gershwin did study rhythm, harmony, melody, counterpoint, form, and semantics (program or story content). A widely circulated anecdote, invoked as tribute to Gershwin's intuitive genius, was Schoenberg's witty comment that probably he should be studying with Gershwin. According to the story, it occurred when he found out the size of Gershwin's Hollywood paychecks, as opposed to his own.

Thus came the final orchestration of Gershwin's popular jazz overture, based on his turbulent, primal, exotic Afro-Cuban materials through, of all things, the abstract, esoteric, Euro-American Schillinger system. Call it applied, scientific, even mathematical musical theory imposed upon a novel experiment, characteristic of a host of twentieth-century attempts across the arts—music, dance, painting, sculpture—to remake Western cultural tradition through new syntheses of the classical arts and a raw primitivism. (Two analogous European names that come immediately to mind here would be Stravinsky and Picasso; in the Cuban arts themselves of the era, one might further cite the notable examples of the composer Ernesto Lecuona and the Afro-Chinese painter Wilfredo Lam.) Or on both counts, just call it modernist genius transmuted through the alembic of the popular American musical imagination.

However one chooses to describe it in the abstract, for Gershwin, in practical terms, the encounter with Piñeiro on one hand and Schillinger on the other set in motion a kind of creative convergence of the planets. The quickly resultant concentration of the creative process down to critical mass seemed to partake of its own temporal inevitability: two weeks in Havana; two months in New York, July and August, of composition and orchestration; ten minutes, on the night of 16 August 1932, at the City College of New York Lewisohn Stadium, of pure modernist musical energy.

Of the occasion overall, Gershwin himself later wrote, "It was, I really believe, the most exciting night I have ever had. . . . 17,845 people paid to get in and just about 5,000 were at the closed gates trying to fight their way in—unsuccessfully." Within that frame, it now seems possible, perhaps, to imagine the debut performance of the one original composition presented that night—the *Cuban Overture*—and somehow re-create the thrill of genius just as surely as it is now experienced every time the work is heard or played. This, after all, was the New York of the 1920s and early 1930s, the capital of the twentieth century in the popular arts, where everything musical must have seemed possible. F. Scott Fitzgerald surely sensed it in *The Great Gatsby*. At one of Jay Gatsby's parties, he has a complete orchestra, transported out to Gatsby's West Egg mansion from the city, play a totally impossible composition, by one Vladimir Tostoff. It is entitled "The Jazz History of the World." The sense of the moment is also captured beautifully, if heartbreakingly, in a Hollywood movie biography of George Gershwin himself—where Gershwin is played by Robert Alda, but many other musical collaborators of the era are played by themselves. (The *Cuban Overture*, happily, is one of the featured performances; less felicitously rendered now is Al Jolson, singing "Swanee," in blackface.) In the final scene, at a memorial concert given just after Gershwin's death, a pianist steps onstage to give a performance of *Rhapsody in Blue*. He is a real pianist, Gershwin's friend and close collaborator, Oscar Levant. He is accompanied by Paul Whiteman's jazz orchestra, with whom the real Gershwin himself played the work in its debut performance.

The first of these scenes takes place in a 1925 novel. The second takes place in a 1945 movie. Somewhere about halfway in between, there would have been that great night at the Lewisohn in 1932. Was any particular announcement made about a new, original composition amid the program of Gershwin favorites? Was any explanation made of the work's Cuban inspiration? Was the original short title, "Rumba," expected to speak for itself? Did the audience accordingly expect some kind of quick novelty exercise in a flashy popular genre? Were they puzzled instead to hear a fairly short but highly intricate and musically challenging orchestral composition, so pointed and complete that it may have seemed to have ended barely after it began? How did they hear the scintillating first measures? How did they mark the passages in the tripartite structure? How did they respond as the concluding notes were played? We will never know any of this save something that actually did happen, by Gershwin's explicit instruction, at the point in the program just before the *Cuban Overture* was played. Actually, he had written it on the score. "Conductor's Note," it read: "The Cuban instruments should be placed right in front of the podium." Beneath, they were labeled, with little sketches of each: "claves," "bongo," "gourd," "maracas." These were duly brought before the orchestra on stage and displayed to the audience during the playing of the composition. The incident, along with accounts of the Piñeiro and Schillinger influences, would become part of the *Cuban Overture*'s musicological history. Of Gershwin's particular joy in his Cuban classic, the gesture still seems to speak volumes beyond. At the forefront of its great cosmopolitan debut, Gershwin wished to honor the simple island instruments at its elemental beating heart.

6

THE SECRET LIFE OF RICKY RICARDO

Somewhere around the end of 1957, Fidel Castro became the most famous living Cuban in the world. Before that, the title was held by a US show business celebrity costarring in the nation's favorite TV comedy show, and doing so largely, it was assumed by most viewers, by playing himself as a Cuban. An immigrant singer and bandleader, he was a dark, charming, gorgeously handsome Latin male, with a square jaw, blazing white teeth, flashing eyes, gleaming hair, a volatile temperament, and a tendency, when excited, to comic mispronunciation. Some twenty-odd years after his arrival in the United States, he was famous as the husband of Lucille Ball, America's favorite comedy actress, and her costar on the aforementioned comedy show, *I Love Lucy*. On the show he was known as Ricky Ricardo. Offstage he was known as Desi Arnaz. Those familiar with his show business background knew that he had enjoyed an earlier career in theater and movies and previous to that as a musical performer with Xavier Cugat before going on to found his own Latin orchestra. In Cuba, the homeland he left when he was sixteen, he was remembered as Desiderio Alberto Arnaz y de Acha III, the celebrity son of a family of great social and political importance in the easternmost province of the island—with its city, Santiago de Cuba, so far from Havana as to be a grand and historical place with its own distinct life and culture.

In his adoptive country, his rise to fame and fortune perhaps could not have seemed more an abstract or epitome of the immigrant dream. Having come here as a young political refugee, he served in the army in World War II, pursued a highly successful entertainment career in music, stage, and film, married a glamorous Hollywood star, parlayed the celebrity marriage into the most successful TV domestic situation comedy of the era, and grew rich as an entertainment business entrepreneur; he was an American success story. In the broadest sense this was true. For those who knew the complexities of Cuban identity then and now, in his secret soul he remained Cuban with personal and cultural dimensionalities no amount of fictionalized acquired identity could assuage. Ricky Ricardo was a Cuban created by mid-twentieth-century American TV. Desi Arnaz was a Cuban carrying together at once the mid-twentieth-century pride and sorrows of a complex Cuban-American history. There was a tremendous difference. What that came to humanly entail within the fabric of a life is the subject of this essay.

An insightful 2008 feature profile by Liane Hansen of National Public Radio provides a set of working outlines. Ricky was from Havana; Desi was from Santiago. Ricky immigrated to New York; Desi to Miami. Ricky married Lucy McGillicuddy; Desi married Lucille Ball. Ricky's wife wanted desperately to be in show business; Desi's wife was already a successful radio and film actress. Ricky eventually owned a nightclub; Desi eventually owned television and movie studios.

Ricky was from Havana. Few, if any, current viewers of reruns—after decades of embargo and travel prohibitions—would now know what that meant. During the 1951–57 period of the show's greatest popularity, American television audiences would have had quite vivid and highly developed ideas of what that meant. Generally speaking, these years were also those of the last golden age of Havana decadence, pleasure, and corruption, at the end of a long reign of American corporate bankrolls, political stooge ambassadors, client political strongmen, and celebrity gangster ownership of a vast empire of earthly pleasures. Glamorous hotels flourished, the Nacional, the Sevilla-Biltmore, the Capri—and later, toward the end, the Havana Hilton and the Riviera—along with their thriving casinos and dazzling floor shows, most of them run by the US Mob in lucrative partnership with the Batista government. Exotic bars, restaurants, and night clubs, racetracks, and gambling emporiums were joined by elegant houses of prostitution and theaters featuring famous sex shows. *Havana Nocturne*, the popular historian T. J. English has called it in a recent book: "Neon, glitter, the mambo, and sex." Music was everywhere; Latin orchestras were the rage, with famous bandleaders including Xavier Cugat and Pérez Prado. Booze was cheap and endless, frequently in glorious tropical concoctions. "Mi mojito en La Bodequita, Mi Daiquiri en el Floridita," Ernest Hemingway is said to have written on the wall of one of his favorite watering spots. The art deco Bacardi building was a downtown landmark.

Desi Arnaz's grandfather, in fact, had been one of the founding directors of Bacardi. Only that did not happen in Havana. That happened in

Santiago de Cuba, the old and equally historical city, nearly eight hundred miles away at the far eastern end of the island, where the Bacardi and Arnaz and Acha families were from. There it was that Desi Arnaz, born in 1917, grew up, in a place traditionally known as the home of a Cuban culture and people in many ways so different from Havana that it is hard to think of them as being on the same island. Though both were presided over at the time by old gallego/peninsulare and criollo elites, Havana still remained the western, European, Atlantic City of Cuba; Santiago was the eastern, Afro-Indian, Caribbean city of the island. There, on the landscape of the old province itself once called Oriente, with the movement of freed and escaped Africans to the deeply wooded and mountainous tropical landscapes of the region, in the wake of the 1791 Santo Domingo rebellion, the great nineteenth-century slavery struggles had begun, and with them the broader debate over Spanish power, colonial rule, native independence, national identity. There, with the religious assimilations of African and native traditions of life, had arisen the cult of Santeria and the larger cultural legacy called *Afrocubanismo*. There it was, that the contestation over the meaning of Cubanness thus came to be between eastern planters, African slaves, freed blacks, impoverished white farmers, and urban workers one the one side, and western peninsulares and criollo elites on the other. There, with Céspedes and the freeing of his slaves in the cause of universal human liberty, and the issuing of the *Grito de Yara*, which called for complete freedom from colonialism along with gradual and indemnified emancipation of slavery, had begun the first great military struggle for national independence, the 1868–78 Ten Years War. There, the struggle continued to renew itself, with the rise of new revolutionary leaders, not least the mixed-race hero Antonio Maceo and his sainted mother Mariana Grajales Coello. There again, in 1895, beginning with the early death in battle of the returned patriot-hero José Martí, had broken out the final phase of what came to be called the great War of Cuban Independence, with the revolutionary belligerents, now the legendary Mambi army, this time equipped with a better organized civil organization and a more aggressive military strategy under such skilled leaders as Maceo, Gómez, and García. Here too, in the new, concurrent, but largely separate war, this time of a US colonial opportunism—called by Cubans to this day la Intervención—came the landings and major battles of the Americans, the heralded conquests of the strategic heights surrounding

Santiago harbor, including Las Guasimas, Siboney, and San Juan Hill, and shortly thereafter the naval action resulting in the complete destruction of the Spanish fleet.

From this would ensue the Americans taking over their own new imperialist governance of the island, albeit, as with the Spanish, from the other end, administered from the old colonial capital of Havana—in the palace, in fact, of the old Capitanes Generales on the Plaza de Armas. Most humiliating in the east would remain a ninety-nine-year lease on a naval base at a fine anchorage called Guantanamo. Accordingly, throughout the twentieth century, Oriente would remain a hotbed of nationalist sentiment and thereby a peculiar idea of Cubanness founded on distinct ideas of resistance to foreign influences of culture and ideology. As is well known, Santiago was to become the site of Fidel Castro's first attack on the Batista regime, with the 26 November 1953 revolutionary assault on the Moncada Barracks. Three years later in Oriente would come the *Granma* invasion, initiating the anti-Batista guerrilla campaigns in the Sierra Madre that would culminate in the 1959 final victory of the revolution.

So in this eastern seat of Cuban history the grandly named Desiderio Alberto Arnaz y de Acha III, himself rather grandly descended from an Oriente family of wealth, holdings, and political influence—albeit at the time of increasingly complex affiliation—was born and spent his childhood and teenage years. His paternal grandfather had been a physician, serving as a Cuban revolutionary medical officer for Theodore Roosevelt during the 1898 war. His father, educated as a pharmacist in Atlanta, became the mayor of Santiago, serving for nine years in this quite powerful position amid the shifting vectors of early twentieth-century island politics. As noted, his maternal grandfather had already gained wealth in equal measure as one of the three founding directors of the Bacardi Rum Company. Accordingly, Arnaz spent a privileged youth and early young adulthood, enjoying family properties including a handsome *palacio* in the city and a vacation home on the Bay—where he barely avoided being caught by his grandfather, he happily recalled in his autobiography, in his first sexual escapade with the compliant teenage daughter of the cook. This all came to an end, however, in the 1933 coup of the sergeants under Fulgencio Batista, with Alberto Arnaz, having for years managed to navigate the terrain of Oriente high elective politics during the Machado dictatorship, and recently gaining election to the Cuban Congress, suddenly considered of uncertain loyalties. Their properties confiscated, the family, including Desi, was forced to flee to the United States by way of Key West, eventually settling in Miami. Held in prison for six months because of Machado associations, Alberto was at length freed and able to make a hasty, ad hoc departure through Puerto Rico to join them. A proud and dutiful son, Desi shortly made a perilous return to the island as a teenager, to have his father's papers cleared officially in Havana. It was a Cuban matter, after all.

From there the story took on a new set of American turns every bit as colorful as the foregoing times in Cuba. Finishing secondary school in Miami, Desi was an athlete at St. Patrick's Jesuit High. Among his favorite classmates and teammates was a boy named Alfred Francis Capone, known to the family as Sonny. In his autobiography, Desi would recall phoning his friend, instead getting the father, recently returned from Alcatraz, on the other end. What he would remember, he said, was the strange, highly pitched voice. Capone seemed to approve of Desi. Desi is said to have returned the favor with the colorful casting and portrayal of the gangster chief in what would eventually become the first great syndicated show of Desilu Productions, *The Untouchables*. It also seems to have earned him the interest of J. Edgar Hoover's FBI, where the series became the subject of an extensive file.

In Santiago, Desi had grown up immersed in music at the place where it is said to come from in Cuba before it migrates to Havana, where it goes to become famous. His lifelong theme as a musician and as a celebrity entertainer, *Babalú*, is testament to its own origins in Afro-Cuban and Caribbean legend. It is a song, it is a dance, it is a virtuoso solo conga drum performance, in its popular renditions, as written by the modern composer Margarita Lecuona, accompanied by a full Cuban orchestra. Babalú Ayé is a god of Santeria. It begins as religious invocation with the singer contemplating a statue of the god and requesting that seventeen candles be lit in the shape of a cross and that a cigar and aguardiente be brought as offerings:

> *Babalú/Babalú/Babalú ayé*
> *Babalú ayé*
> *Babalú*
> *Ta empezando lo velorio*

Que le hacemo' a Babalú
Dame diez y siete velas
Pa' ponerla' en cruz.
Dame un cabo de tabaco mayenye
Y un jarrito de aguardiente,
Dame un poco de dinero mayenye
Pa' que me de la suerte

In the chorus, endlessly repeated, he prays for good luck, the love of his woman, and the god's special attention to them as opposed to presumably undeserving others:

Quiere pedi
Que mi negra me quiera
Que tenga dinero
Y que no se muera
Av! Vo le quiero pedi a Babalú 'na negra muy
santa como tu que no tenga otro negro
Pa' que no se fuera/Yo.

In greatly transformed English, Desi turned it into a wild ritual song of tropical worship:

Jungle drums were madly beating,
In the glare of eerie lights;
While the natives kept repeating
Ancient jungle rites.
All at once the dusky warriors began to
Raise their arms to skies above
And a native then stepped forward to chant to his Voo-
doo Goddess of love.
Ah!

In the chorus, again with great liberties to the earthy Spanish, it becomes a passionate lament of lost romantic rapture:

Great Babalu!

I'm so lost and forsaken.
Ah, great Babalu!
Bring back the love you've taken.
You can restore all the dreams that once were mine
If only you'll use some mystic sign.
Ah! Great Babalu!
Bring her back to me.
Ah!

In Miami, music became Desi's passion and his choice of career. Rising quickly as a singer-entertainer, with conga drums, or *tumbadoras*, his specialty, he joined the popular Xavier Cugat orchestra. Then, with permission of the leader, he formed his own orchestra, in something of what we would now call a Cugat cover band. Desi's novelty, for which he quickly gained celebrity, was a new popular music and dance form itself called the conga, frequently involving performers and the audience forming a line in a long, shuffling, rhythmic carnival march. Soon, he had outgrown Miami.

It is at this point that we may briefly return to the opening outline. According to Hansen, Ricky Ricardo was a Cuban in New York. This turned out to be at least briefly the case for Desi as well, with his casting in a Broadway college show, on the model of *Good News*, set on an American campus and entitled *Too Many Girls*. Desi played a hunky Argentine football star, Manuelito, recruited to play for the college. On acting merits alone, he is said to have stolen the show. Nor were his musical talents wasted. Director George Abbott had the musical writing team of Richard Rodgers and Lorenz Hart configure the first-act finale, "Look Out"—a stirring football march, mentioning prominent college teams of the day—into a dance number joining the entire cast in a conga line. Walter Winchell called the gimmick "the Desi chain."

It was also at this point, however, that the life of Desi Arnaz quickly took one of its most radical and permanent shifts: from New York to California. *Too Many Girls* was contracted to be made into a movie version. Desi was signed to the cast in a reprise of his Broadway role. With this, he once and for all became a Cuban in Hollywood.

There, working at the RKO complex on the Hollywood film version, he met the female star. Her name was Lucille Ball. Known at the time as "the Queen of the B Pictures," she had established herself as a movie figure of a certain glamour and celebrity, although not reaching the stardom to which she aspired. The standard story casts this as the dazzled Latin American newcomer's meeting with the Hollywood woman assigned to play the part of the movie ingénue. "Miss Ball?" he is alleged to have inquired. (In some versions, seeing her from a distance, he is also described as exclaiming "Watta honka woman!") "Why don't you call me Lucille," she replied, "and I'll call you Dizzy."

He called her Lucy. Within a year, presumably she had gotten the "Desi" pronunciation part right because by then she was also, after an elopement to Connecticut, calling him her husband. On the other hand, the phrasing of the news broadcast announcing the match remained telling: "Actress Lucille Ball" had married "band leader Desi Arnaz." As telling was entertainment gossip about their choice of names for a new place to live, called Desilu. The roles they would play, so it seemed, had already been scripted for life.

Lucy resumed her career in popular movies. Desi tried to pursue his own Hollywood acting ambitions. After World War II began, having worked in a series of forgettable movies, he tried to enlist in the US armed forces. Initially rejected, he took one more film role, where he gave a moving dramatic performance—maybe the best of his career. Now it is hard to remember that this was before he became Ricky. To viewers at the time, it must have come as a small gift of revelation. The movie was the 1943 classic of doomed heroism, *Bataan*. As part of a grab bag detachment of thirteen Americans thrown together on a hopeless patrol mission to delay the advancing Japanese, Desi plays a Mexican American California National Guardsman, Pvt. Felix Ramirez. He knows they are all going to die. Nonetheless, he does his duty to the end, refusing to reveal his serious illness to the detachment commander. Amid a cast including Robert Taylor, Thomas Mitchell, Robert Walker, and Lloyd Nolan, Desi Arnaz plays his "outsider" role with immense pathos and dignity. After this, Desi succeeded in being taken into the army but remained stateside, serving as USO entertainer for hospital wounded and organizing Hollywood starlets to visit them and serve refreshments.

After a 1945 discharge from the real army as sergeant, Desi found a new Latin star competing for attention on the Hollywood movie scene, Ricardo Montalban. He accordingly returned to front-line nightclub bandleading work, at Ciro's in Los Angeles, and at the Copacabana in New York. As the *Babalu* guy again, Desi seemed willing to become a caricature of himself, even down to one last film, from the novelty song, "Cuban Pete." Marital troubles had sprung up during the war years and continued during Arnaz's new travels with his orchestra, attributed to Latin American male womanizing. Lucy meanwhile mined a newly emerging talent for physical slapstick in widely popular films such as *Sorrowful Jones* with Bob Hope and *The Fuller Brush Girl* with Eddie Albert. On this basis, during the final late 1940s heyday of radio shows, Lucy, having acquired a reputation as a comic actress, was offered a weekly program, about a married couple, entitled *My Favorite Husband*.

Her popularity in the role of a humorously addled wife led to an offer to develop the show as a television series. Meanwhile, she and Desi had seemed to find both happiness and success as a show-business couple on a vaudeville tour. For the TV show, she insisted that the husband of the zany spouse be played by Desi. Given the intimate visual quality of the new medium, not to mention the domestic setting, there arose a certain anxiety about an Anglo-European redhead married to a swarthy, temperamental Latin—almost a scenario, by the racial views of the era, for something like miscegenation. The worry was unwarranted. Lucy and Desi quickly found the secret. They created themselves as a couple playing themselves as characters in a TV show about a marriage.

Or, to return to the Liane Hansen PBS outline, Desi Arnaz became Ricky Ricardo and Lucille Ball became Lucy Ricardo. To be exact, the New York Cuban nightclub bandleader Ricky Ricardo married Lucy McGillicuddy, a hare-brained, red-haired, Irish hoyden. The world of Desi Arnaz and Lucille Ball became the world of Ricky and Lucy Ricardo, along with the funny, but rather dim and dyspeptic neighbors Fred and Ethel Mertz—played, for the record, by William Frawley and Vivian Vance, who from the outset disliked each other with almost as much energy as Desi and Lucy spent trying to stay in love. The dynamics of the show, real and imagined, played out as a ceaselessly volatile chemistry of tempers. The sheer loudness of it was off the chart. At the source of the noise, of course, was the battle of the sexes: sputtering, exasperated men dealing with plots hatched by conniving, dizzy women.

One does not want to make too much of this in the context of popular American golden-age radio and TV. Predictable plots were played to predictable gendered types: Fibber McGee and Molly; George Burns and Gracie Allen; eventually Archie and Edith Bunker—the woman was the dingbat. As often, with the frequently clueless male, she could be the sensible one, the stabilizing maternal influence: Harriet Nelson, June Cleaver, Margaret Anderson. The shows were marital and connubial. As this one wore on, however, something happened. With all the noise and pratfalls and howling arguments, something got oddly gendered about the TV Lucy. Even in the controversial late periods of the show with the actually pregnant Lucy going through on-screen, relatively late-life childbearing, she suddenly seemed too old for Ricky. The red-haired bombshell became increasingly sexless, even mannish. Meanwhile, in the outbreaks of temper, the signature meltdowns that accompanied every episode of the show, Ricky strangely got remade as a gender figure as well. The playing of the volatile Latin male with the machine-gun Cuban Spanish, the chattering, the grammatical incompetence and mispronunciation seemed to get something childish and even feminized about it. Lucy became the marital schemer; Ricky became the irrational, emotional partner in the match.

On the show, this is what became of the passionate marriage of Desi and Lucy, by all accounts a genuine Hollywood love match—in the glamour era of the '50s newspapers and gossip columns, the popular movie and TV magazines, the handsome Cuban bandleader and the sexy redhead Queen of the Bs. As the marriage itself evolved, even this now seemed to be negatively imaged in the '50s TV sitcom. Ricky's Lucy wanted to be in show business. Desi's Lucy was meanwhile making her way toward a new, composite concept of Hollywood status—stage, screen, and television celebrity, now coupled with heavy business involvement—that would make her one of the most powerful and established figures in the American entertainment industry. Having navigated the evolutions of twentieth-century American popular media while rising higher toward stardom, she eventually came to reign over large portions of it both as grande dame and as a studio executive, in the Desilu Corporation founded with her husband during their early days of marriage, with a string of well-known and lucrative hits. On the TV show, during the sixth and final season, Ricky became part owner of the fictional Tropicana nightclub, where he had been the star performer. He renames it the Club Babalu. In Hollywood, Desi got to own, briefly, half of the entertainment conglomerate that, in nearly all accounts, he had founded on a notably independent and forward-looking corporate model. Somewhere at that point, one imagines that both the show and the marriage just got merged into the business end of it, and at the business end of it the relationship between Desi Arnaz and Lucille Ball broke under the strain of it all. In the late 1950s after the end of *I Love Lucy*, darkness set in. Out of the house, Desi had extramarital affairs. At Desilu, there were what the industry likes to call "creative disagreements." In the end, Lucille Ball is alleged to have called her husband, besides a drunk and a philanderer, a spic, a greaser, a wetback.

Such was the story of Desi Arnaz and Lucille Ball who played themselves again once they were no longer Ricky Ricardo and Lucy McGillicuddy. While the relationship briefly maintained a stable public face, it played out in a set of evolutions—corporate in the fullest sense of the term—that could only end badly. The real Desi Arnaz continued to be touted—as noted above, not without justification—as the distinctly un–Ricky Ricardo–like brain, a highly respected media executive known for business acumen, the organizing genius of Desilu, in many ways revolutionizing television with the studio's new breakthrough dramatic series, *The Untouchables*. By 1957 the studio bought RKO. In the 1960 divorce, the couple split interests. Lucy bought Desi out in 1962. In 1967 Desilu was sold to Gulf and Western. Meanwhile, Lucille Ball became the ex-business partner who exploited the full potentialities of the Desilu empire, producing hit programs as diverse as the *Dick Van Dyke Show*, the *Andy Griffith Show*, *Make Room for Daddy*, the *Real McCoy*, and many others.

The breakup—of the marriage and the business—besides deriving from the kind of sexual infidelity that somehow, someway, always managed to make itself inconceivable for all the TV ups and downs of the New York TV Ricardos also had its other secret curse in booze. To put it directly, Desi Arnaz, throughout his life a heavy drinker, evolved throughout the marriage into an alcoholic of the sort that partners just stop trying to deal with. Even in the late-stage development, to be sure, he remained at what Alcoholics Anonymous calls the social or professional high end: not a derelict, not a lunatic, not a danger to society; just the kind of person who gets drunk to the point—talking too much at the table, telling the same old stories, passing out somewhere around bedtime—where family members say they just can't do it anymore. After a considerable period of being on his own, even that façade broke. Picked up by the police outside a well-known Hollywood bordello, he was described in the *Los Angeles*

Times as "a common drunk." In good Hollywood fashion, his driver was dispatched to come get him.

At this point, the secret life of Ricky Ricardo began to move inexorably toward its conclusion. In the early 1960s, he quickly remarried. He stayed active in the entertainment business with various projects, including a TV musical special on which he performed with his children, Luci and Desi Jr. In 1976, to promote his newly published autobiography, he served as a guest host on *Saturday Night Live*, again accompanied by Desi Jr. The program included parody segments of both *I Love Lucy* and *The Untouchables*. He recited Louis Carroll's "The Jabberwocky" with a heavily caricatured Cuban accent. He sang "Babalu" and "Cuban Pete." The show ended with a conga line of cast members snaking its way around the studio.

In 1986 Desi Arnaz was diagnosed with lung cancer. He died on 2 December. One of his last telephone calls is said to have been from Lucille Ball. They said "I love you," one last time back and forth. She supposedly concluded the conversation by saying, "All right, honey. I'll talk to you later." Ricky Ricardo was married to Lucy McGillicuddy. Desi Arnaz was, or so it seemed, still married to Lucille Ball.

One wishes to imagine alternative scripts less sadly irreconcilable in art and life. Remarkably in the present case, regarding the strange double life of Desi Arnaz at the height of the 1951–57 *I Love Lucy* era, this has actually been done by the well-known fiction writer Oscar Hijuelos—himself the son of Cuban immigrants who came to America between the wars and a novelist who has specialized in re-creations of the New York somewhere between the one that must have greeted the young Desi Arnaz and the one imagined for Ricky Ricardo—in a number of works frequently written across the boundaries of language, attempting to honor the vanished worlds of both early to mid-twentieth-century Cuban immigrant New York and of the vibrant life and culture of the island during the same era. The particular novel is entitled *The Mambo Kings Play Songs of Love*, which attempts to re-create the family and cultural life of the vibrant Cuban community of upper Manhattan, centered on the west 90s to upper 120s, on the fringes of Harlem, in the region extending from Riverside Park to Washington Heights. It further explores in particular the Cuban musical scene of the era, extending from George Gershwin's 1930s orchestral popularization of rumba in the *Cuban Overture* to contemporary Latin American musical figures of the time including Xavier Cugat and Pérez

Prado. The central figures are two immigrant musician brothers, Oscar and Nestor Castillo, trying to make it with their band on the nightclub and recording scene. Their countryman, Desi Arnaz, is at height of his career. *I Love Lucy*, in which he costars, is the top TV show. But they still see Desi/Ricky as a bandleader, a club owner, a Cuban fellow artist influential in music circles. To them, Desi/Ricky is a living Cuban embodiment of the American Dream. But throughout the novel, he is more than a symbolic idealization. Indeed, in the very first scene, a young Cuban boy runs to a next door apartment to awaken his Uncle Oscar Castillo—old, fat, and dying from a life of sex and drinking and unhealthy Cuban food—from his drunken stupor long enough to look again at an umpteenth rerun of the TV moment when he and Nestor have actually gotten the chance to appear in a guest shot on the *I Love Lucy* show as aspiring new immigrant musicians, fresh from Cuba—in this case cousins of Desi—where they get to play in a first scene of arrival at the famous Ricardo apartment; and a second, at Ricky's club, with the band, where they get to perform Nestor's signature song, "The Beautiful Maria of My Soul."

In the novel, this has eventuated from a personal encounter at a grimy, obscure Cuban music club, where the great man has dropped by to survey the talent, perhaps indulge in a little island nostalgia. Lucy is with him. In person, the two of them seem to be quietly happy in their marriage. Desi is an important man without self-importance. A powerful influence in the music industry, he is pleased to give fellow Cubans a good word. He behaves with generosity, sincerity, quiet humility. They address him with guajiro/peasant deference appropriate to the aristocratic peninsulare/criollo from Oriente. He responds with quiet *dignidad*/dignity. Lucy, in the extended scene, radiates star power but also comes off as gracious, kind, and, above all, patient. Desi and Lucy accompany Oscar and Nestor home to their loud, gritty immigrant-neighborhood apartment after the show for a late night Cuban meal of beans, pork, rice, plantains. The Kings eventually get to go on the Lucy show. That is, they are *in fact* invited to Hollywood and participate in the filming of their own guest appearance on *I Love Lucy*, where they play recently arrived Cuban kinsmen of Ricky Ricardo who visit his home and later make a musical appearance in his nightclub show. Their featured song, "The Beautiful Maria of My Soul," is one that Nestor, now with a New York Cuban immigrant wife and two children, has written about a former love from his youth on the island whom he has never been able to forget.

The experience is the highlight of their careers, possibly even the event of their lives. It is also an abstract or epitome of the larger imaginative project. Two Cuban brothers from Pinar del Rio, Oscar and Nestor Castillo, gain modest celebrity as Havana musicians and move to New York, where they spend the rest of the lives as part of the immigrant life and culture of the city but mostly with real, major success as performers and recording artists just slightly beyond their grasp. Their great moment comes with their appearance on *I Love Lucy*. Soon after, Nestor is killed in an automobile crash on winter roads outside New York. The novel then relates the later story of Oscar as he sinks, after years of hard living and dissipation, into old age and decline. Told from the point of view of Nestor's son, Eugenio, a young Americanized, college-educated Cuban American attempting to reimagine the lives and histories of the Mambo Kings from a Cuba he no longer knows, as well as the earlier New York life he must somehow reconstruct from his relationship with Oscar, the uncle, in old age moving into a dismal, run-down tenement where he awaits his inevitable death. At the end the work thus comes full circle, weaving the multiple narratives of the past into the imagined present.

As is happily, if infrequently, the case with great novels, the movie gets nearly all of this brilliantly. The Mambo Kings, Oscar and Nestor Castillo, are Armand Assante and Antonio Banderas. The meeting with Desi Arnaz occurs in a nightclub, where he has come with his agent. In the movie version, Lucy is not present. It is Ricky's happy time with his compatriots, and a moment for him to give attention to his fellow immigrant strivers. He introduces himself. (It is the only instance, to my knowledge, in an English-language setting, when the name Desi Arnaz has been properly pronounced in Spanish.) In the movie, as in the book, the Desi character behaves with quiet grace, generosity, magnanimity. You can see the Mambo Kings' eyes popping out of their heads. Desi goes home with them. He eats a Cuban meal. The wife, the baby, all the neighbors come out at the end, an impromptu middle-of-the-night fan gathering in the middle of the street.

The movie/TV splice of the *I Love Lucy* show appearance is a miracle of *Zelig-* or *Forrest-Gump*–like seamless integration, only better in every way—visual, dramatic, historical, emotional. The movie is in gorgeous period color. The re-creation of the TV episode is in black and white. The *I Love Lucy* video is in flickering 1950s kinescope. The movie reproduction of the guest visit is fitted into the contemporary recording of a Lucy routine in one of the episodes of the show where she is trying to make conversation. The boys, who speak only Spanish—sitting on the couch, endlessly smiling and nodding, hilariously crossing and recrossing their legs in unison—pretend to understand. Everything one does, the other does. The physical comedy is as good as anything that ever happened on *I Love Lucy*. The ensuing musical appearance on the show goes beautifully. The Assante and Banderas characters blossom into figures who could be romantic actors in a movie. It is a beautiful memory for everyone, the young Cuban musicians achieving their immigrant dream playing Nestor's "The Beautiful Maria of my Soul" on the *I Love Lucy* show. As importantly, the movie-created Desi seems to have made peace for a moment with the TV-created Ricky. Or, rather, it is the imagined moment when the real Desi was able to remember that he was Cuban. But there is more. He is played in the movie, as well as in the television interlude—that is, as both Desi and Ricky—by his own son, who is well known like his sister, Luci, because their mother actually carried them and they were born on the show while they were being born into the real world.

"Lucy, I'm home!" These remain some of the most familiar words of golden-age TV, uttered by Desi Arnaz playing Ricky Ricardo, like the character himself, somehow suspended between worlds, fact and fiction, art and life. In 2008, Felix Contreras did a US National Public Radio musical feature piece on Desi Arnaz entitled *"Mr. Babalu" Next Door*, reminding us that Ricky Ricardo may have been a fictional character, but he played very *real* music. As it turns out, Desi Arnaz's son and daughter now themselves have recently promoted the vision of their father in his own musical career in a show called *Babalú—A Tribute to the Music of Desi Arnaz*. The thrust in both cases is to recall a certain kind of musical genius—an art, so to speak, that found its true home—in being a certain kind of Cuban from Santiago de Cuba by way of Havana, a young peninsulare/criollo simultaneously and deeply immersed as only a true artist can be in the spirit of Afrocubanismo so central to any understanding of the life and culture of the island in literature, music, and the arts.

To be sure, as pointed out by Contreras, it is now hard to figure out where the *Babalu* musical legend itself fits into the strange mix of fact and fiction threading itself through the intertwined identities of Desi Arnaz and Ricky Ricardo. Written, as noted earlier, by Cuban composer Margarita Lecuona, it was first recorded by Cuban vocalist Miguelito Valdés in 1941—and among fans of more traditional Latin music, Valdés remained the real Mr. Babalu. Further, even when Desi Arnaz sang it in his early musical career, he changed the English lyrics to those quoted earlier, tailoring them to Cuban floor-show American audiences and making them have little or nothing to do with the cultural intricacies of the strange cult of an Afro-Cuban Santeria god. When in turn, it became the signature song of Ricky Ricardo, it was further homogenized and abridged to '50s New York TV nightclub fare, with "Mr. Babalú" a pale, domesticated version of his earlier musical self and the song a quick musical novelty feature to break the slapstick and briefly showcase the talents of the costar. As noted above, eventually it became just a plot reference, a piece of TV trivia. In its sixth and final season, Ricky becomes part owner of the fictional Tropicana nightclub, where he was a regular performer, and renames it Club Babalú.

If Ricky Ricardo was surely not the original Mr. Babalú, one wonders at least how close the original Desi Arnaz got to it. What was Mr. Babalú like with his song, at least, back before he was Ricky? Fortunately, almost magically one wants to say—appropriate to this figure who also so adeptly navigated for so many years American entertainment technologies—we now have our own technologies of video engineering, concurrently historical and imaginative recovery literally at our fingertips. The technology is called YouTube. The YouTube item is a 1946 film short *Desi Arnaz and His Orchestra*. It is a complete performance of *Babalú* and a ghostly reminder of the stunning beauty, vitality, and true entertainment genius of the young Cuban, not quite yet thirty. One recognizes it also as the source of the astonishingly beautiful photograph chosen for the cover of the autobiography, poised over the drums. Accordingly, the camera here truly acts as a magical instrument of the sort that untutored peoples fear will capture their souls. Here, indeed strangely, almost magically, one does feel for all time the impress of his genius, his personality, his energy, his youth. In the beauty of the person and the joy of the performer, we do actually see someone, for a shining, youthful moment, eternally blessed by the great island gods.

7

GOOD NEIGHBOR BATISTA

Diaz, Machado, Gómez, Ibarra, Perón, Trujillo, Duvalier, Somoza, Stroessner, Pinochet, Castillo-Armas, Batista: for the better part of the twentieth century, US policy makers held their noses and cozied up with politically useful tyrants in Latin America. Somewhere back in junior high civics, most of us knew they were the neighborhood thugs; but at least they were *our* neighborhood thugs. At the height of the charade, we actually called it the Good Neighbor policy. Now little known—or at least little remembered—is the bizarre local interlude when one such figure also enjoyed domestic notoriety as the neighbor just down the street. To be exact, from 1944 to 1948, and then off and on again during the 1950s, even after he had reassumed the Cuban dictatorship in 1952, Fulgencio Batista was the good neighbor who made his home at 139 Halifax Avenue in Daytona Beach, Florida. As late as 1956, the city held a Batista appreciation day, complete with a parade, banquets, and toasts. In 1957, presumably in gratitude and happy memory, the dictator and his wife in turn announced to a visiting Florida delegation the eventual bequest—with a phrasing still carefully noted as "a gift to the city and people of Daytona Beach"—of the family residential properties, along with the couple's personal acquisitions of Cuban art. Today, the properties are no longer recognizable as such, with the original sites occupied by new construction. Meanwhile, trailing the increasingly shadowed vestiges of their place in history and memory, the Batista art treasures themselves remain there as the centerpiece of a museum collection unrivaled outside the island for its cultural value and beauty—at once the less than savory legacy of a community's eager embrace of a despised tyrant and the glittering cultural reward of his civic benefaction.

Various accounts are given of how Batista went from being absolute dictator of Cuba to being a homeowner in Daytona Beach. As to events on the Cuban side, the generally accepted explanation is that, having held power for more than a decade behind a series of presidential stand-ins, he had miscalculated the outcome of the 1944 election, somehow allowing his handpicked candidate, Carlos Saladrigas Zayas, to lose to an old rival, Ramón Grau San Martín, and deemed it best to leave the country for a while. Often cited as equally important, however, was a parallel development in the dictator's personal life, namely a desire to end his first marriage, to Elisa Godinez Gomez, mother of his three children, and begin his second, to his twenty-year-old mistress, Marta Fernandez Miranda, by whom he would father four more.

If so, this was duly accomplished through the making of a new domestic life in Florida, albeit one that was not without its own residential complications. The American part of the narrative indeed begins with a story that his original choice of destination, Palm Beach, made it clear that, rich ex-dictator or no, a new resident of mixed Spanish, black, Indian, and Chinese racial ancestry would be decidedly unwelcome. According to this account, Batista and Marta, still his wife-to-be at that juncture, just pointed their car northward on US Highway 1 and chose Daytona Beach as the first place where people seemed cordial and welcoming. What is known for certain is that he quickly bought a typical large 1920s stone and stucco house on a riverside lot—as can still be discerned from dwellings of similar vintage along Halifax Avenue, a place of size and substance, but not of particular ostentation—and settled in as an accepted member of the community. His next-door neighbor was the retired industrialist and automotive pioneer Ransom Eli Olds, who had, among other things, put the town on the map at the turn of the century as an automobile mecca with its wide, flat beaches especially suited to speed racing. Presumably, they got on well enough for Batista eventually to be given the opportunity to buy the adjacent Olds property and riverfront acreage. Meanwhile, according to a *Time* magazine article of 12 April 1948, the resident dictator became known among fellow residents of the municipality for his brisk early morning exercise rowing on the river in a nine-foot dinghy, his tennis at the Daytona Beach Bath and Tennis Club, his twice or thrice weekly movie outings, and his occasional speeches to the Rotary Club. Driving about town on his own, he was said to have become a familiar figure in his yellow convertible. On one occasion, mistaken for a cab driver, he was even said to have given some visitors a friendly lift. Meanwhile, he also seems to have found contemplative time enough for the composition of a book attributed to his authorship while there, *Sombras de América* (*Shad-*

ows of America)—an account of his earlier life and political career. To be sure, as noted by the article, political travels took him frequently to meetings around the state—Orlando, Tampa, Fort Pierce—with fellow exiles, as well as to New York, where his hotel of choice was the swanky Waldorf Astoria. Still, it was with a distinct sense of folksy familiarity (not to mention a cheery nod from conservative publisher Henry Luce) that the piece headlined itself—the occasion being his surprise election in absentia to the Cuban legislature—"The Senator from Daytona."

So for both the city and its resident dictator, an early first period of relatively quiet and unheralded domicile came to an end accordingly when Batista, elected on the Liberal-Democratic ticket, reentered island politics and worked actively against Grau's successor. This time, however, a return to absolute political mastery rule was not the only motive. For now power would also hold out the prospect of nearly boundless wealth, with new North American connections in a US Mob initiative well underway, following a legendary 1946 meeting at the Hotel Nacional, to convert Cuba into a new Las Vegas–style version of its prewar identity as a gambling, drinking, and sexual paradise. Specifically, he had been beckoned by a call to direct financial opportunity issued by US gangster Meyer Lansky, an old partner and associate from the 1930s, initially brought in to manage such affairs after the "Revolt of the Sergeants" that had first elevated Batista to power. Now, in the dictator's absence, Lansky had begun rebuilding the earlier vice network into a postwar empire of crime in collaboration with former US Italian American mobster Salvatore "Lucky" Luciano, released from prison for shadowy contributions to World War II homeport security but deported to his native Italy as an undesirable alien. Luciano in turn had secretly entered Cuba to work with Lansky and other Mob associates but by 1947 had been once again banished from the Americas, this time by the Grau government under US pressure. The way now lay open for a new Lansky-Batista partnership essentially centered on the creation of a fabulously lucrative criminal state within a state.

The consummation of the project, of course, would require Batista's eventual return to absolute power. Accordingly, facing defeat in a third presidential election two decades after first installing himself as behind-the-scenes dictator, he this time brazenly reassumed both total de facto control of government *and* the official role of president in 1952 through a preemptive, second military coup. Nor from here on did there remain any further necessity to disguise the complete cementing of relationships between Mob operations and the regime. The government itself now became a complete criminal enterprise, a state founded on its own unrestrained capabilities for repression, cruelty, arrest, imprisonment, torture, murder, and ceaseless self-enrichment. Though no record exists of Batista ever meeting Lansky or other prominent Mob figures, the seamlessness of the criminal collaboration became the central fact of everyday Cuban life. The senator from Daytona (to the credit of Henry Luce, Inc., a cycle of post-coup 1952 articles, headed "Cuba's Batista: He Got Past Democracy's Sentries," proved notably absent of the earlier chummy approval) had become openly the president of Gangsterland.

As if scripted in a long tradition of bloody response, in the eastern regions far from Havana, the course of Cuban history quickly began its celebrated march toward revolution. Within a year of the old dictator's return to power, in Santiago de Cuba, the island's second city, came the famous 26 July 1953 Moncada Barracks attack launching the Castro Revolution. To be sure, it proved a local disaster for the insurgent forces, with many attackers dead, those not killed in the attack summarily executed, and its two leaders, the brothers Fidel and Raúl Castro, tried and imprisoned. Yet it also remained an event—even with post-1959 mythologizing set aside—seen by the general populace as one of extreme political significance, an active beginning of organized military resistance at the far eastern end of the island, the traditional hotbed of patriotic revolt. In turn, almost inexplicably in 1955, came the biggest mistake of the dictator's career—releasing Fidel Castro, along with his brother Raúl, from prison to prove he was not a tyrant. Clearly this was an attempt to defuse revolution by commuting the sentence—and thereby compromising the notoriety—of its charismatic figure, the author of the famous "History Will Absolve Me" declaration. Or perhaps the US sojourn had strangely left a residual concern for image. If so, in the role of merciful tyrant Batista must have felt gratified a year later to receive an invitation back to his former place of exile—his last visit back to the mainland—for an official Daytona Beach celebration in his honor. Accordingly, as recorded in the local media and elsewhere, 4 March 1956 was duly proclaimed Batista Day, with gala events including a parade, speeches, toasts, and a banquet.

Further, as it turns out, the adoptive hometowners themselves would shortly be given even greater cause to celebrate their ongoing civic friendship. In gratitude, special arrangement was made by the Batista regime for a return in late 1957 by a junket of sixteen Daytona Beach dignitaries, including Mayor J. H. Long and wife, to Havana. And there, the highlight of the trip for the American guests surely came with the 28 October 1957 announcement in the Hall of Mirrors of the Presidential Palace (now the Museo de la Revolución) of the aforementioned gift of the Batista properties to the city and people of Daytona for a "Cuban Foundation and Museum." The real estate alone was said to be valued at $125,000. An endowment was also established of $50,000. On this basis, the museum would become, it was happily proposed, a showplace for illustration of "Cuban progress in art, history, culture, science and technology."

Then, at midyear 1958, came a dazzling additional payoff with the 4 June arrival at Daytona Beach municipal airport of two heavily loaded Cuban Air Force C-46 transports. The cargo included "paintings, ceramics, photo murals, a bust of José Martí, and a working model of a sugar mill." All addressed "To Señor Presidente Fulgencio Batista," they were shortly installed at the two addresses on Halifax Avenue until the eventual sale and demolition of the original structures. Today, they can all be seen in the large and substantial Cuban Foundation sections of the Volusia Museum of Arts and Sciences (MOAS).

By any measure, this final play of events could not have been more complete in its self-compounding ironies. Celebrated one last time in Florida by his former fellow citizens as Good Neighbor Batista, in Cuba the dictator now stood at the height of his homicidal cruelty and criminality. Meanwhile, the zenith of the island's status as an empire of illicit pleasure had also been achieved through a complete symbiosis of state terror and Mob corruption. Dissidents and rivals died or simply disappeared regularly at the hands of the regime's SIM (Servicio de Inteligencia Militar) operatives and various army and police death squads. Those not handled thusly often fell as the victims of Mob enforcers.

Across Cuba, however, events of the same period were playing out their own domestic version of the beginning of the end. By 2 December 1956, barely six months after the Daytona festivities, Fidel Castro and his military revolutionaries, this time including the estimable Che Guevara, would be back in Oriente, to be sure barely surviving yet another tactical military disaster in the *Granma* invasion, but this time making it into the hills of the Sierra Maestra, where an army of assembled guerrilla bands would gradually fight their way across the island to ultimate revolutionary victory. And so on 13 March 1957, in his presidential offices just down the hall from the site of the October gift ceremony six months hence for the Daytona visitors, Batista himself would barely escape assassination by a heavily armed contingent of Havana student revolutionaries. On 2 December of that year came the opening on the Malecón of Meyer Lansky's glittering Las Vegas–style Riviera Hotel, the new jewel in the crown of seething, murderous, criminal Havana, with the event given a US media commemoration with a special live telecast of the *Steve Allen Show* back to the mainland—the longest TV show ever made, Allen quipped, to be shown as part of a commercial. By now it was all too late. The grotesque channeling of Cuban spectacle into US Sunday-night family TV became a dread harbinger of imminent collapse.

A year later, the dread dictator-impresario himself would be preparing for departure. Meanwhile, ever attentive to his own cultural prestige, he already seems to have been assembling his personal treasures. Among these were the pick of his favorites from the new Museo Nacional de las Bellas Artes, a pet project of Marta's following the return, newly styling herself, her husband, and the regime at large as major patrons of the arts. In retrospect, the 4 June 1958 removal of art and other artifacts thus seems clearly in anticipation of a possible new Florida exile. Historical accounts indeed suggest this remained possible until nearly the end. But at some point the clock stopped ticking. By the time of the New Year's Eve 1959 downfall, Batista would no longer be allowed to enter the United States for political asylum. Years of exile followed in new places of residence including Portugal, Madeira, and eventually Spain. In Daytona, the old home of the dictator, now a museum, continued to honor him in his role as civic benefactor. Eventually the original structures were torn down and the collection moved to a new Daytona Beach municipal facility, the Museum of Arts and Sciences. There, to this day, Good Neighbor Batista continues to honor his adoptive city in a payoff with immense cultural dividends.

Even as civic capital, the collection, from the outset, as with anything post-1959 Cuban in Florida *or* on the island, has proven a subject of more or less permanent political controversy. In 1962 came an official demand by the revolutionary government that the art be returned as lawful property of the Cuban people. Such contention has been renewed over the years as the museum's Cuban holdings have become increasingly prominent with additions of new art and island artifacts. In 1980, the core collection, augmented by small numbers of works from other collections—the New York Guggenheim Museum and Museum of Modern Art, and the Washington, D.C., Museum of Modern Art of Latin America—became the basis of an illustrated exhibition volume, jointly published by the Daytona Beach Museum and the John and Mable Ringling Museum of Art in Sarasota, in the latter case with the official support of the Florida Department of State. Whether by political or aesthetic circumscription, or some combination of the two, the text was tellingly entitled *Two Centuries of Cuban Art: 1759–1959*. Meanwhile, on the overtly anti-Castro side, the museum and its collections have retained a high political profile on the part of major roles played in its operations and activities by exile Cubans. As late as 1999, media reports noted a museum visit by three of four living Batista brothers, Ruben, Jorge, Robert, with Ruben noted as the president of the Cuban Foundation. (Ruben was said to live in Coral Gables, Jorge in New York, and Robert in Madrid. A fourth brother, Fulgencio, was also in Spain. Three daughters were also reported, one in Palm Beach and two in Miami.) Eventually a granddaughter, Tere, would serve as the new foundation president.

In 2007 came a fiftieth anniversary celebration, in this case augmented by a new collection, entitled *Art of the Cuban Republic, 1902-58*, with the latter assembled by two brothers, Roberto and Carlos Ramos. Themselves wealthy late twentieth-century exile-entrepreneurs and patrons of the arts, they are said to have actually escaped the island in an open boat with fourteen prized paintings, thus beginning a project of acquisition devoted to "rescued" work by artists who had fallen out of favor with the regime. This, too, resulted in a comprehensive volume, *Cuba—A History in Art*, coauthored by Gary R. Libby, editor of the earlier text, and Juan A. Martinez, author of a definitive scholarly book on the group of significant twentieth-century Cuban modernists, highly represented in the Batista collection itself, known as the Vanguardia Cubana.

Some Ramos work can still be seen on permanent display in main public spaces of the museum. But now, what still catches the political eye, not to mention the artistic and the historical imagination, lies in its own, small, carefully designed gallery. It is the Batista legacy: surely the most precious collection of Cuban masters outside the island—a small, pristine, gemlike treasure surrounded by other gaudy bagatelles.

Within the collection space itself, for individual paintings, information on the artist, the title, and in some very few cases, a post-1959 provenance, is offered on demure wall tags. Some items reveal the display to have been slightly expanded over the years, with small borrowings or additional gifts. The priceless Batista paintings themselves are what immediately command the attention, assembling themselves before one's eyes into an abstract or epitome of Cuban modernism. For one who has visited the dazzling Vanguardia sections of the Museo de las Bellas Artes Cubanas in Havana, there is a distinct sense of flashback. To be sure, here, among works from well-known individual painters, there often appears just one, perhaps two, possibly three. But each becomes at once its own story while invoking the larger vision of the whole.

One recognizes immediately the achievements of three pioneering twentieth-century figures. The works of the soldier-patriot painter and muralist Armando Menocal, with his characteristic evocation of Cuban landscape and people of early independence era, are recalled with his Monet-like "Peasant Child." His contemporary Leopoldo Romanasch is represented with two portraits, "Italian Peasant" and "On the Way to Mass," as well as a third, uncompleted, markedly less classical "study for a head," the face of a woman haunting both for her own mysterious beauty and for the manner of its new style of impressionistic evocation. Completing the triad of best-known figures, two signature abstract works appear by Amelia Pelaez, characteristic experiments in vivid color and geometric shape.

Transitional modernists include Victor Manuel (sometimes Victor Manuel Garcia) and Antonio Rodriguez More, both famous landscape artists, the first shown in the artful primitivism and simplicity of "Landscape with Figures," the second in his lush, almost primordial "Symphony in Green."

The only major twentieth-century modernists from the island missing from the display turn out to be two big ones. The first is the Afro-Cuban expatriate modernist Wilfredo Lam, with an absence likely explained by his lifelong sympathy for leftist causes, including service with the Republican forces during the Spanish Civil War. (In the aforementioned 1980 exhibition—though interestingly not in the resultant MOAS volume—this major problem was remedied by inclusion of Lam's "Zambesia, Zambesia," a signature work borrowed for the occasion from the Guggenheim holdings in New York.) Second, and probably for similar reasons, is the Italian Cuban futurist Marcelo Pogolotti, throughout his career a critic of state power and capitalist exploitation of workers.

Of the group called Vanguardia, at once exponents of a cosmopolitan twentieth-century modernism yet each in his way unmistakably Cuban, many major figures are represented by examples of signature work. Eduardo Abela, with long periods of residence in Italy and France, shows in *Promenade* the movement from an earlier soft impressionism to a linear abstraction combined with a crowded figural scheme, in something of the busy gaiety of a Chagall or a Klee. (Again, in the 1980 exhibition, as well as in the resultant volume, this was complemented with rounded qualities of caricature and humor typical of Cundo Bermudez with the unmistakably Cuban domesticity of *The Balcony* and *Barbershop*, borrowed for the occasion from the Museum of Modern Art.) The experimentalist Mario Carreno, a playful imitator of many styles, is here represented by a bold Picasso-like abstract construction of bright colors and sharply delineated geometric figures. In *Harlequins*, Carlos Enriquez presents a characteristic Daliesque synthesis of the surreal and the vividly erotic, at once menacing and disturbingly sensual. In contrast, Rene Portacarrero's mystical *Figure in Grey* seems to pay homage to Picasso while inflecting the titular image with an iconography distinctly religious in its sharp medievalism. Daniel Serra Badue, the youngest of the artists, is represented by a 1957 still life of a dish of candies, whimsically entitled *Cuban Sweets*.

Included among the paintings are a few of historical significance. Two important eighteenth-century painters are represented: Jose Nicholas de la Escalera with a classic religious work entitled *Coronation of the Virgin by the Trinity* and Vincente Escobar with the aristocratic colonial *Portrait of Don Tomas Mateo Cervantes*. Also present are romantic late nineteenth-century landscapes by Miguel Arias and Esteban Chartrand. In a similar vein are *Landscape* and *Seascape* by Valentin Sanz Carta. A last classical representative of European classical academic style is Miguel Melero, with *Portrait of Aurelio, Son of the Artist*.

In the works of other gifted twentieth-century figures, sometimes considered within the traditional assemblage of Vanguardia, sometimes not, one encounters a host of free-standing masterpieces. *Corner in a Cuban Garden* by Emilio Rivero Merlin is unmistakably of the island, with its lush, thriving vegetation, at home in its own portion of a happily enclosed domestic space. Likewise Cuban to its guajiro soul is the domestic primitivism of Lorenzo Romero Arciaga's famous *The Cup of Coffee*. Two ocean landscapes appear by Enrique Crucet, one each from eastern and western regions of the island. Of abstract expressionism, perhaps explicably, one finds a single, solitary selection, *Composition* by the mid-twentieth-century expatriate Guido Llinas.

Thus one struggles to summarize barely the arresting beauty of individual works while attempting to evoke their collective testimony to a powerful upsurge of Cuban creativity—the true flowering of a distinctive national modernism in the early twentieth-century arts. Indeed, as noted, the only dimension finally lacking is the Afro-Cuban strain of Lam and others—perhaps a function of Batista's politics, but also of his sensitivity to his own racial heritage. Even so, a complete volume remains largely captured before our eyes in this single pristine collection—an abstract or epitome, available to the common US viewer, of what can only be called the glory of *Modernismo Cubano*. Meanwhile, other features of affiliation to a larger cultural modernism lie equally far beyond enumeration. Deeply embedded in the collection throughout is an awareness and assimilation of the great currents of the twentieth-century arts. All the figures and movements are imaged and refigured, a who's who of stylistic influences and invocations. From Europe, one finds Matisse, de Chirico, Picasso, Dali, Chagall, Monet, Renoir, Magritte, Mondrian, Modigliani, Juan Gris, Joan Miro; from Mexico, Diego Rivera. Cubism, fauvism, surrealism, futurism become assimilated into new forms of distinctly Latin American primitivism and constructivism. The list of artists and -isms could go on indefinitely.

Yet what unites the works of the Cuban Foundation collection and the painters represented is not their homage to the twentieth-century art world but their common distinctive quality of national heritage. As is well known, we now live in a world of art and art criticism in which one is no longer supposed to talk about essences and/or essentialisms. At the same time, one is impelled here to assert that an exception may still have to be made for the Vanguardia Cubana, both in the outlines of their individual projects and in their manifest creations of large and enduring bodies of distinctive work. Whatever the style or the politics of the artist, the character of the individual work or its place in the larger body, to look at a work of the Vanguardia is to see nearly always a creation ineradicably and unmistakably possessed of the essence of Cubanism.

It is just this singularity of the collection—its monetary worth to be sure, to some degree its historical provenance, but beyond all else its nearly priceless artistic and cultural integrity—that also continues to uniquely politicize its very existence and identity now coming up on a century after many of the major works were produced. There is still, after all, the stamp of Batista notoriety—like a painting by Hitler or a hat worn by Somoza, the small historical frisson of a touch of evil. Still, outside the claims of Cuban community, or the occasional charge of favoritism or elitism against the administrators and trustees who seek city funds to maintain the MOAS facility, such issues seem increasingly dealt with as things better left alone. Perhaps testimony to the relative lack of interest shown by Americans to the past generally or to art in particular is the way the city attempts to deal with the Batista connection at the level of published popular history. On tourist and vacation websites, local legend begins with the customary obeisance to Ponce de Leon's dropping by to investigate a natural spring. Time then jumps to the city's founding by one Matthias Day, an Ohioan. (Day, a native of Mansfield, seems not to have had anything to do with Dayton.) Among early civic worthies, a Commodore Charles Burgoyne is also cited as an early guiding spirit and municipal promoter. Much is made of late nineteenth- and early twentieth-century auto racing on the beach, leading eventually to the construction in 1959 of the Daytona Beach Speedway by NASCAR legend Bill France. Also blazoned is a proud twentieth-century civil rights history, including the work of pioneering black educator Mary McCleod Bethune and the fact that Jackie Robinson, as a minor leaguer, was allowed to play there in one of the first integrated games of spring training. No mention is made whatsoever of quondam citizen Batista.

Thus it now stands with the physical evidence of Batista history as well. The houses are gone. One wonders what the city of Daytona would have made of them had they survived. Just a few miles up the Halifax River in Ormond Beach, for instance, stands the residential legacy of another splendid mid-twentieth-century civic benefaction, John D. Rockefeller's grand winter vacation house, the Casements. Besides making a lot of money and styling himself a philanthropist, Rockefeller was a notorious cartel builder, monopolist, and general-purpose robber baron. Still, the Casements remains a widely advertised tourist attraction and civic achievement in architectural preservation. To be sure, the Batistas living in a similar riverfront pile a little south on the Halifax proved definitely another story—particularly after 1958. Accordingly came the attempt over the years to move the collection away from its dictator provenance even down to nomenclature, with an attempt to subsume the Batista core legacy into the neutral-sounding Cuban Foundation Collection.

Thus does the local story, now nearly forgotten, become a fable of how to read art, history, memory. The last physical traces of Batista's life as citizen Batista, the dictator down the street, now nearly gone: the properties sold for development; the houses torn down, and in one instance replaced by a large Greek Orthodox church; the addresses no longer corresponding with the original numbers. While no secret to local historians, the whole sojourn continues to be not much mentioned outside occasional feature story, or as part of the little known facts of a style piece on Florida popular history. The Cuban Foundation art collection now seems something like a last haunted political trace, the vestige of a story not unlike that told in Milan Kundera's *Book of Laughter and Forgetting* about Clement Gottwald and Vladimir Clementis and a ghostly hat. In 1948, Kundera tells us, the two appeared before a mass gathering of the Czech people, Gottwald as the new communist dictator and Clementis as his vanquished rival. The day was bitterly cold, and Clementis found his old comrade hatless. In a generous and graceful gesture of amity, he took off his own fur hat and put it on Gottwald's head. Hundreds of thousands of copies were made and distributed by the government of an official commemorative photograph taken that day, Kundera goes on, of Gottwald speaking to the Czech people while wearing a fur cap. Four years later, Clementis was tried and executed, eliminated at once from history and memory. This included the airbrushing of his person from all public photographs. Now all that remained of Clementis was the hat on Gottwald's head.

Actually for the Batista collection in the Museum of Arts and Sciences in Daytona Beach, not nearly so metaphysical a story of shadowed memorialization is required. As it turns out, for the viewer leaving the collection space, one last painting remains to be seen. Given by the Marta Fernandez

Batista estate, it is of course a handsome full-length formal portrait of the dictator himself.

As noted, when no Elian Gonzalez is available, or somebody goes on trial in Cuba or Florida for illegal revolutionary activities, the Cuban Foundation collection finds occasional renewed visibility as the focus of a half century of bitter political hatreds. Anti-Castro Cubans see it as a historical patrimony, something saved from the Castro debacle. Meanwhile, the Cuban government periodically renews claims to the collection as a dictator's plunder to be returned to the people. (The visitor to Havana, it must be said, senses something of a corresponding atmospherics of theft in the splendid, glorious, extensive collections at both locations of the state Museo de las Bellas Artes—themselves in many cases likely the product of revolutionary confiscation.) Not even these probably connect the art much with the queer interlude in local history from which the whole business originated—when the ultimate American spring break destination also became the site of a dictator sabbatical a half century ago.

The friendly dictator down the street, Good Neighbor Batista never got back to Daytona after the gala events of 1956, finally dying in Spain in 1973. As to Marta, who began her official married life with him and became his fellow arts patron and civic benefactor during the happy Daytona days, she chose to return to Florida and was granted residence, dying in her own home, it was reported, in 2006. According to her obituary, she had continued to maintain a reputation as a lover of the arts and supporter of the needy, in both Cuba and the United States, giving to south Florida charities that fought cancer and leukemia. Brief mention was also made of the 1940s and '50s domestic interlude, that Fulgencio and Marta Batista had earlier had a home in Daytona Beach and had donated an extensive art collection to the city. The obituary noted she had died at her residence seventy miles north of Miami, substantially down the coast from Daytona in the traditionally pricier and more prestigious south Florida precincts where she and her husband had once tried to settle back in 1944. Still, the dateline would have been a giveaway to anyone in the know about Florida money, real estate, civic philanthropy, and social prestige. After all these years, and with all that money, on the geographies of history and memory, Marta Batista may have been allowed to return and take up residence in the neighborhood of the once-glamorous southeast Florida Gold Coast; but she had still made it only as far as West Palm Beach.

8

THE TWO ERNESTOS

The actual first name of Che Guevara, the legendary international political figure still most familiarly associated with mid-twentieth-century Cuba, was Ernesto. (According to one theory, in the street vernacular of his native Argentina, "Che" is a common nickname, translating as "pal" or "buddy;" according to another, it is a common conversational interjection, something like "hey" or "yeah.") The first name of Ernest Hemingway, the legendary international literary figure still most familiarly associated with mid-twentieth-century Cuba, likewise translates into Spanish as Ernesto. (Though by the time he arrived in Cuba, a biographical detail not without importance, "Papa" seems to have been the preferred term of address.) These two pieces of information would be merely interesting as facts of linguistic curiosity were it not for the highly visible ways, at once startling and mystifying to the contemporary visitor, in which Ernesto "Che" Guevara and Ernest Hemingway continue to inhabit twenty-first-century Havana as strangely twinned icons of popular-culture myth.

To be sure, despite coming from vastly different political eras and cultural backgrounds, the two share a number of distinctly visible traits. Both were renowned expatriates, heroic citizens of the world: the first an Argentine military and political adventurer enshrined as a revolutionary hero-saint; the second an American literary and cultural adventurer renowned as a creator of larger-than-life artistic legend. Both made their homes in places they sought out as the epicenters of the great cultural and geopolitical conflicts of their eras. Both were exemplars of the twentieth-century warrior intellectual, the man of action united with the man of thought; and both sought to invest their images as cultural cosmopolites with a hard edge of violent machismo. In early adulthood both eschewed traditional education—though Guevara eventually returned home long enough to complete his medical studies—to go off in quests after direct, firsthand knowledge of the world. With a fellow youthful adventurer, Alberto Granado, Guevara, as is now well known, set off to see the real conditions of human existence across South America in what became a life-changing motorcycle odyssey that committed him to a career of social and economic liberation. Hemingway volunteered for overseas World War I service with the Red Cross as an ambulance driver on the Italian front, where he was severely wounded and initiated into the mysteries of love and death. Both became obsessively attracted to involvement in the great military and political struggles of the century. Guevara, having played small roles in a failed revolution in Guatemala against a US-supported military dictatorship, wound up in Mexico, the site of his fated eventual meeting and alliance with Fidel Castro in the wake of the latter's imprisonment following the 26 July 1953 attack on the Moncada Barracks. He then found his larger revolutionary destiny in Cuba, home of the nation and people with whom he would be most permanently associated, in the 1956–59 war of revolutionary liberation. Hemingway, while cementing his career as a major literary and cultural celebrity, likewise pursued an adventurous migratory early existence as a newspaper and magazine correspondent, chronicling twentieth-century conflicts ranging from the Spanish Civil War to World War II in China and Europe. Meanwhile, after frequent periods of extended stay during the 1930s, he also established a more or less permanent home in Cuba from 1940 onward until his death two decades later.

Accordingly, during their lifetimes, both in Cuba and in the larger world, the two may be seen to have developed a number of parallels as figures of popular-culture mythology. Both possessed a certain fatalistic glamour in their quest after dangerous geopolitical trials of personal bravery. Following experiences in Guatemala, Mexico, and Cuba, Guevara continued to serve as an apostle of revolution, first in the Congo and then in Bolivia, where he finally met his death. Hemingway followed journalistic assignments in the Spanish Civil War and Sino-Japanese War into World War II missions with the RAF bomber force, the Normandy invasion, and the infantry campaigns of Western Europe including the liberation of Paris and the battles of the Huertgen Forest and the Ardennes. Both developed carefully cultivated legends of military prowess. Moreover, both partook of the extra cachet of the irregular warrior, the figure of special knowledge and expertise standing outside conventional military doctrine and regimentation. Rightly or not, Guevara was always regarded as the irregular-warfare brains of the 1956–59 guerrilla campaigns that succeeded in finally toppling the Batista regime and as the imaginative genius without whom victory would not have been possible. Fully undeniable was a reputation for nearly insane bravery, an uncanny ability to lead, inspire, face death in combat with personal example. Hemingway, as is well known, was likewise always quick to publicize his possession of what he called "the true Gen"—the special knowledge of warfare frequently not vouchsafed to the plodding, tradition-bound, professional military functionary. As to personal bravery, Hemingway fostered a genuine—if progressively embellished—cult of hard-won perilous encounters as a true citizen of the wars of the twentieth century, including volunteer service as a freelance intelligence operative in Cuba and much-publicized stint as a World War II sub chaser in Caribbean waters.

Similarly, as icons of a certain sort of twentieth-century masculinity, both were invested with a distinct sexual charisma. For Guevara, the operative phrasing was media idol, with the proximate image enshrined forever in the famous Alexander Korda portrait, *El Guerrillero Heroico*, possibly the most famous celebrity photograph of the twentieth century. To cite a recent commentator, Che was sexy, with rumors of hundreds of female conquests to his credit, though Fidel often got more credit for being the lover boy. Had Guevara looked like Churchill, Roosevelt, or Stalin, he goes on, there would still be unsold T-shirts all over the world. Hemingway, with his many marriages and swaggering exhibitions of maleness, occupied a kind of movie-star status not unlike that of his friends Gary Cooper and Humphrey Bogart. Ingrid Bergman, Marlene Dietrich, Lauren Bacall, Ava Gardner all called him "Papa," though his own interests were surely more than paternal.

"Grace under pressure": in all these respects, to use Hemingway's signature phrasing, both Guevara and Hemingway seemed personifications of twentieth-century existential heroes, high priests of male adventure and romance, with their own ritual codes and conceptions of identity validated by the presence of death. It is necessary only to endure, said Hemingway in a favorite quote: "Il faut d'abord durer." And then there is a time to die: "We owe God a death." For Guevara, as for his fellow Cuban *guerrilleros*, the code was even simpler. Life was truly *"patria o muerte"*—with the homeland in his case being in the largest sense always the cause of revolution.

Both, to their admirers at least, found ways of leaving the world in keeping with such personal codes as two of the twentieth-century's most legendary suicides, one might propose. In 1967, after capture in guerrilla combat, Guevara faced his death resolutely, allegedly taunting his murderer to get it over with. Hemingway was his own executioner, tripping both triggers of a favorite double-barreled shotgun. In death, both became icons of their own myths of heroic masculinity. Guevara, in surviving photos, remains unmarked, with peaceful features, the revolutionary martyr; with the removal of hands for identification, their permanent separation from the body, mutilation became elevated to the status of religious mystery. Prefigured in similarly religious terms through the ritual drama enacted by the old fisherman Santiago in *The Old Man and the Sea*, the final passion and death worship of Ernest Hemingway could have had only one outcome. The suicide itself may have been a terrible mess, blowing out the back of his head. Hemingway was certainly making sure it got done. As Che made one last defiant obeisance to the revolution, Hemingway determinedly faced one last reunion with the figure he called just another whore.

At the same time, given the radically opposed cultures of pre- and postrevolutionary Cuba, the circumstances and conditions underlying these strangely twinned associations of place with legendary historical personality could hardly seem more different. Guevara, after all, was a figure of distinctly post-1959 Cuba, a true hero of the revolution, and friend, comrade, and loyal right hand of the Comandante. Accordingly, for all his own machismo glamour, he was also the hard, uncompromising, doctrinal Marxist-Leninist, the ideological conscience of the revolution and also its cold-blooded executioner—selfless, austere, ultimately drawn to revolutionary martyrdom and heroic self-sacrifice. Hemingway, in contrast, seems now as then the prerevolutionary arch-representative of decadent (read capitalist) ego-driven celebrity modernism, with all its rewards of wealth and fame: the legendary drinker, big-game hunter, sport fisherman, war lover, womanizer, finally undone by his own bogus cult of heroic personality, a death by suicide with paranoiac delusions about the Internal Revenue Service.

Yet there they are, still, for anyone who arrives today in Havana, the two of them—*los dos Ernestos*, one is tempted to say—comparably celebrated and strangely ubiquitous, with their stories continuing to be told and their images equally and concurrently promoted. And so the ways in which they are remembered and represented reveal their own bizarre confluences of vectors, political and commercial, at times saying less about the two personalities than about the political and commercial complexities of today's Cuba. Paired icons from two halves of a broken, tempestuous, Janus-faced century, both have been essentially colonized by postrevolutionary Cuban culture and reconstituted in the Cuban image as icons of the twenty-first-century nation. "Ironically, Che's life has been emptied of the meaning he would have wanted it to have," asserts Cuban author Jorge Castañeda. "Whatever the left might think," Guevara is now far less "an ideological and political figure" and more "a symbol of a time when people died heroically for what they believed in. People don't do that any more." Something of this might now be said of Hemingway also in his symbolic relation to the intense, vibrant, colorful island culture of the pre–Cold War Cuba, the old glamour and excitement of the international celebrity days when people knew how to live, eat, drink, gamble, dance, make love, and die. And so the personalities of both come to be enlisted as images of memory in service of new stirrings of Cuban cultural pride, the irrepressible energy of industry, enterprise, resilience, ingenuity, creativity. Guevara recalls the era of revolution without the failed experiments of Socialism, the Russians, the Missile Crisis, the "special period;" Hemingway recalls the era of the Pearl of the Antilles, the excitement of the glamour decades of the century without the big corporations, the dictators, the Mob. Now, as then, in the environs of gleaming, restored twenty-first-century Havana, the images of Ernesto Che Guevara and Ernest "Papa" Hemingway seem easily harnessed as twinned cultural icons in a culture where the spirit of *Patria o Muerte* seems newly compatible with that of *Patria y Dinero*.

Regarding Guevara first, as anyone can report who spends time in the streets of Havana—stores, restaurants, public buildings, souvenir stands, offices, and party headquarters—images of Che continue to show up everywhere, vastly exceeding those, for instance, of el Comandante, Fidel Castro. In fact, one rarely sees a likeness of Castro—for a number of reasons later discussed—either alone or accompanied, save in some historical collection such as that at the Museo de la Revolución or at the national photo archive, La Fototeca. Even then, it is usually a picture from the '50s or early '60s, the great years of revolutionary struggle, idealism, and triumph. Moreover, Che is usually with him; alternatively, as with the occasional building decoration, one may also see *el Lider* as part of a fairly familiar mural design of three faces in silhouette, still featuring the original triad of youthful heroes of the revolution, Fidel, Che, and the late Camilo Cienfuegos.

But it is mostly Che one sees, still Che, the ever-youthful, undying spirit of Revolución. Indeed the *Cuba Libre* of the vanished glory days indeed now mainly seems to live on, in the autumn of the Comandante, through the ubiquitously displayed images of the charismatic sidekick, the eminence grise, the alter ego, even sometimes the necessary evil twin, but still Che forever alive and forever young. The details, themselves many of them less than glorious, have ceased to matter: the joining with Castro's ragtag band in Mexico, after the 26 July 1953 Moncada Barracks disaster, Castro's imprisonment, and his release during a surprise amnesty; the survival, after the *Granma* invasion, along with a handful of others, including Fidel and Raúl, of a defeat nearly as disastrous as Moncada; the long guerrilla struggle in the mountains of Oriente, where besides serving as Castro's closest comrade and revolutionary advisor, Che had also already become, along with Raúl Castro, the ruthless executioner, facilitator of drumhead court martials, summary shooter of traitors, defectors, cowards, informants; then, finally, with the Revolución consummated, second in power only to el Lider himself, Che, the commander of *la Cabaña*, presiding energetically and remorselessly over the mass trials and firing squads, the elimination of Batistianos along with turncoats, counterrevolutionaries, and other enemies of the state; finally the emergent ideological genius in the Marxist-Leninist tradition, the Red Richelieu, at home, Castro's chief commissar, abroad his geopolitical guide, mentor, monitor. With Fidel as the idealistic socialist liberator of the Cuban people, masking his own ideological commitment with his political coyness and international hijinks—spirited trips to New York, the United Nations, secret Washington meetings with Nixon, John Foster Dulles, and others—Che embraced the role of ideological heavy and rigorous enforcer of party discipline.

Indeed, it remains telling in this connection, but unsurprisingly remarked on, that the only Che Guevara residence site maintained by the government—equivalent to Hemingway's much-visited Finca Vigia, his pastoral retreat in the hills outside the city, though touted with rather less touristic cheery enthusiasm—lies within the sinister, overwhelmingly massive walls of Fortaleza de la Cabana—to this day the largest military fortification in the Western hemisphere. (His actual burial site, after the much-publicized return of his remains to the island in the 1990s, was chosen to be not the capital and seat of Communist government, but Santa Clara, the site of the culminating late 1958 "battle" where forces led by Guevara, at least according to revolutionary legend, opened the gateway to final victory in Havana.) In a "cottage" reverently preserved on the Cabana site, within quick walking distance of the wall used for the mass firing squads, was the place Che chose to make his dwelling in the months following the final revolutionary victory (officially appointed commander of the fortification by Castro), with his office and living quarters now devoted to a major collection of his personal memorabilia, even exceeding that, for instance, at the Museo de la Revolución. In official brochures, the quarters are described as those from within which Guevara "consolidated the revolution"—essentially reviewing and in most cases confirming the death sentences of its enemies. Identified also on the tourist map of the fortress is the aforementioned wall—noted as once the execution site of nationalist martyrs—where appropriate revolutionary justice was handed out.

On the personal, romantic, reflective side, while still in life Guevara himself was fostering something of an alternative textual legacy in various works of fictionalized self-mythologizing combining revolutionary history and political autobiography. These too remain ubiquitous at countless historical and commercial venues. His *Reminiscences on the Cuban Revolutionary War*, widely translated, remains a bible of guerrilla warfare and is now bookended by the early *Motorcycle Diaries* and the final *Bolivian Diaries* lies an ever-enlarging body of political and personal testament, published and republished in a host of languages, preserving and memorializing the words of Che, the great martyred evangelist of revolutionary world liberation.

Now, in Havana, as elsewhere, it is most often the risen, defiant, ever-inspirational Che one sees in the very image of revolutionary apotheosis. Made famous, ironically by '60s US radical youth, and thereby becoming the symbol of Socialist Liberation movements worldwide, reproductions of the Korda photograph especially seem ubiquitous, on caps, T-shirts, prints, posters, scarves, banners, pencils, pens, postcards, paperback covers of every size and description, in shops, museums, galleries, photo exhibitions, and displays of Cuban art. Decidedly less publicized are the images of the later Bolivian death and martyrdom or even ceremonious Cuban reburial. One has to read websites to find out about the shrine of final entombment.

A number of fairly obvious explanations may be suggested for all this, most having to do with the ever-increasing divorce over the years of the youthful, heroic promise of the early years of revolutionary victory from the dispiriting course of political and ideological history as it actually turned out for the makers of the revolution and their inheritors. First of course is the fact that Che the revolutionary hero had the good manners to die young in yet another war of world-historical liberation, a martyr to world Socialist revolution. In the Korda image and those of the other revolutionary photo chroniclers; even in the death photos, something seems just unkillable: a fierce, defiant beauty mixes with a serene, heroic beatitude. Meanwhile, there has now passed before the eyes of Cubans and the world a lifetime of photographs of Fidel, growing older with each failure of the promised revolution. The celebrated gallego profile, the masculine energy that made the Soviets call him *el Caballo*, may still help Castro live on as the last of the great twentieth-century dictators. But within a few years of victory, even the fatigues, the beard, the black framed glasses, had gotten old for el Comandante, as the familiar revolutionary costuming never would for Che. The former, in movies like Woody Allen's *Bananas* and on the drawing boards of editorial cartoonists around the world, had become a caricature of himself, trying out other designs. Soviet-style military getups would be followed by the occasional suit, eventually the odd guayabera. Even Che himself, one thinks, could hardly have imagined Fidel now this old, hidden away and years in his dying, or Raúl, still holding on.

Although crucially influential as an advocate and agent of the revolution's Russian misalliance, the creation of Cuba as the Western hemisphere satellite of the Cold War Soviet Union, neither did Che of course live long enough to have to take the rap for the long, torturous unraveling of that disaster: the American embargo, a long string of disastrous experiments in managed economy, the dire times of shortage and want of the "special period" following the fall of bankrupt Soviet Communism. It is a handful of old men who have outlived the revolution who now fully bear blame for the prolonged agonies of the great casualty of the revolution, the Cuban economy—a colossal material and human failure, completely ruining, for no one will know how many years, the richest country in the Caribbean, not to mention plunging generations of Cubans, comprising who knows how many individual lives and aspirations, into a long malaise of poverty and nearly universal deprivation.

As to official reasons for Che's ubiquity as a symbol of revolution and Fidel Castro's invisibility—even before the geriatric travails of the past decade—Cubans themselves will explain that there is a proper ideological reason. Indeed, they say, for a doctrinally sound Marxist-Leninist society such as their own, a true dictatorship of the proletariat, it is not only ideologically improper but in fact illegal to promote images of el Lider. For that would be to foster, as did Mao Tse Tung, or Stalin before him, a cult of personality. Che, on the other hand, along with the sainted Camilo Cienfuegos, is safely and faithfully in that great good place of all ideological correctness, the grave.

The simplest explanation possible, however, for such enduring appeal is one apparent to nearly any French semiotician or American teenager. To put it directly, for certain historical or cultural figures, in certain circumstances, particularly in a mass-media world of instant visual and verbal information, image takes on a life of its own. Like a Nike swoosh or a Mercedes star, Che is at once a historical product and a brand, in the fullest sense a popular-culture logo: a name, a face, a photograph, an icon of revolutionary heroism. If anything, in Guevara's case, the persona remains continually enriched and enlarged by additions to the legend, including a recent revival of interest in the United States and elsewhere through books and movies. With the rediscovery of the *Motorcycle Diaries*, Che now becomes something like a young Jack Kerouac, with Granado playing his Neal Cassady. The cover picture on the popular paperback, as well as the inevitable movie poster (2004), both spotlight a boyish, prerevolutionary, almost prep-school looking Che, square jawed, well barbered, unbearably handsome. Meanwhile, at the more recent end of the legendary history of an image now lies the recent Benicio del Toro movie characterization, showcased in a 2008 two-part, four-hour bio-epic by director Steven Soderburgh.

Books, movies, a long history of lifetime and posthumous media representations in their relation to celebrity legend certainly may be said at least to begin to explain Cuba's corresponding embrace of the Ernest Hemingway legacy in twenty-first-century Havana. The drinking, the meals, the celebrity guests, the movie stars, the Cuban cronies, the favorite watering spots, the sport fishing expeditions—all these became recurrent subjects of feature newspaper and magazine journalism. In 1949, *Life* magazine sent the renowned critic Malcolm Cowley to chronicle literary and personal life at the Finca Vigia. In 1950 it would publish *The Old Man and the Sea* in its entirety.

Out of such records of the times, the significance of the Hemingway image in both pre- and postrevolutionary twentieth-century Cuban popular culture likewise remains curiously invested in a single famous photograph, taken in this case by Oswaldo Salas—along with his son Roberto, among the other legendary photographers of the revolution. It is not nearly as known to the world as the Korda image of Che; in Cuba, however, one sees it frequently and with comparable effect. The only known photograph in existence of Ernest Hemingway with Fidel Castro, it commemorates their friendly meeting at a notorious fishing tournament, sponsored by the former, and won by the latter. The "competition" itself is the source of a much retold story in Cuba that speaks volumes about both the boyish Comandante and the aging Hemingway, depending on your sense of humor. In one version, the tournament (if a pun may be excused) was rigged with a modestly prize-winning sailfish secretly attached to Castro's line. The other is that the fishing was utterly terrible anyhow and the meager specimen actually caught by Castro did indeed weigh in as the winner.

As important are the ways in which the photo and tournament anecdote comprise equally a story about Hemingway's relation to Cuba and Cubans. Though he is described then and now to have loved the island, thinking himself even an honorary citizen, the consensus remains that he did not particularly care about its everyday inhabitants, save those who enhanced his celebrity or provided him with "character." Here the popular and journalistic record rings true. Virtually all photos of Hemingway during the era, when he is shown associating with Cubans at all, reveal his relations with a handful of privileged hangers-on, most of them socially well placed and extremely wealthy as a result of family holdings or commercial fortunes, or his everyday pleasures with ostensibly beloved menials.

Still, in life, as posthumously, the Cubans remained large in their admiration for Hemingway, and some of the reasons remain fairly simple and obvious. In many of his works, characters find their purpose in life in sacrificing individuality to some larger struggle against social or political injustice. (He is said by some witnesses to have expressed sympathy for the revolution; others suggest that his demise was hastened by his knowledge of the likely expropriation of his property.) Fidel Castro seems to have been an informed reader, allegedly claiming that *For Whom the Bell Tolls* helped serve him as a primer on revolutionary insurrection. Castro is also said to have admired the author's ongoing quest for an adventurous life. And the legendary life itself was no small matter for many Cubans. The fact was that the most celebrated American writer in the world, when he could have been a celebrity anywhere, chose Cuba; and by doing so he made Havana at once the exotic celebrity and cultural capital of both the Caribbean and to some degree of the Western hemisphere at large. Along with Italy, France, Spain, Africa, the Florida Keys, Cuba became a place of residence made to order for the Hemingway persona, with its history of romance and excitement linked to a vibrant tradition of native writers, composers, painters, and in the glory days of between the wars attracting musicians, entertainers, literary and artistic figures from America and Europe.

So Cubans also embraced the literary and popular-culture evidence of Hemingway's honoring of Cuba as the home of a host of avatars of Hemingway "code" heroes—including himself. Even before taking residence, Hemingway had created in the 1930s the convincingly proletarian Harry Morgan in *To Have and Have Not*, in large passages a deeply felt and honestly rendered book about Depression-era Key West and Machado-era Havana, the poverty, the violence, the danger, the desperation. (In deference to the wartime Rick Blaine characterization in *Casablanca*, on the other hand, the Bogart movie role as the hard-bitten skipper would be transferred to Martinique.)

The height of Hemingway's connection with the island, of course, both personal and literary, would be marked by *The Old Man and the Sea*. In that last great fable seemed to be a complete transfer of heroic interest from an autobiographical self to a simple Cuban fisherman, his catching of the great fish, and his battle with the savage, devouring sharks, the sun, the sea, and the sky. An instant world classic, winning for its author the Nobel Prize, and eventually appearing in the great Spencer Tracy movie version, it was eagerly embraced then as now in Cuba, with a kind of quasi-scriptural veneration. Everyone knows where Cojimar is; everyone knows who Grigorio Fuentes was; everyone knows that the *Pilar* is up there next to the house in San Francisco de Paula, just the way the *Granma* is in the park in front of the Museo de la Revolución.

Less known, still happily ignored, is *Islands in the Stream*, a posthumously published World War II chronicle of sculptor Thomas Hudson, another Hemingway stand-in. This time the hero is found living initially on Bimini, where he creates art, drinks, fishes, bonds with his sons, makes love to his beautiful ex-wife, eventually takes his boat to sea, finds adventure, fights bravely, and dies. Along the way, in this late, mendacious book, one gets again at least a vivid nostalgic rendering of Old Havana, the Floridita, the Bodeguita, including one of its denizens as the legendary prostitute Diamond Lil; styled on Hemingway's own wishful wartime activities, there are secret intelligence operations working out of the US embassy and vivid action scenes of hunting down a shipwrecked Nazi submarine crew amid the *bahias* and inlets of the northern Atlantic coast. In an even more mendacious late '70s movie, Thomas Hudson becomes a rescuer of Jews from Hitler's Europe; Cubans are Fascist collaborators. When Hudson takes a fatal slug in the movie, it is not, as in the book, from a desperate fugitive Nazi submariner; it's from a collaborationist Cuban coast guardsman.

More generally for the writer Hemingway in the nearly two decades he spent off and on in residence at the Finca Vigia and in Havana, the Cuban world seems to have been deeply inspirational. Among texts produced while living on the island, he began and wrote major portions of his most popular book, *For Whom the Bell Tolls*, with Robert Jordan, a heroic American serving with the Republicans in the Spanish Civil War modeled on his own experiences as a journalist. He also dreamed himself back up, this time at his most vaingloriously macho and self-parodic, in an aging US colonel, as the protagonist of the World War II novel *Across the River and into the Trees*. During the postwar years he also began work on a trilogy to be called "The Land," "The Sea," and "The Air," which he intended to combine in one novel known as *The Sea Book*. (Less known, in 1946 he also began work on *The Garden of Eden*, at the height of his masculinist celebrity posturing, a book about androgyny and sexual transference.) Increasingly, Cuba became and remained for two decades the place where he lived and wrote the Hemingway myth and found inspiration to further it, even as the Cubans helped make it come true in the way they idolized him as an adoptive son, brother, papa, favored elder. Toward the end at the Finca seemed to come a mood of mellow nostalgia, enabling Hemingway to finish writing much of *A Moveable Feast*, a posthumously published volume about his formative years as an expatriate writer in Paris.

For all this, in today's Cuba—there is just no other way to say it—one is just stunned by what seems the bizarre ubiquitousness of Hemingway references, markers, images, memorials, historical and commercial commemorations. The state-sponsored, reverential promotion of the Finca Vigia, the writer's country home in the hills twelve miles outside Havana, places it as a tourist site in a league with many of the city's other most prestigious attractions. It is far more heavily publicized, for instance, than the birthplace of José Martí. Books, magazines, furniture, and everything else remain in place, left as if he is going to walk back in at any moment. Inside visits are given to those culturally privileged, or otherwise well connected, with government agencies in charge of preserving the site. Indoors or out, notable is the evidence of how fully the great author enjoyed displaying his trophies as the great hunter. A shocked Graham Greene got it just right: "Taxidermy everywhere, buffalo heads, antlers . . . such carnage."

The Finca remains the crown jewel of the Hemingway memorial trail. But it is surrounded by a host of complementary sites. At Cojimar, in a specially constructed beachside pavilion, a bust of Hemingway, placed on a pedestal and facing out to sea, commemorates the author of *The Old Man and the Sea*. The Terraza restaurant next door naturally specializes in Hemingway drinks and dishes. Until a few years ago, the actual centenarian Grigorio Fuentes himself could be visited and paid to hold forth on the author he accompanied as first mate of the *Pilar* and the novelistic protagonist he allegedly inspired. In old Havana, on the harbor a block from the Plaza de Armas, at the Hotel Ambos Mundos one can pay a small fee in tourist currency to see his room, number 511. Downstairs, the bar is walled with pictures, as is the case with everywhere else he stayed or ate and drank—the Plaza, the Sevilla, the Nacional. Among the legendary bars, the Floridita and Bodeguita still compete for watering-hole nostalgists, swilling overpriced daiquiris at the former, to this day home of the Papa Doble, or at the latter, production-line mojitos. At the Floridita, amid all the celebrity knickknacks, one may have one's own picture taken with a bronze statue of the great man, permanently seated at his favorite corner on his favorite barstool. At the Bodeguita, more vintage pictures accompany a display of the definitive Hemingway endorsement, alleged to have been written in his own hand on the wall: "Mi mojito en La Bodeguita, Mi Daiquiri en el Floridita." For deep archaeologists of heroic Hemingway drinking, Internet directions are easily available for tracking down the former site of the original Sloppy Joes.

So, to one's wonder, the reach of the celebrity Hemingway presence today extends from the familiar precincts of Habana Vieja, Habana Centro, Vedado, out beyond Miramar to Jaimianitas and Cubanacoa, still the old Beverly Hills of Havana, home of all the confiscated yacht clubs and pleasure palaces of the prerevolutionary elites. In luxurious precincts where Batista could not enter because he was insufficiently "white," where Fidel and Raúl Castro maintain their homes, one now finds an area now converted into international resort properties, American-style townhouses, and office developments. Closed to all but the most privileged everyday Cubans, one is proudly called the Marina Hemingway. It features two deluxe hotels. The first is actually called El Viejo y el Mar. The second has a bar named Massai; the restaurant is called Ernie's.

Actually, it is amid so surreal a setting, out beyond where the revolution seems no longer much to pertain, that one finds something of an answer about the ongoing Guevara-Hemingway connection in today's Cuba as well. And that too has to do with new relationships being forged between history and commerce in both official and popular-culture Cuban memory. The great glistening restored clubs themselves, the new international hotels, the four-star restaurants serving food Cubans cannot buy, turn out to have everything to do with the restoration of Habana Vieja, the rehabilitation of Habana Centro and Vedado. As Che Guevara remains the shining, youthful face of the revolution, a Cuba without the later failures, the bizarre posturings and adventurings, the humiliations and the fiascos, the corresponding Hemingway image represents a renewed cultural connection with the glory days of prerevolutionary Cuba, purged of their own corruptions and failures. As phrased by Valerie Hemingway, the writer's secretary during the Cuba years and eventual daughter-in-law, on a brief 1999 return, "The Hemingway I encountered on my ten-day visit was both more benign and more Cuban than the one I knew, with an accent on his fondness for the island and his kindness to its people. There seemed almost a proprietary interest in him, as if, with the yawning rift between the

United States and Cuba, the appropriation of the American author gave his adopted country both solace and a sense of one-upmanship."

To put this most directly, in the Cuba of what might now be called the pre–post Castro era, several generations removed from the eras of their particular historical and ideological associations, both Ernesto Che Guevara and Ernest Papa Hemingway have undergone twinned resurrections as major tourist attractions. Reconceived as heroic citizens of the world who chose Cuba as their adoptive home, in their legendary lives and deaths, both now showcase Cuba as the place where their legends would most happily rest. To be sure, both appeal to distinct target audiences and capture identifiable market shares. Guevara, with his revolutionary political cachet, appeals to European and Latin American social democrats and North American left nostalgists. Hemingway, with his modernist artistic prestige, appeals to the more conventional literary-cultural traveler. Guevara attracts the kind of person who would visit Lenin's tomb in the Kremlin or Trotsky's house in Mexico City; Hemingway attracts the kind of person who would visit Jefferson's Monticello in Virginia or the Globe Theater in London. The chief appeal of both, now coming up on nearly fifty years in the grave, would now seem to be a certain permanence as attractive celebrity images of cultural memory in a new world of instant information where a week is a geological epoch.

For all the great archaeologies of the past, stretching back through five centuries, Cuba as a nation is slightly more than a hundred years old and moreover divided into capitalist and communist eras almost exactly in the middle. Accordingly, both Guevara and Hemingway represent a subset of Cuban thinking about modern history as a kind of serial time warp: Guevara from the victory days of revolution still in some perverse relation to wheezing '70s and '80s Ladas and Fiats, the grotesque deserted Soviet embassy building, the vast baking asphalt desert of the party square in Vedado, the Cold War junkyard of the *Granma* memorial in front of the Museo de la Revolución; Hemingway from the prerevolution glamour era in some perverse relation to the '50s Detroit automobile behemoths still on the road, the old Mob hotels still flaunting their notorious history of seedy glamour, the now-dismantled monument to the American sailors of the USS *Maine*, with even its fragments relocated to the former office of the American proconsul in Palacio de los Capitanes Generales.

Somehow standing apart from all that now are the two Ernestos, images of twentieth-century culture heroes become icons of twenty-first-century national pride. Che, the eternally young; Papa, *el Viejo*. Both become emblems of romantic reprise for a hundred years of mostly bad history: the first representing, from the recent five decades, a chance at glory as a cynosure of revolutionary world liberation, now largely failed and abandoned; the second recalling, from the five decades before that, the promise of an earlier glory as the showplace of a culturally vibrant and teeming independent nationhood corrupted and betrayed. Poised on the edge of a century deeply in need of new heroes, the nation builds its historical image through the iconic adoption of two strangely disparate, yet parallel, outsiders who found in Cuba affirmation of their own sense of romantic destiny and whom Cubans came to embrace on equal terms: twentieth-century men of the world in the tradition of the conquistador, the freebooter, the patriot, the revolutionary *guerrillero*; but also warrior intellectuals in the image of Céspedes, Martí, Gómez, Maceo, Garcia. In a Janus-faced broken century, both remain heroes appealing to a poet's and—if one may be so crass—a publicist's soul, and thereby heroes whom the Cubans still gladly recognize as their own.

9

STEVERINO IN GANGSTERLAND

My purpose here is to recount a curious episode—a representative late anecdote, it might be called, of post–World War II US-Cuban commercial and popular-culture relationship—connecting golden-age American television programming with Mob-era Cuban tourism and entertainment on the eve of revolution. Specifically, it centers on the record of a little remembered January 1958 broadcast of the *Steve Allen Show*, a popular Sunday night variety program devised by CBS as a lively, innovative, frequently offbeat competition to the staid and venerable Ed Sullivan's *Talk of the Town*. The unique concept involved here was for the show—like Sullivan's, based in New York—to originate live as a midwinter special from tropical Cuba, and specifically from American mobster Meyer Lansky's new Las Vegas–style hotel and gambling palace called the Riviera, on the Havana Malecón—the final glittering evolution in a chain of Mob-dominated properties extending from the venerable Hotel Nacional and Sevilla-Biltmore to the more modern Capri and Havana Hilton. The result, slightly less than a year before the triumphal entry of the Cuban revolutionaries into Havana, comprises a vision of Cuba at one last surreal intersection of American show business and American gangster history, a mythical lost world of garish pleasure on a luxuriant tropical island now all the more legendary for the loss of its mythicality.

Havana Nocturne, the writer T. J. English has called the era: a hedonistic high roller's dream, an hour's flight from Miami, Las Vegas with palm trees and tropical beaches, *anejo* rum, and *Montecristo* cigars. The designs of such an empire of forbidden pleasure, even down to the allocations of the spoils, had been all sorted out in the beginning after World War II, in a vast collusion between the Batista regime and a gathered pantheon of US underworld figures including Charles "Lucky" Luciano, Meyer Lansky, Vito Genovese, Santo Trafficante, and Albert Anastasia, to name the most prominent. Everybody got his share. A greedy apostate, Anastasia, was duly gunned down in 1957 in a barber's chair at the Park Sheraton Hotel in faraway Manhattan. There was plenty for everybody—the running take on a vast, open-twenty-four-hours, all-you-can-put-on-your-plate buffet of unimaginable earthly delights: the luxury hotels, the nightclubs, the strip shows, the booze, the drugs, the women. A short, sunny plane ride from the mainland made for an easy launch into a long trip on the nightside of exotic pleasure, risk, and, for a few lucky ones at the tables, at least, reward. In the gambling was the enormous money. The lavish entertainment was the come-on and the sweetener. Cuba gained a reputation for high-end audiences with a taste for live US entertainment star power. Representative figures ranged from opera performers such as Enrico Caruso and Mario Lanza to popular musical celebrities including Frank Sinatra, who notoriously flew in to give a private show for the celebrated, original 1946 Mob convention called by Lansky and Luciano at the Capri Hotel, and Ginger Rogers, who gave the opening show for Lansky at the new Havana Riviera. Major bandleaders of the era playing the island included Tommy Dorsey, Woody Herman, and Benny Goodman. In 1956 alone, headliners were Dorothy Lamour, Maurice Chevalier, Billy Daniels, Nat King Cole, Eartha Kitt, Edith Piaf, Ilona Massey, Cab Calloway, Dorothy Dandridge, Tony Martin, Tony Bennett, Ginny Simms, Connee Boswell, and Vicente Escudero.

As a multiracial culture, mid-twentieth-century Cuba also proved notably hospitable to African American and Hispanic American musicians, singers, bandleaders, dancers, and variety show entertainers. Those who came to enjoy particular celebrity on the island included Paul Robeson, Dizzy Gillespie, Josephine Baker, Cab Calloway, Nat King Cole, Pérez Prado, Celia Cruz, Carmen Miranda, Eartha Kitt, Sarah Vaughan, Ella Fitzgerald, and Johnny Mathis. (To be sure, as late as 1956, like Josephine Baker in 1950, Nat King Cole, contracted to perform at the Tropicana, was denied a room at the Hotel Nacional. As to the latter, the current establishment has atoned with a Nat King Cole corner, featuring a bust of the entertainer and a classic 1950s jukebox.)

Even when they weren't on the entertainment bill, mainland celebrity visitors were likewise trumpeted by the flashy resort hostelries, casinos, and nightclubs claiming them as guests: Errol Flynn, Cesar Romero, Ernest Hemingway, John F. Kennedy, Marlon Brando, Ava Gardner, Tyrone Power, Gary Cooper, Barbara Stanwyck, Esther Williams, William Holden, Rita Hayworth, Fred Astaire, Liberace, Elizabeth Taylor, Eddie Fisher,

Pier Angeli, Vic Damone, Debbie Reynolds, Anne Miller, Eva Marie Saint, Frankie Laine, Jimmy Durante, Rocky Marciano, Jack Paar, Diane Carroll, and Sammy Davis Jr. In many of the famous old entertainment venues, the celebrity picture gallery remains a main-lobby fixture. As opposed to the swanky Nacional, a traditional destination for dignitaries such as Winston Churchill and the Duke of Windsor, at the old Sevilla-Biltmore, for example, one still finds Ted Williams next to Al Capone, Joe Louis beside Santo Trafficante. At the Capri, where Hollywood gangster George Raft was the house greeter, the pictorial roster includes Betty Grable, William Holden, Ava Gardner, Nat King Cole, Esther Williams (in the rooftop pool, of course), and the boxers Joe Louis and Kid Chocolate.

The glossy façade of the happy glamour-getaway for US celebrities, television and movie stars, political figures, and entertainers, barely covered a well-known underside of imported first-tier US vice and criminality feeding its own bursting coffers, those of Cuban associates, and that of the brutal Batista dictatorship. Well known were the notorious strip clubs, sex shows, nude reviews. Prostitution flourished. Showgirls from the Tropicana, the Montmarte, and the Sans Souci were recruited to entertain visiting worthies, as were professionals from Havana's most elegant brothel, the Casa Marina. Reports of such lurid attractions were featured in 1950s magazines with names like *Stag*, *Eye*, or *Modern Man*, often accompanied with grainy black-and-white photo documentation.

The genesis of a late 1950s scheme for getting the idea of a "new" Havana out into the world by putting it on Sunday night US TV lay largely with the main architect, there from the beginning along with Lucky Luciano, of the original late 1940s to early 1950s empire of glittering, tawdry delights, Meyer Lansky. In Lansky's case, this was connected with a project envisioned as providing the ultimate marker of his personal fiefdom, his ambitious design for a totally new, state-of-the-art, American-style hotel: on the Malecón itself, just down from the grand old Cuban flagship Nacional—even after the latter's 1956 gala additions of a Las Vegas–style Casino Parisien and Starlight Bar—a place that would truly represent the jewel in the crown, the newest bright star in the constellation. Dominating the beachfront with the old city to one side and the high-end suburbs of Vedado and Miramar on the other, it would be something totally his, from start to finish, top to bottom, design to execution. To be sure, he would have a complex of investment partners, legitimate and otherwise, ranging from a Miami hotel group to old Mob associates from the Las Vegas casino-resort syndicate; a further large chunk of the eight million dollar construction cost would also be supplied by the Bank for Economic and Social Development (BANDES), a state-run development apparatus set up by the regime of Cuban dictator Fulgencio Batista. Once set in motion, however, it became signature Lansky, the full Las Vegas effect, even down to the choice of name—the Riviera—on tropical shores mirroring in image and reality the lavish, spectacular, much-heralded project with the identical name at the same moment actually going up in the desert thousands of miles to the west. The latter, ironically funded by a Miami syndicate, was to be and now remains the first high-rise on the Las Vegas strip. Its headline act for years was Liberace.

As things turned out, such a jumble of style and image would characterize the evolving, hybrid architecture and entertainment design of the Havana Riviera. At the earliest stages of his audacious conception of a glittering, fully modern, Las Vegas–style hotel on the winding, beautiful, completely Havanese Malecón, Lansky had tried but failed to secure the services of architectural giant Philip Johnson. Next he tried Las Vegas celebrity architect Wayne McAllister, pioneering creator of the 1941 El Rancho Vegas, but best known for the classic 1950s strip properties including the Sands and the Desert Inn; he finally got Miami giant Boris Polevitsky. Either way, he split the difference—with a promise by Polivetsky that the building could go up in six months. The resultant main structure is classic mid-twentieth-century resort high-rise, a tall, clean rectangle of concrete with large windows and outdoor balconies highlighted in a color design of aqua and white. The attendant facilities emphasize curve and clamshell, with statuary of ocean wave and marine motif, including, at the entrance to the grand automobile porte cochere, an elaborate design featuring the interwined figures of a mermaid and a swordfish. The grounds are flat, paved, contoured with automobile entrance and exit lanes. One could be at the Las Vegas Riviera; one could as easily be on South Beach. To this day, to enter the building, with the glass and steel openness provided by the original design for its lower-floor public expanses, is to feel some uncanny sense of transportation to earlier dimensions of time and space. As to openness of design, one experiences something like the ultimate glassed-in Vegas-style pleasure palace transplanted from the desert by way of Miami Beach to the majestic Malecón, with its crashing waves, almost blinding sunlight, shimmering heat, all silenced and damped with the inside air-conditioned chill. As a complete interior space, it feels less carved up than sectioned into separate but connecting spaces and venues. In general décor, the interior remains late '50s deluxe, open staircases, architecturally coordinated statues, paintings, sculptures, hangings, wall pieces, murals. At some point, one is nearly overwhelmed by the sense of a whole garish interconnected, unfolding panoply, in which one space outdoes the over-the-top vulgarity and garishness of the last. Still the centerpiece of the interior, corresponding to the marine statuary just outside the entrance, is a large lobby sculpture entitled *Ritmo Cubano* (*Cuban Rhythm*), depicting intertwined male and female dancers in bronze. In the main dining room known as L'Aiglon, billing "dining in the grand manner," were murals allegedly depicting native Cubans at carnival time. The main cocktail lounge was called L'Elegante. The coffee shop and dining terrace, in full polyglot riot, were respectively Primavera and Al Fresco. The casino sunken bar was Doble or Nada (Double or nothing). The main performance space, in honor presumably of its New York counterpart, itself named by way of Brazilian inspiration, was the Copa Room.

It was from here that originated in January 1958 the live US television broadcast of the *Steven Allen Show* that may be imagined, in culmination of Lansky's audacious design, of the hotel's true grand opening to the world. And here as well, completing the time/space figure, one now reimagines what seems in retrospect an almost surreal assemblage, an abstract or epitome in strange, various caricature of American Sunday night variety-show programming. Well-known guest stars on the show, as the saying went at the time, included Mamie Van Doren, a gushing, platinum-haired, curvaceous, second-rate Jane Mansfield or third-rate Marilyn Monroe, in the huge-breasted, bursting-out-of-her-tight-dress style of the era; comedian Lou Costello, late of Abbott and Costello, without straight man Bud Abbott; ventriloquist Edgar Bergen with Charlie McCarthy and Mortimer Snerd; young singer Steve Lawrence, fresh from his Las Vegas heartthrob marriage to musical partner Eydie Gorme; to interject a Latin/tropical note, the cast also included the dance team of Augie and Margo, mambo dancing regulars at the Palladium and Roseland and moderately famous as the opening act for stars including Harry Belafonte, Tito Puente, and Sammy Davis Jr. Local auditions brought aboard the Afro-Cuban dancer Tybee Afra. The New York format was topped off by

Cuba-themed interview encounters with Allen-show "man on the street" regulars Don Knotts (Mr. Morrison, "the nervous man"), Tom Poston (the man who can't remember his name), and Louie Nye (the effete advertising executive, Gordon Hathaway). One can nearly still hear the last, on the *Prado* perhaps, with a Cuban turn on the standard opener: "High-ho, Steverino!" "Que pasa, Esteban?"

Though the setting was supposed to contrast warm, sunny, tropical Havana with New York in the dead of winter, the night of the show failed to honor the script. The sky was overcast and notably dark; a chill breeze blew intrusively off the seawall, rippling the water in the swimming pool. Nonetheless, the Riviera show went on.

From the outset, the hotel was itself a feature attraction. A long mobile shot at the opening came in on a limousine pulling up at the curb under the porte cochere. One by one, cast members were revealed emerging, walking toward the camera and into the hotel. Next, a donkey cart pulled up carrying Steve. He got out to the accompaniment of the familiar New York musical theme. The usual emcee, Gene Rayburn, did the usual opening program announcement—in makeshift Spanish. The camera then continued to travel with Steve, shaking hands and greeting bystanders, through the vast lobby to the front desk. Passing through the casino on the way, Steve encountered his wife, Jayne Meadows. Commenting on all the pretty women in Cuba, he kissed her and remarked on how familiar she seemed to be. At length arriving at the reservation desk, he found he had no reservation. Eventually he collected his wits. Shortly there followed the opening lines of the standard monologue, "We are in Havana, home of the pineapple and Meyer Lansky," he announced to a no doubt on both claims somewhat stupefied world. "And we're happy to be here," he quickly added.

The shamelessness of it all seemed to daunt even the irreverent Allen. According to *Time* magazine, there had been an alleged exchange during a wrap-up script conference. "Is there any hotel plug in this script?" somebody asked at the final review of the lines. Cracked Allen: "Is there any script in this hotel plug?"

The acts themselves ran the standard variety gamut. Steve Lawrence sang "Begin the Beguine" as a strolling mobile production number with background visuals taking him through the casino out to the pool area. Edgar Bergen, seizing on the sybaritic reputation of the Cuban metropolis, interviewed dummy Charlie McCarthy about the latter's boozing and carousing the night before. Back in the casino, Lou Costello did a rendition of his famous "dice game" sketch with Allen regulars Tom Poston and Louis Nye. Mamie Van Doren, in a swimsuit, sang "Sand in My Shoes," while lounging on a raft in the pool. Still outside, Augie and Margo performed a dance number, followed by music by the Facundo Rivero Cuban vocal quintet and then another dance by Tybee Afra. As the theme of the "Man on the Street" segment, Steve posed the question, more than slightly loaded, of what most attracts American tourists to Havana. Characteristic answers were supplied by Knotts, Poston, and Nye, joined by Edgar Bergen's Mortimer Snerd.

The show got subsequent publicity at home in a lighthearted *Time* magazine feature of 3 February 1958 entitled, with goyish misspelling, "Borsch and Bongos." The writer was impressed by the elaborate preparations, expense, and logistics of the enterprise in an opening account of the preparation long on facts and figures. After a two-month reconnaissance of the site, eventually there had been an airlift of a cast and crew of fifty (along with ten wives, the writer duly noted). Cargo shipments included sixteen tons of lights and more than five miles of cable. In-country technical assistance was provided by "three dozen technicians from Havana's TV station CMQ." As to financing, the hotel was noted as paying twenty-five thousand of the show's forty thousand dollars in extra costs and supplying "its bellhops as extras." Lighting alone, the technical summary concluded, required electricians "to string out the lights the length of almost four football fields and use more kilowatts than the same NBC lighting men once used to illumine Niagara Falls."

Human interest was provided in accounts of special preparations made by various stars. Mamie Van Doren and singer Steve Lawrence practiced lip synching their musical numbers with renditions prerecorded in New York just in case of technical problems. The producer was said to have beaten the bushes for supporting local talent, finding some bongo drummers and a singing quartet. Tybee Afra, as it turned out, was a lucky late minute addition who happened to be on the island. Her usual venue was the Jewish Catskill circuit.

The article enumerated unforeseen problems at various points in the visit. The frail regular Don Knotts, cast as the perpetually "nervous" interviewee in the weekly Allen "Man in the Street" feature, passed out in the coffee shop; a doctor flown in from the United States diagnosed "nervous exhaustion." The bearded bandleader Skitch Henderson, dressed in an outdoorsy pullover sweater and denim pants, was said to have "created consternation" by his resemblance to a Fidelista revolutionary. Mamie Van Doren's strapless swimsuit was adjudged too risqué to play in "East Cupcake, Iowa." Louis Nye, lacking a garish tie of the sort worn by a gambler, was provided with one sufficiently vulgar taken from an unsuspecting guest in the lobby. During the show itself, the whipping wind unmoored Van Doren's pool raft, levitated announcer-pitchman Gene Rayburn off the diving board, and nearly sent the luckless Don Knotts headlong into the water. According to Knotts, in a later oral-history recollection, they were all expendable anyway as far as the Cubans were concerned. For the latter, the only real celebrity in the visiting cast, was Lou Costello, since they had of course seen all the Abbott and Costello movies.

The *Steve Allen Show* from the Meyer Lansky Havana Riviera: thus did golden-age American television write a kind of absurd popular culture coda to a long tradition of US entertainment and entertainers partaking of the allure and opportunity of an exotic Cuban setting. It brought neither of them much good. By the next year, Allen was out of the coveted prime-time Sunday night variety-show slot. Even more drastically, by the next year, with the triumph of the revolution, Lansky was out of the hotel. "I crapped out," he is said to have mordantly remarked.

To put this in the vein of publicity images and headlines accompanying events of the time, with the triumphant entry of revolutionary forces a year later, the Allen show at the Riviera was permanently eclipsed and erased from memory by the Castro show at the Hilton, where he held his first raucous postvictory press conference and allegedly turned loose a herd of pigs in the lobby. Renamed the Havana Libre, it would soon welcome new Soviet-era celebrity guests, including Nikita Khruschev's daughter, Salvador Allende's widow, and the parents of Che Guevara. Younger star power would be provided by US Black Panther heroine and Marxist revolutionary *passionaria* Angela Davis and Valentina Tereshkova, the first Russian female cosmonaut.

In a kind of shabby valedictory the Copa would play its own brief postrevolutionary role in a subsequent 22 January 1959 press conference where Castro formally laid out his response to the world concerning the aims and directions of Cuban Revolution. Shortly, all casinos were closed and all major hotels nationalized, including the Riviera. A last moment of fleeting pictorial fame would come during the 1962 Cuban Missile Crisis, where it appeared in photographs surrounded by Cuban Revolutionary Army–manned antiaircraft defense positions. In the 1990s, with the reopening of tourist initiatives in the wake of the withdrawal of Soviet economic and industrial support, the major surviving hotels attempted to reopen themselves to the outside world. At the Riviera, the Copa Room became the Palace of Salsa, "where the best salsa orchestras in the country perform." Now, in the new century, the hotel bills itself as "Su casa grande in la Habana" and as "charming in its nostalgic preservation of 50s style and glamour." Everything is still there. Photographs beautifully cast in perspective relief, the high-rise core with the spectacular views of Havana, Vedado, and the Malecón standing out against the outbuildings with their curves, ellipses, clamshells. Time also seems to stand still in shots of the facing designs of outdoor and indoor abstract sculpture. Interior photos emphasize a décor with distinctly vestigial tones, designs, lighting, and furniture of the original glamour era. The whole effect would seem not at all out of place in a back to the future segment—even down to a parking lot full of cars with enormous chrome grills and bumpers, goggling headlights, jet-age tailfins.

To catch that most fully, one may also go to a website facsimile of the lavish promotional brochure. Here, the initial slogan turns out to be not so different from the present one. "Havana in the Grand Manner," it proclaims. The thoroughly modern amenities are noted, including air conditioning. But what catches the eye are the reproduced artist's illustrations of the public and entertainment spaces, the bar, the restaurant, the nightclub. And of course, the casino. In the glamorous crowd depicted, not unlike the opera goers in a luxury car or diamond jewelry advertisement, the women are all fashion-model beautiful, immaculately coiffed, fabulously rich but also somehow cultivated looking in their floor-length evening gowns and fur pieces. The men, straight out of *Esquire*, are models of sophistication in tuxedos or, since it is Cuba, immaculate white dinner jackets. One suddenly sees that Lansky's original design was not just to span the distances between the island and the gambling palaces of the American West but also to invoke the imagined elegance of their European counterparts. The place in the illustrations looks not so much Las Vegas east as Monte Carlo west. Indeed, digging through the records of the financing and construction, one discovers that the place itself in Lansky's original plan was to be called the Hotel Monaco. The Riviera indeed.

On a recent visit to Havana, I visited the grand old place on the Malecón. Myself a scion of the American 1950s and early 1960s and the quintessential homogenized tastelessness and banality of the era, I, at first, stood back and tried to take it all in at some length from the outside, essentially a huge, blank, shadeless parking lot, with car lanes everywhere, yet notably absent of traffic. It was hard not to remark on the exterior as quaint, dated, typical fifties showy glitz, all space-age jutting sharpness and verticality—the standard high-rise of concrete, glass, and steel, ocean aqua and sunshine white, of the hotel and condominium developments now crowding the beaches of the world from the Greek Isles to China, from Belize to Abu Dhabi—in this case still surrounded by all the little old domed annexes and kitschy statuary. (In retrospect, it must be said, the swordfish with the mermaid now looks distinctly like a seahorse. Was that the covert sexual style of the era, or is it just age?)

When I walked in, on the other hand, I was astounded at the sheer beauty of the place from the inside. In the chill of the air conditioning, the white, glaring sun was transmuted by the glass walls into a wonderful Malecón blue. It seemed as if one could pass invisibly through any surface and be at one with the air and water. Every room in the original floor plan was still in its place. Though they had brightened up, there was enough left of American 1950s design and décor, coupled with the old Cuban murals and wall relief to recreate an arriving guest's strange wonder at the place. Indeed, if anything, through such museum-like vestiges of the original, the suspension of time seems intentionally maintained—not unlike, one imagines, the continuing preservation of the rooftop pool at the Capri, or the room at the Ambos Mundos where Hemingway lived and wrote during his first extended stays on the island. It is all part of what seems a certain kind of carefully cultivated tourist nostalgia. A daiquiri at the Floridita, a mojito at the Bodeguita, a floor show at the Tropicana—a ride in a 1953 Packard Clipper or a 1958 Oldsmobile Starfire. Strangely, the Riviera has outlived this in significant ways. With its clean but not completely antihistorical restorations, it is not unlike something preserved in amber. The imagination easily falls in with the effort to catch what it was like.

As I walked around and stared, I was approached by a person who, while not occupied in any particular hotel business, gave the impression of being a hotel staff member, inviting me, even if I was not a registered guest, to enjoy an "executive massage." Apparently, amid all the reclaimed luxury and beauty and glamour of the Havana Riviera, not everything had changed regarding the other, less savory entertainments available should one be so desirous. I declined. I was not there anyway. I was back in 1958. Who would ask such a thing of a teenage American boy who finally got to see Cuba after all these years and just wanted to see the place where they once did the Sunday night *Steve Allen Show* he enjoyed so much on television live from Havana?

10

WHY NO ONE IN HAVANA SPEAKS OF GRAHAM GREENE

Among the unique features of Cuban culture over the centuries is the readiness with which people of the island have taken to their hearts and honored in historical memory the various writers, painters, and composers of other nationalities who have come there and embraced the life of the nation, frequently memorializing their associations in works of great beauty and power in their own right. Even a small but representative list suggests the diversity of such recognitions: the great nineteenth-century explorer and natural philosopher Alexander von Humboldt; the Swedish feminist and social reformer Frederike Bremer; North American literary travelers such as William Cullen Bryant, Richard Henry Dana, Julia Ward Howe, and John Muir; the painter Winslow Homer; the journalist, short-story writer, and novelist Stephen Crane; the photographer Walker Evans, the composer George Gershwin; the African American poet and translator Langston Hughes; and, not least, two major literary figures of international twentieth-century modernism, Ernest Hemingway and Graham Greene.

For readers of the modernist canon in English, it is the latter two who come immediately to mind as making well-known fictional representations of mid-twentieth-century Cuba. Most prominent, to be sure, as discussed in the foregoing chapter, is the celebrated American adventurer-celebrity Hemingway, who made his home there for two decades and wrote a number of works during the period depicting life on the island, most notably his spare 1953 fable of struggle against nature, *The Old Man and the Sea*. Fifty years later, he remains revered by the nation, with memorials rife in the Havana environs particularly where he lived and wrote. Of comparable popular notoriety would be his expatriate British counterpart Graham Greene, author of *Our Man in Havana*—a late 1950s spoof of Cold War espionage fiction that probably remains the best known popular political novel of the century in English to deal with Cuba and Cubans just on the edge of the defining moment of revolutionary liberation. By contrast, one seeks vainly in Havana or in Cuba at large for a single form of public remembrance.

Both Hemingway and Greene may be said to have literarily capitalized on the island, its people, and its long, rich, and complex history. Socializing mainly with the wealthy and the well placed, though affecting public warmth for everyday Cubans, Hemingway in many ways promoted an image of local identity as a kind of honorary citizen. In his art, he tended to use Cuba itself as a mythic backdrop for adventure featuring avatars of the Hemingway hero ranging from Harry Morgan in *To Have and Have Not* to Thomas Hudson in the posthumous *Islands in the Stream*. As is well known, he seems to have been awarded the Nobel Prize—with the moment marked in a contemporary interview still famous on the island where he returned credit to the Cuban people—largely on the basis of his late depiction of the simple, courageous Cuban fisherman Santiago and his battle for the great marlin in *The Old Man and the Sea*.

All three Cuban books, it might be noted, are remembered as sources for well-known Hollywood movies, featuring such major actors as Humphrey Bogart, Spencer Tracy, and George C. Scott, and for various reasons have had continuing appeal to Cubans then and now. *To Have and Have Not* replaces 1930s Cuba in favor of World War II–era Martinique as a Caribbean Casablanca. The Machado police are replaced by the Vichy French, with Cubans in wartime thus remaining unsullied. *The Old Man and the Sea*, while of the Batista era, is markedly devoid of political statement, with the fisherman Santiago and his battle with the great fish evoking a purity of elemental struggle and manhood. *Islands in the Stream*, following the posthumously assembled novel, casts Cuba in the light of World War II heroics; Havana is replete with a gaudy nostalgia—of a piece with the glamour and adventure of Hemingway's Cuba years, themselves a kind of epic movie scenario of life imitating art. Accordingly, for such depictions of the island and its inhabitants in literature and film, Hemingway remains Cuba's favorite twentieth-century international literary citizen, a kind of prerevolutionary gringo icon of a glamorous, if mythologized, past.

Though traveling to the island somewhere between eight to ten times, both pre- and postrevolution, Greene, in contrast, experienced Cuba mainly in the form of pleasure trips and journalistic visits, none longer than several weeks. Nor did he ever relent in describing his extended serial-tourism affair with the island as largely devoid of any particular interest in the beauty or the people and history of the Cuban nation. Self-described, he was altogether the decadent cosmopolitan pleasure seeker. Regarding his particular attraction to the notably corrupt and seedy version of Havana and its environs depicted in the novel and the film, Greene was callously direct. "I enjoyed the louche atmosphere of Batista's city," he confessed, "and I never stayed long enough to be aware of the sad political background of arbitrary imprisonment and torture." "I came there," he went on, "for the sake of the Floridita restaurant (famous for Daiquiris and Morro crabs), for the brothel life, the roulette in every hotel, the fruit machines spilling out jackpots of silver dollars, the Shanghai Theatre, where for one dollar and twenty-five cents one could see a nude cabaret of extreme obscenity with the bluest of blue films in the intervals."

Thus Greene boasted, surely in a way offensive to many Cubans then and now, of the glorious corruptions of the island and the vast array of open depravities available to visitors in the mid-1950s, after a long reign of American corporate bankrolls, political stooge ambassadors, client political strongmen, and celebrity gangster ownership of hotels, casinos, clubs, and houses of prostitution. Nowhere could one find a compensating word about the beauty of the island or the bravery and passion of its people and their history. Postrevolutionary pronouncements showed some small increase in popular political awareness. While applauding advances in health care and literacy education, he eventually came to disapprove openly of the government's intolerance of homosexuals, artists, and political dissidents. Even here, hedonism seems to have remained an important gauge. In the first days of Castro rule, he urged a friend to explore the Havana brothels before it was too late. "When communism starts, Puritanism immediately follows," he wrote. "You ought to see what is on offer here before it goes." Even as Greene publicly embraced the new regime—eventually calling attention to its advances in education, health care, economic security, he lamented its prim repressiveness of the flesh.

As a term of political critique, the choice of vocabulary is revealing. Puritan. It was the worst thing he could call the new regime—not unlike the Saigon US do-gooders in his previous novel of revolutionary Indochina, *The Quiet American*, where the idealistic titular character, Alden Pyle, is the latest ideological incarnation of the American New England puritan hemorrhoid, a pain in the ass. It might be remembered as well that Greene spoke with equally unadorned hedonistic fondness of Saigon, the setting of the former novel. There the operative drug was opium. Oddly, he did not reserve equal disappointments for the Hanoi moralists. Perhaps it is because the war took so many years and cost so many Vietnamese their lives. The Cuban insurrection turned out to be a matter of months by comparison. At no time did Castro have more than three thousand to four thousand soldiers in the field. Militarily, the US-supported Batistianos proved a predictable joke. The great enemy was to the north, the puritans with nukes. According to the moral calculus so expressed, before or after the revolution, one of the worst things that can happen anywhere in the world is the takeover by a confederacy of prigs. What this view of things amounted to, in the larger Cold War geopolitical context of Greene's anti-Americanism, was a novel that refused to take very seriously either the tyrannies and tortures of the Batista regime or the heroism and sacrifice of the revolution. Among the Cuban intelligentsia who likely read the book, the difference in treatments did not escape their attention or their long-term resentment.

Even down to Cuba's historical or geographic role as a setting for the novel he planned, he was equally open about what seemed an almost cynical literary utilitarianism. Havana seemed simply to deliver itself up as the perfect locale for an intentionally surreal Cold War espionage caper about a bumbling British intelligence agent—a kind of feckless anti–James Bond, about whom his creator, Ian Fleming, had already contributed five novels—who manages to set up an entire fictitious spy network, growing rich on payments from his masters for reports from the imaginary agents. The plot, Greene went on, was itself borrowed, with the germ of the original story having taken place in World War II Lisbon. There, a clever alleged Nazi Axis operative, code named Garbo, had spent the war directing a complete phony "agent" network for which he had been lavishly rewarded by his clueless German masters. Then there had also been the local operative he had known during his own time in East Africa, actually quite illiterate, who had done much the same thing with the Vichy French. (Further, as he surely must have known, Cuba could boast its own oddball story of the capture and execution of one Hans Luening, whose almost pitiable ineptitude revealed him to be surely the most hapless operative in the *Abwehr*.) Whatever the origin of the story, Greene went on, his initial concept had been to transplant the concept to Tallinn, Estonia, but simply found the place and attendant Cold War atmospherics too cheerless for his comedic designs. It was thus, he said, that Havana beckoned as suitably absurd. "Suddenly it struck me that here in this extraordinary city, where every vice was permissible and every trade possible, lay the true background for my comedy. . . . [I]n fantastic Havana," he went on, "among the absurdities of the Cold War (for who can accept the survival of Western capitalism as a great cause?) there was a situation allowably comic." The front matter of the book, he insisted, told the simple truth of his intentions: "A fairy story . . . set at some indeterminate date in the future."

A borrowed spy story in a second- or third-choice setting, with an intentionally absurd, perhaps even farcical plot: this called for a cast of characters on which Greene happily gave himself license to exercise his considerable powers of invention. Accordingly, the text itself introduces us without delay to the unlikeliest of protagonists ever recruited to Her Majesty's Secret Service anywhere. He is James Wormold, the Havana representative of Phastcleaner, a British vacuum cleaner company, whose store, attended by a Cuban employee during Wormold's absences at various neighborhood bars, is nearly always deserted. His wife has left him for an American. A figure named Hawthorne shows up at the shop. He is on a mission from London. After many mishaps, the recruitment pitch gets made. In need of money for the expensive wants and pursuits of an attractive teenage daughter, Wormold becomes MI6's man in Havana. To satisfy his employer's insistent requests for information, he basically invents his own network of agents, bankrolling himself and his daughter's aspirations as an equestrienne—a horse, riding lessons, a fancy stable at an elite country club—by sending the made-up characters (with names initially taken from the country club membership list) on equally fictitious spy missions. He "enlists" others he sees on his various travels. All given new identities as fictitious agents, they begin sending in "reports" forwarded by Wormold and eagerly read and paid for in London. Afoot on the island, the members of the vast network allegedly discover mysterious secret installations, the construction details of which Wormold documents by sending on traced-out technical drawings of various vacuum cleaner assemblies—all taken from the factory specifications of a model named, with particular aptness, "the Atomic Pile." With every report, Wormold gains prestige, and London keeps buying and paying even more eagerly than before. Wormold secretes the bulk of the money in a trust for his daughter. His activities shortly draw the attention of the head of the Cuban security police in Havana—a notorious torturer and murderer, said to possess a wallet made of human skin, named Segura who has already shown a menacing sexual attraction to the daughter. Meanwhile, in good Cold War fashion, a competing intelligence network—we are never really told whose—also enters the action. An array of opposite numbers begins to emerge, not least, Wormold's longtime geriatric drinking companion Dr. Hasselbach, a mysterious German physician with few patients and great affection for the old Pickelhaube empire. Carter, a professional assassin with the assignment of killing Wormold arrives in the guise of a fellow vacuum cleaner salesman flown in by a competing firm. He chooses an official trade association dinner as the occasion at which Wormold will be poisoned. Forewarned, the latter avoids both lethal food and drink. The chief casualty of the evening is a dog belonging to a waiter involved in the plot. Soon, a lot of people begin to die. "Raul," a drunken Cubana Airlines pilot picked at random by Wormold and about to be launched on an entirely fictitious "reconnaissance" flight over the island confirming the mysterious construction actually gets killed in an auto accident on the way to the airport. Engineer Ciefuegos, picked from the country club roster and quietly minding his own business, nearly suffers the same fate in a drive-by assassination attempt. From the same list, Professor Sanchez turns out to be leading his own double or triple life, having a girlfriend he is trying to hide from his mistress, both of whom he is trying to hide from his wife, who herself turns out to be the sister of the Catholic bishop of Havana. Meanwhile, on the other side, casualties also begin to mount. Hasselbach dies in punishment for his attempt to warn Wormold that he is about to be murdered by Carter. Carter in turn is eventually murdered by Wormold.

Meanwhile, as revealed in inter-chapters set in London, MI6 is pouring in the money and the personnel. In due response of central headquarters to what seems his rapidly expanding operation, Wormold gets sent a secretary, Beatrice, whom he falls in love with. He gets a radio operator, who carries his equipment in a huge suitcase and sleeps on a cot in the office.

Segura knows about all of this, and Wormold knows that he knows. To implicate him in the espionage plot, Wormold engineers an evening checker match between them with whiskey miniatures, a drinking game in which the first man to win the most checkers wins the checkers but probably loses the drinking match and passes out. While Segura is unconscious, Wormold uses his gun to kill Carter. Segura is now compromised as to the political situation and also discredited as a suitor. In a Casablanca-like final scene at the airport, as the Wormold party prepares to board a plane to England, Segura makes a final appearance and drops the spent murder bullets into Wormold's palm. The three arrive safely in London, where, British intelligence, chagrined at Wormold's duplicity, promote him to a supervisory position in the home office.

Set amid the decadent atmospherics of the city in the waning days of the Batista dictatorship, the book was published in late 1958—as it turns out—a bare three months before the victory of the Socialist revolution. Then, ironically—a bare three months after that, to be exact—in early spring 1959, it became the source of a postliberation British-American film collaboration, starring the distinguished actor Alec Guinness. Greene himself was also present, this time as a celebrity guest of the new revolutionary government, still playing coy about its possible Communist affiliations. So, of course, as revealed in various publicity stills, was Fidel Castro.

The director was Carol Reed, famous for his classic version of Greene's first great work of Cold War espionage, *The Third Man*—with Greene, as revealed in publicity photos, looking expertly over his shoulder. The result was a curious admixture of styles. The language was English, with Spanish subtitles. The filming was black and white. The geography of the centuries became a gritty tourist map of mid-twentieth-century Havana. Wormold hears the wolf whistles beginning at the corners of Virtudes and Compostela, signaling his teenage daughter's daily return home from school. The meager vacuum cleaner inventory, with its pseudo-American atomic-age branding, gathers dust at the pathetic shop on Lamparilla. Meanwhile, the developing action launches itself on a tour of the city's basic social geography: the quaintly labyrinthine and claustral Habana Vieja of the shops and shadowed, quiet *palacios*; the teeming, hucksterish Habana Centro of the Parque Central and Capitolio, the swanky, upscale, residential Vedado of the tropical villas, resort hotels, and country clubs. The plot comes to encompass action at nearly all the great tourist places: the Wonder Bar; Sloppy Joe's; the elegant Hotel Nacional; the Tropicana with its lavish music and dance spectacles; the Barrio Chino with the Blue Moon and its sex shows. (In prophetic image of the opening Mob-convention scenes of *The Godfather II*, the opening scene views the city from the rooftop pool of the Havana Hilton.) At some point, the viewer then as now must have wondered at the choice of filming in black and white. In a Technicolor world, how could there be a more Technicolor place than 1950s Cuba? Then one sees the logic of the Cold War plot, the need for the erasure of the colors of history. Nonetheless, there must have seemed to Cubans of the era particularly an encasement of their life and culture in an overlaying of political and cinematic conceits. The view from the Hilton may be from a beautiful rooftop pool, but the streets are sweaty and grimy. The opening scenes at ground level follow at length an unknown street couple in the process of making an assignation. The mood is film noir, gritty, Latin. At the Wonder Bar, on a corner open to the noisy, teeming street crowds, we shortly meet Guinness, playing the central role in his signature '50s British oddball/amiable nincompoop. It is as if for a moment *La Strada* or *The Bicycle Thief* has met *Kind Hearts and Coronets*.

The other male British cast members helpfully invest the spy atmospherics with a Cold War Anglo-European espionage panache—as in Reed's *The Third Man*, set in Vienna, or Le Carré's *The Spy Who Came In from the Cold*, set in Berlin, playing the operative role to type: Noel Coward appears as Hawthorne, the inscrutable handler; Ralph Richardson back in London is M. Among the film's many curiosities, political and otherwise, is the venturesome inclusion of Americans. The old German doctor, Hasselbach, is played by Burl Ives, known to American music audiences as a rotund, genial folksinger; to American movie goers as Big Daddy in *Cat on a Hot Tin Roof*; and to followers of political events, as among the show business figures who had named names for the McCarren committee. By now considered a signature American movie queen, Maureen O'Hara proved a brilliant piece of casting, playing off type in her original Irish glory as steady, quick-witted Beatrice, unflappable as a beacon of sturdy womanhood even amid the sordid wreckage of the Tropicana, the Blue Moon, the Shanghai. In contrast, the US starlet Jo Morrow was a case of simple bad casting as Wormold's daughter Milly, playing against the novel not as a postpubescent ingénue but a Hollywood teenage sexpot. But above all, for Cubans surely, the strangest casting must have been the high-profile, offbeat US TV and movie comedian Ernie Kovacs as Segura. This is not to say that, for an audience unattuned to the realities of Batista terror as were most Americans of the era, he did not achieve a complex, interesting performance in the role, with an exquisite combination of menace and obtuseness, the absence of anything resembling human emotion. For Cubans on the other hand, he must have seemed an inconceivable monstrosity, trivializing the Batista horrors and, more particularly, the justly earned reputation for genuine monstrosity of Ventura, the figure on whom he was modeled. The problem with Kovacs was, of course, that they had seen too many American movies and watched too much American TV. Even when viewing the original film fifty years later, it is not hard to escape seeing Segura even thus cleverly played as just another Ernie Kovacs weirdo, along with all the American grainy kinescope footage and the TV laugh track to go with it. Perhaps inspired from the standpoint of art, this Butcher of Havana portrayal as a menacing dimwit—complete with a seltzer-bottle scene with Maureen O'Hara at the Tropicana—was doomed from the outset in the Cuban context of known totalitarian horrors.

As to Cuban responses within such a history of textual evolutions in *Our Man in Havana*, it is impossible to know how many Cubans read the novel, before or after the movie. There was a 1958 Spanish translation of the book. The film was played with Spanish subtitles. As to Greene's own widely printed and reproduced commentaries on his attitudes toward the choice of setting and his attempt to divorce serious geopolitical questioning from his farcical purposes, no information exists on whether any of the text cited above found translation.

What is known is that Greene had chosen to write *Our Man in Havana* about a nation and a people actually on the verge of a Socialist people's revolution. From start to finish, if only to the Cuban cultural intelligentsia who may have read it, left or right, the novel accordingly must have seemed a notably odd if not downright callous and opportunistic production from a major artist with a history of sympathy to third-world revolutionary movements and caustic denunciations of a blundering and naïve American imperialism. There had been, for instance, his recent excoriation of destructive, callow US geopolitical arrogance in his previous novel of Indochina, *The Quiet American*. Wasn't the Castro insurgency against Batista corruption and tyranny at least as worthy of literary seriousness as the Ho Chi Minh anticolonialist struggle in Vietnam? For those more than prepared to take cultural umbrage, Greene's next Caribbean political thriller, *The Comedians*, providing a highly racialized caricature of Duvalier's Haiti, must have seemed to bookend Greene's general depiction of the region as a third-world shithole. Then, in the personal sphere, there had also occurred more recently Greene's black-comedy, late-Caribbean traveler's run-in with the US McCarran Act, making him, because of youthful radical Socialist flirtations and brief Communist Party membership at Oxford, "a prohibited immigrant to the United States." Through the dreadful earnestness of American functionaries, both government and commercial, he had somehow managed to get detained in Puerto Rico, reemplaned for Jamaica, and then rerouted, albeit quite happily, to Havana. In all this, Americans had seemed not so much dangerous as silly and contemptible. One wonders, on the other hand, if the general farcicality of the situation rubbed off on his attitude toward the larger politics of the Caribbean.

One tries now to reconstruct particular objections in this vein. Both the book and the movie of *Our Man in Havana*, in their distinctive ways, it must be admitted, do give short shrift to revolutionaries and revolution. In the book, as part of an annual tour of Phastcleaner branch offices, Wormold takes a trip across the island to Santiago, the capital of revolutionary Oriente, where he innocently runs afoul of a local police patrol and is roughed up and interrogated. (The incident is founded on a trip Greene himself made as a minor-league courier for Castroite acquaintances.) Literarily and historically, the setting could not have been, at the time, more ripe for the political moment, with the 26 November *guerrilleros* up in the hills, at the time of the novel's writing, about to culminate the long struggle beginning with the near disasters of the 1953 Moncada barracks and the 1956 Granma invasion. The fictional emphasis, however, is completely on the thuggery and stupid officiousness of the Batistiano minions. In the one arguably brutal scene in the novel—Wormold's sudden, random beating, arrest, and interrogation—two brutal cops, more than six hundred miles away on the other end of the island where an insurgent could blow them up on any day, wind up cravenly backing off because they are scared of Segura. Otherwise the uprising out in the hills of Oriente gets a sentence: "The usual rebels held the mountains and government troops the roads and cities, blocks were frequent and buses were less liable to delay than private cars." In the movie, even the side trip itself to the far-off land of insurgency is eliminated. A subtitle in the beginning, overlaying the panoramic shot of the city taken from the rooftop pool of the Hotel Capri, simply provides a silent legend: This film was completed after the recent revolution.

Though risky to assume any party functionary spent much official time parsing the literary-cultural implications of *Our Man in Havana* in the heady days just after victory, there does seem to have been sentiment among some few who saw the film script in Spanish that the cruelty of the Batista regime had been underplayed. The general seediness of the depictions of Cuban life came in for brief comment. Beyond this, the only explicit postrevolutionary objection to the movie—one that must have delighted the antipuritan Greene—was that the strippers needed to take off fewer items of clothing.

According to Peter Hulme, asked once whether he wished he had written a book like *The Quiet American,* "which would have carried more weight" than an "entertainment"—if adding insult to injury was needed, the Cuban novel was in fact, the last one on which the author used the term as a canonical way of distinguishing his serious books from his lighter or more popular ones—Greene replied: "Not in the least. I think that *Our Man in Havana* is a good comic novel. The object was not to talk about Cuba but to make fun of the Secret Service. Havana was merely the background, an accident—it had nothing to do with my sympathy for Fidel." Nor obviously did it waste much time on any other political complication. "In poking fun at the British Secret Service," he said, he had intentionally "minimized the terror of Batista's rule." He could appreciate the feelings of "those who had suffered during the years of dictatorship," but his "real subject was the absurdity of the British agent and not the justice of a revolution." It was all simple enough: "The Cuban government is corrupt; the British Secret Service is inept." The representation of actual politics beyond any of this was beside the point. For Cubans, then and now, that was just the point, entirely.

Apparently it remained a point lost on Greene. In 1992, an interviewer asked, "In the Preface to *Our Man in Havana*, you say the Cubans after the revolution rather disliked the book because its nature, its lightness, prevented you from exploring Cuba in depth . . . . Have they forgiven you?" Greene answered, "They've forgiven me since, yes." The comment is astute. In conversation, recollection, guidebook citation, humorous anecdote, he is correct, as is worthy and characteristic of Cubans. As for public commemoration or inclusion in official history, on the other hand, the answer remains a dour and unequivocal no.

To be sure, there had been the eventual falling out with Fidel, the revolution itself, with Greene's particular criticism of the revolution's treatment of Catholics, homosexuals, and intellectuals. As to a certain affectionate respect for the Comandante, Greene proved still capable in 1983 of writing a politely official letter on behalf of imprisoned writers.

Timing is everything. In the 1939 *Wizard of Oz*, MGM studios took a turn-of-the-century children's book addressing now obscure questions of populism and bimetal currency and made it into a classic allegory of the beauty and resilience of common humanity in the face of totalitarian fear and threat. The same may be said to a lesser degree of Greene's curious text. A tragic-comic hybrid, an entertainment by a serious artist, a prerevolutionary novel that became a postrevolutionary film, it came to express the state of the Cuban nation, the people, their history, their mid-twentieth-century centrality in the great geopolitical struggle of east and west, Communism and capitalism, revolution and reactionary imperialism; caught between identities, pre- and postrevolution inhabitants, first literary and then cinematic, of a kind of floating island, not unlike that visited by Swift's Lemuel Gulliver, Greene insisted that he had simply exercised his right to put them to his own fictional uses—though interestingly, as it turned out, in many cases, especially as Cold War and Nuclear Age events in the region and the world took their course, such uses proved to be far more serious than he let on. Time has actually served this dimension of the text well. It is, of all his novels, absurd in setting and tone, the most Kafkaesque/Koestlerian—to be distinguished from the black comedy atmospherics of *The Comedians*. As to history within the text, even as he wrote, he had an important point on fictional temporality, frequently missed in subsequent readings. He had set the novel "a few months in the future." Eventually a lot of strange things came true. Most directly and proximately, given the basic elements of the main political characters, there came a quick turn in British/Cuban relations, with the UK culture of official secrecy being embarrassed and rattled by controversial revelations over the foreign office sale of military aircraft to the Batista regime. And, as to the plot device of secret "weapons installations" hidden across the island, it, of course, also proved eerily prescient of the actual geopolitical machinations eventuating in the Cuban Missile Crisis a few years later—even down to the intentional dispersion of installations to remote sites across the island and the pattern of intelligence gathering by aerial reconnaissance overflight that eventuated in their being revealed. Whether as a book or a movie, much of the critical puzzlement about *Our Man in Havana* would remain that, even as popular entertainment, it was a book before its time, anticipating the imminent explosion in popularity of the serious spy spoofs such as the James Bond series and thus eventually moving it beyond into complete absurdity. The former Pearl of the Antilles joined a host of other exotic locales harboring increasingly far-fetched and even comic scenarios of strange sinister plots of world domination by warring Cold War powers and their outriders. Without anyone much noticing, *Our Man in Havana* could be mentioned in the same breath as *Our Man Flint*.

The afterlife of Greene's novel played out most extensively in the movies. "Spy farce." "Espionage Caper." "Cold War fantasy." (And then later, in reprise of the shot from the Capri rooftop pool, would come the further godfatherization of the old black-and-white classic.) Whether or not Cubans liked it, they and their most wonderful of all cities, by implication themselves and their proud history as a nation, by way of a Graham Greene "entertainment," had become a basic movie property. Thirty years after the subject had been more or less forgotten, Hollywood felt compelled to reinvent the city as imaged by Greene for a Robert Redford–Lena Olin–Raul Julia love-triangle potboiler set against a period backdrop of Mob corruption and imminent revolutionary victory entitled, of course, *Havana*. "Cuba, December 1958," reads the breathless IMDb header: "The professional gambler Jack visits Havana to organize a big Poker game. On the ship he meets Roberta and falls in love with her." The casinos are in full glory. The vintage '50s American cars are everywhere.

It all may be said to have begun with Graham Greene. About all this, Cubans of sundry political persuasions, proud of a rich and vital history and culture, would themselves the next fifty years to the present be wondering why anyone should be interested in the story of the twentieth-century nation suffering under the last days of the Batista tyranny played as a goofy espionage fable played for laughs. To be sure, read any English language/culture guidebook to Havana, and you will find a section on Graham Greene, his novel, and the movie. With maps, commentary, and photographic illustration, for the latest Havana pilgrim interested in the city of the literary imagination who might search out the Hemingway orbit of the Ambos Mundos, the Floridita, the Bodeguita, and the like, the vivid geography of Graham Greene and his novel is still available chapter and verse: the old Wonder Bar, the Barrio Chino, the Tropicana, the legendary bordello of Doña Marina; for that true archaeologist aficionado of the novelistic mind, even the shadow addresses of the former Sloppy Joe's, Sans Souci, Club Zombie, Shanghai Burlesque Theater, Havana Country Club, and all the rest. Look, on the other hand, anywhere in Havana, and you will find no annotations of memory whatsoever concerning the author or his book. His compounded offense seems to be that not only had he sold the political moment short, he had betrayed the character of Havana as a symbol of the humanity and spiritual vitality of the Cuban nation. A people who felt they deserved to be treated with historical and political seriousness, their most wonderful of all cities had become a squalid, off-key, film noir backdrop. Like Vienna, Saigon, or Leopoldville, Havana had become just another piece of Greene-land, and not even a serious one at that.

11

INSPECTOR RENKO ON THE MALECÓN

Twenty stories high, a monument to the totalitarian gigantism favored by twentieth-century dictators worldwide, from Benito Mussolini to Mao Tse Tung, Adolf Hitler to Kim Jong Il, the former Soviet Embassy in Cuba to this day dominates the otherwise shining and resort-like skyline of the Miramar section of Havana like a finger stuck in the tropical blue eye of the twenty-first-century nation. If one works at it, the thing can seem vaguely Aztec, Mayan, Toltec, though with jutting angularities of make-believe arms and head looking also like some huge, monstrous Lego or Transformer movie toy, perhaps upreared during a remote geological era now long forgotten.

It is largely abandoned now, as it has been for coming up on twenty-five years. A skeleton staff, the story goes, has barely the resources to pay the electric bills that keep the lights on. Though little notice otherwise seems to be paid to it, no one can dispute its centrality to a whole cultural symbolism of USSR abandonment—at the time of the 1991 dissolution of the Soviet Union itself—of a loyal Marxist-Leninist Cuban government and people crucially dependent on military materiel, foreign aid, international trade assistance, and high-level state investment. Showing that homegrown government propagandists had at least not forgotten their acquired talent for Soviet-style totalitarian euphemism, the Cuban regime put its own historical tag on the economic catastrophe that almost immediately ensued. "The Special Period," it was called. El Período Especial. What the phrasing actually describes is the nearly complete domestic cultural and economic collapse of a centralized Marxist-Leninist–controlled production system that had already been sputtering for three decades, plunging the whole of the nation into a lean, joyless, unstable era usually described as occupying the decade of the 1990s—though with ravages unabated to the present day. Overnight, the nation is said to have lost both four-fifths of its imports and four-fifths of its exports. The gross domestic product plunged by a third. Oil imports were reduced to a tenth of pre-1990 levels.

Transportation, industry, and agricultural activity dependent on petroleum-based fuels came to a near standstill, with technology replaced by manual labor. In the face of a continuing US embargo, came a breakdown in delivery of the most elementary necessities of everyday life: electrical power, transportation systems, basic consumer goods, essential food, in some cases, potable water. Hunger and malnutrition were ubiquitous, and health, education, and social services had to be radically curtailed.

The nation still struggles visibly to recover more than twenty years later. Indeed, for many Cubans, it still seems a shock so recent, so stunning in its inconceivable rapidity and devastation, that people who went through it can barely talk about it. "It was awful," one will hear someone say. "It was unbelievable." "It is impossible to make you understand how bad it was." "Everything was gone; you couldn't get anything; people had nothing." At the same time, almost nothing is written about it outside the technical academic literature of politics, economics, international affairs; nor is there yet permitted, it would seem, any published internal description concerning what everyday life was like there in autobiography or popular social history, imaginative literature, or film. It therefore comes as a queer surprise, albeit a welcome and revealing one, as noted by Jacqueline Loss, that the student of the period is able to find a singular, extraordinarily detailed depiction in popular US fiction—to be specific, in a detective novel/espionage thriller by the American writer Martin Cruz Smith, part of a larger series featuring the adventures of the Russian detective, Arkady Renko, and centered itself on the downfall of the Soviet Union, the rise of a corrupt capitalist plutocracy, the evolution of a brutal, bloodthirsty, and utterly lawless Mob system, and not least the collapse of the police and intelligence functions into a shadowy, violent, mirror-image nexus of secret cabal and conspiracy. The title of the proximate text, as well of the center of all the novel's main actions, is *Havana Bay*. The resultant genre might be best described as murder mystery and police procedural engrafted upon international criminal conspiracy thriller. Where once, on the eve of Marxist revolution, Graham Greene wrote *Our Man in Havana*, now, at the end of the great Soviet experiment, in *Havana Bay* Martin Cruz Smith gives us the adventures of Arkady Renko on the Malecón.

Accordingly, as to the representations of a particular time in a particular place, the opening chapters inform many English language readers for perhaps the first time concerning some things about which Cubans need no reminding. For the rest of the world, the fall of the Soviet Union and quick dissolution of Iron Curtain satellite governments marked the end of the Cold War; for Cubans it marked the beginning of a new era of suffering in a history already replete with tragedy: elevated briefly into twentieth-century international major-nation political status and rapid Soviet-style economic and industrial development, the island, we find, has been plunged back into a social and even environmental nightmare. The former Caribbean people's paradise has become postindustrial hell.

The early chapters of the novel plunge us into a panoramic spectacle of this world of nightmarish reversal and/or inversion. The place is Havana Bay; but now, amidst the dark national passage into a new era called el Período Especial, the action of the opening scenes is in the middle of an impenetrable night, on the "wrong" side, across the water from the old city just barely beginning to be visible in the first hours of a foul-smelling, humid dawn. We are on the eastern industrial side, below the cliffs of Casablanca and the menacing walls of the great prison fortress of La Cabaña. Further along lie the dismal port towns lining the interior bottom, Atares, Regla, Guanabacoa. The bay proper, the oily inner harbor, is pollution streaked, garbage strewn, a vast collocation of rotting docks, abandoned loading piers, shipyards, refineries. The night glares with gas flames and police spotlights, and the illumination is absorbed into strange patterns of movement and shadow. Across the bay, it is as if the dawn itself struggles to break against the luminous whites and pastels of the old city, the stately seawall girding the grand historical government buildings, fortresses, mansions, harborside parks, plazas, and promenades. Over there, one can still imagine Habana Vieja—the Fuerza, the Punta, the Avenida Céspedes, and the beginnings of the Malecón—and then move westward into Habana Centro, with the Paseo, the Capitolio, the Parque Central; Vedado, with the University, the Martí Tower, and the Plaza de la Revolución; and then westward still into the high-end luxury beachfront Miramar with the abandoned Russian embassy and Jaimanitas with the Havana Yacht Club and Marina Hemingway. The whole scene projects the atmospherics of a barren energy field, a topography of loss and menace, the landscape of a dark star that has just imploded within a blighted paradise. Even when we get across the bay, the first destination is a police mortuary, a technologically run down and increasingly makeshift forensic pathology lab, to which has been borne a rotten, disintegrating corpse fished out of an inner tube. Havana itself becomes a post-Soviet version of the gothic nightmare city, out of Dickens, Balzac, Dostoevsky, by way of the detective landscapes of Sherlock Holmes's London, C. Auguste Dupin's Paris, Raymond Chandler's Los Angeles, and simultaneously those of the secret agent dark places of the earth in Joseph Conrad, Graham Greene, and Robert Stone. In the proximate case, Havana has become the post-Soviet extension of Arkady Renko's Moscow and the latest postmodern version of itself, now, in the words of one of Robert Stone's burnt-out cases, "Somewhere south of cliché." Yet as with figures as disparate as Cirilo Villaverde, Walker Evans, Ernest Hemingway, Graham Greene, and others, this fictionalized place remains a deeply recognizable Havana that is a topography of history and of the imagination. On the inside cover of *Havana Bay*, not surprisingly, to be recognized by anyone who knows the place, is a simple, familiar guidebook map, marking what are to be the novel's major locations of conflict and action.

The mise-en-scène is recent history, in the broadest sense, after the revolution, the Americans with their embargo, the Russians with their promises and their lavish assistance programs, now with these too, after the breakdown of the former Soviet Union, now nearly all gone away, leaving behind their former client nation to the old vicissitudes of poverty, hunger, social and economic decay, and geopolitical isolation. Assembled on the actual opening scene, we find all of the individual figures—a collection of police, security operatives, subordinate functionaries, gawking locals, and other hangers-on that seem to represent a microcosm of the new post-Russian order—contemplating a single, slimy, stinking, disintegrating corpse in a wetsuit crammed into an inner tube washed up against a rotting pier. They are nearly all of them Darwinian evolutions for bad weather. The official types seem determined to crawl out of the disaster with some kind of status, power, or identity, just something they decide they want, can say at least, this is mine, this is my portion of what is left. The attendant figures largely turn out to be specialists in blackmail, robbery, assault, and murder, practiced in the various nether worlds they navigate as ways to keep from getting blackmailed, robbed, assaulted, or murdered.

Renko, himself, in the aftermath of the Soviet collapse at home, and now of the nearly complete abandonment of their great failed experiment in Western hemisphere Communist nation-building, is a Moscow-based Russian inspector who flies to Havana to investigate the death of a Russian friend and colleague—one of the last Russian operatives remaining and quite likely now the two-week-old dissolving corpse in the wetsuit crammed into the inner tube. The Russian counterpart, Sergei Pribluda, once Arkady Renko's own deadly enemy and would-be assassin within the shadowy Russian security network, has worked in Cuba for the embassy, from which someone has sent Renko a fax message simply saying that Pribluda is in trouble.

Arkady Renko, the Russian police inspector who has now inexplicably arrived in a Cuba that is decidedly "not a good place for a Russian," is nothing if not in trouble. With the fall of the Soviet Union, he has become the strange evolutionary by-product of the bureaucratic system devised to produce the Soviet man. In public life, he has once been a good Russian cop, the son of a Soviet major general and hero of the great patriotic war. Of late, with the collapse of the police apparatus into a tangle of corruption and official betrayal, he has been a chief investigator of uncertain status who can't figure out the difference between the cops and the criminals. In private, he mourns the pointless death of his beloved wife, Irina, killed by the blundering Russian medical system, the victim of anaphylactic shock after being injected, by an incompetent nurse who has carelessly misunderstood the instructions of a harried doctor talking on the phone to his broker, with the wrong allergy medicine. In every sense, Renko could not be more alone with History. Like Gogol's Akaky Akakievich, on whom he is clearly modeled here—even down to an incongruously fine, ostentatiously visible, and highly superfluous cashmere overcoat—a gift of Irina's he wears in the Cuban heat—he is the empty, broken, despairing relic of a complex bureaucratic system that has used him up and spit him out. Like Akakievich (whose name actually invokes the Russian word for excrement, or shit) he bears an empty government title; like Akakievich he has been summarily dismissed of his responsibilities; as if to seal the bargain, now like the ghost of Akaky Akakievich, he shows up in Havana wearing the overcoat, about to be an endless irritant and mystery to those in power and a strange figure of menace and rivalry to those shadowy others operating outside the system. He has just gotten off an Aeroflot plane from Moscow and has been taken to the harbor where the decomposed, waterlogged, nearly liquid corpse, probably of his dead Russian colleague, has just been fished up. The latter, whose full name is Sergei Sergeivich Pribluda, has been a Havana-based security officer, officially listed as an embassy "Sugar attaché," but suspected by Cubans of being a spy, and shortly revealed to Renko as having further mysterious connections into criminal schemes of international finance and market manipulation. At his death, he has seemingly joined a mysterious group of offshore Havana sea scavengers called the *neumáticos* who fish from inner tubes by night to supplement the starvation subsistence economy. The diagnosis as to cause of death seems to have been a sudden, simple heart attack. Beginning, as do most of the *neumáticos*, in the waters to the west at various places off the Malecón in Vedado or Miramar, he has simply drifted unconscious or dead in the tube according to the well-known current patterns of the bay, entering the harbor at the Morro and winding up under the cliffs at Cabanas. Renko, simply by arriving in Havana to investigate the death of the shadowy Pribluda, is immediately suspected of his own espionage and/or international criminal connections. By arriving at the particular time when events have taken place, he simultaneously bears the full outrage of post-Soviet Cubans in their sense of betrayal and abandonment.

The particular Cubans present at the scene, pursuing their own investigation of the death, are representative. To a person, they are a very unpleasant, hostile lot. A small, officious captain of Interior Ministry Security, Arco, can barely contain his fury on the scene at the Russians, live or dead. His great menacing negro sergeant, Facundo Luna, stands by in cold silence. A small, brown, female mulata detective, Ofelia Osorio, conducts the actual investigation for the Policia Nacional de la Revolución. An interpreter-translator, Rufo Pinero, having learned his Russian as a member of the Cuban boxing team, stands by as an embassy representative.

The body, largely disintegrated in its removal from the bay, is taken to the Instituto de Medicina Legal in Habana Centro, just south of the Plaza de Revolución, where an autopsy is conducted by a cynical forensic pathologist, Dr. Blas, who intersperses caustic commentary on Renko's investigative caution with praise of Cuban forensic ingenuity, which has enabled them to outlive both the treacherous Americans and the Russians. In the shadow of the menace and corruption of the state security apparatus, and the vestiges of the Russian diplomatic and espionage mission, Inspector Arkady Renko and Detective Ofelia Osorio form a wary bond as they pursue the story of Pribluda's fate, which takes them from a series of mysterious locations, including an embassy guest apartment, where Renko is nearly murdered by Rufo; the dead man's own rented apartment on the Malecón, where Renko is nearly beaten to death by Luna; and an abandoned mariners' club on the harbor in the old city, the nicely named Centro Russo-Cubano, where they are both nearly murdered, again by the ubiquitous, brutal Luna. Renko's journeys take him to the nearly abandoned embassy, where a frightened junior official directs him to a ghostly handful of embassy troglodytes, vestigial grotesques of the Soviet experiment, including Elmar Mostovoi, a seedy former official photographer with his shabby studio props and porn trove of "art" shots of voluptuous Cuban nudes, and Olga Petrovna, a nostalgic middle-aged embassy mother superior, remembering a proud little Russian colony in Cuba, "protecting socialism on this island far from home in the teeth of the Americans." In the hunt for the secret of Pribluda's last days, amid the labyrinthine processes of Havana, Renko finds Isabel, a Cuban ballerina, the daughter of a party official who has attempted a coup, promised by her former lover Pribluda, she claims, escape to a magical new life at the Bolshoi; Erasmo, a garage mechanic downstairs from Pribluda's secret apartment on the Malecón who rebuilds Jeeps in an illegal workshop; Mongo, a Cuban Army EOD expert who lost his legs in Angola; Hedy, a fourteen-year-old *jinitera* working the tourist brothel, the Casa De Amor, with her picture of a Russian mystery man and her strange connections to both Facundo Luna and Rufo Pinero, who winds up being savagely hacked to death with a machete; George Washington Walls, a '60s American black radical airline highjacker long past his celebrity days in Moscow or Havana; John O'Brien, a fugitive American financier, living on his yacht and working his latest schemes to capitalize upon the economic ruin of the dollar-hungry revolution. Meanwhile "he" is there as well: everywhere, el Comandante, Fidel—on a street mural propaganda poster still proclaiming the eternal Venceremos; passing by in a motorcade; acted out in somebody's quick, humorous, frightened hand gesture under the chin, the fluttery reference to a beard. He is still the one who hears and sees everything.

Renko is the latest postcolonial evolution of recognizable literary forebears, voyagers in the world of Latin American revolutionary upheaval. He is decidedly a Graham Greene burnt-out case. He is a Robert Stone survivor, somewhere out past paranoia, in the world of life on the edge. He has been threatened with police investigation and possible imprisonment simply by showing up at the airport. To the extreme displeasure and suspicion of his new Cuban associates, he refuses to make final identification of a body in near-complete decomposition after two weeks in a floating inner tube. They take it as a patronizing Russian resistance to put professional approval on Cuban findings. Their resentment is only compounded by his shambling, unorthodox, almost perverse attempts to draw out the inquiry. *Idiota*, Orfelia Osorio calls him. Renko has discovered by now that she, like nearly every Cuban he has encountered in his odyssey, is fluent in Russian. For the Spanish term she has just uttered, he needs no translation. Renko's own confused post-Soviet psyche and actions breed their own complication. Attempting, at the embassy apartment, in a place that has now suddenly seemed to become the final destination of his own despair, to commit suicide by injecting empty air with a large autopsy syringe stolen from the forensic lab, he is interrupted and nearly stabbed to death by Rufo, the translator assigned by the embassy. When the police arrive, the syringe is inexplicably sticking out of the base of Rufo's brain. Taking up residence in Pribluda's old apartment on the Malecón, he is savagely attacked and nearly beaten to death by Luna with an aluminum baseball bat. Rufo and Luna, it turns out, are former members of the Soviet-era Cuban boxing team, where they have learned their Russian in Moscow. Luna, it will be discovered, has improved on his as a Russo-Cuban military advisor in Angola. With his batwork, apparently, he becomes something of an expert in certain American skills as well.

Eventually Renko starts to put together a whole complex chain of international, geopolitical, and criminal connections. He has begun on the dark, decayed, stinking, industrial far side of Havana Bay; he winds up all the way to the west, in lavish, upscale Guanabacoa at the Havana Yacht Club, where he has traced the mystery of Pribluda's death to his associations with Walls, the old American black radical plane hijacker, and O'Brien, the fugitive American financier. He now begins closing in on the web of greed and murder conspiracy that unites everything. Under the cover of a sugar cartel has come a related scheme to reopen the club as a luxury resort. The main attraction of the result will be a casino. As in the old days with the Batistianos, this will require a fifty-fifty split with the government. To get the cooperation of the government, the country will need a Batistiano-style military coup and a new, compliant leader.

Pribluda, it turns out, under the cover of his sugar attaché assignment with is various international business connections, has been working for them as security. Renko is invited to take his place. By virtue of the new connections with Walls and O'Brien, he finds out that his friend Pribluda has indeed died of a heart attack while in the sea. Only he had not been off the coast at the Malecón. He had been all the way out west of the city on the glittering shores of La Playa, at the new yacht basin called the Marina Hemingway, where a frayed high-voltage dock cable had fallen accidentally in the water. The shock stopped his heart instantly, confirming the diagnosis by Blas, the police pathologist. The Walls and O'Brien people floated him out into the offshore current, where, as they knew, he, or what was left of him, would eventually wind up in the dark, rubbish-stewn, polluted eastern reaches of Havana Bay—where the novel has indeed begun—and probably would be identified, after two weeks or more of waterlogging and decomposition, as just another *neumático*.

Interestingly, it is also here that Smith, once he has arrived at his American characters, turns the novel back to history—with reasons that are soon to be seen—with both Walls and O'Brien, it turns out, modeled on actual people. In his queer exile, Walls closely resembles the African American folk hero William Lee Brent, a Black Panther militant and fugitive from a warrant for the murder of two white sheriff's officers, whose 1969 plane hijacking to Havana was rewarded with twenty-two months in jail. Eventually released and granted sanctuary, he learned Spanish, educated himself in workers' Socialism, and eventually became the author of a memoir of his twenty-five-year Cuban sojourn, *Long Time Gone*. O'Brien similarly recalls the fugitive American financier, Robert Vesco, who, from the 1980s through the early to mid-1990s, was allegedly involved in everything from CIA espionage to narcotics trafficking, in the latter case with the implication of high-level military figures in the Castro government. Allowed to live on his boat at Cayo Largo, an upscale resort under his development, he also boasted involvement with Donald Nixon and Donald Nixon Jr., brother and nephew of the US president, in a pharmaceutical scheme on the island, involving the patenting and marketing of a miracle anticancer drug. He prospered until he was said to have attempted to defraud Raúl Castro. He was tried and sentenced to thirteen years in prison, where he died in 2005.

The most real political characters in the novel, on the other hand, are two Cubans. One of them, recurrently the most representative of the average person's struggle to survive daily life during el Período Especial, is the tiny, beautiful, mulata police inspector, Ofelia Osorio, a single parent of two, sexually harassed by her colleagues, bent on stamping out police corruption in sexual commerce. Accordingly, she and Renko, the lost, despairing post–Soviet Russian survivor, eventually find in each other brief spiritual identification and a few days as lovers. The other is, of course, "him." Fidel. The Comandante. He who sees and hears everything. As the revolutionary conspiracy plot of the novel speeds toward its conclusion, he is to be actually present. A gala event, the reopening of the venerable Havana Yacht Club as a glittering, five-star, international tourist resort, will in fact be a coup of soldiers and politicians, connected by service in Angola and Ethiopia and funded by a Ministry of Sugar scheme Pribluda has helped administer out of the Russian embassy in connection with the fugitive American financier and his Black Panther accomplice. The secret of the grand event is that the club is to be reopened as a casino. To this end, the leader is to be assassinated. At the last moment, the plot is betrayed; the leader vanishes to safety, the conspirators are arrested in the dignitary crowd and carried off one by one. With Arkady Renko aboard, Walls and O'Brien along with Luna try to make off on the financier's yacht, the *Gavilan*—in English, a "small, fierce bird of prey." In the ensuing exchange of weaponry, included firearms and spear guns, Arkady himself comes close to winding up another *neumático*. He survives, floating off the Playa, unlike the dead Pribluda, this time not to be carried by the currents into Havana Bay.

Meanwhile, the reader's mind may come full circle to the song Renko heard that first dawn back at the investigation scene in the polluted waters under the cliffs at las Cabanas while Pribluda's body was being recovered. It is a song played from some onlooker's loud radio. "La fiesta no es para los feos," go the lyrics. "Qué feo es, señor. Super feo, amigo mio. No puedes pasar aqui, amigo. La fiesta no es para los feos." The crowd seemed to be quite enjoying it. Renko was curious about it. Rufo translated: "'The song?' . . .This party is not for ugly people. Sorry, my friend, you can't come." In silent retort came an answer. "Yet here I am, Arkady thought." Where once there were ugly Americans, now it is the Russians who are somewhere south of that in el Período Especial.

What of the Cubans? Renko, again, has asked for a Russian translation, this time from Osorio concerning a big propaganda wall slogan. *"Venceremos!"* she says, "means we will win! In spite of America and Russia, we will win." Replies Renko: "In spite of history, geography, the law of gravity?" "In spite of everything," says Osorio confidently. "You don't have many signs of that in Moscow anymore, do you?" "We have signs," he replies. "We have signs. Now they say Nike and Absolut."

Osorio reminds him of his imminent return flight, and the dead friend who will be going home with him. "Let's hope it really is the Colonel," says Renko. Osorio is stung by his slight of her detective work, also by his tired cynicism. "A live Russian, a dead Russian," she says, "it's hard to tell the difference." For a moment, he seems to have heard in her voice the indomitable Cuban voice, after the Americans, after the Russians. He simply says, "You're right." He is a man who now knows Cuba, and who, by knowing Cuba, knows a place and a people who are still standing after the end of History.

12

THE EXAMPLE OF YOANI SANCHEZ

In theme and chronology, it is appropriate that the last of the chapters comprising the main body of this book on Cuba and the imagination becomes a historical and cultural mirror image of the first. The study began with an essay about the fictionalized early nineteenth-century life history of an imaginary Cuban social and political heroine whose story wrote itself into national legend. It now concludes with an essay about the factual early twenty-first-century life history of a very real social and political heroine of Cuban letters currently writing herself into new legendary status. As appropriately, amid a set of reflections on culture and imagination perforce dominated—through recurrent engagement with themes of war, politics, economic relations, and other systems of male power—by conceptions of dominant masculinities, both the female subject of the chapter that begins this text—Cecilia Valdés—and the corresponding female subject of the chapter that now concludes it—Yoani Sanchez—may be properly seen in just these contexts as acquiring their legendary prominence as cultural and/or ideological disturbers of the peace. In the great nineteenth-century novel of Cuba bearing her name, the literary tragic mulata Cecilia Valdés, the illegitimate offspring of forbidden interracial sex, herself eventually a courtesan, then a wife and mother, dares to live fully and freely at whatever cost in an imprisoning system of gender, race, and socioeconomic and political class relationship. In the global realm of twenty-first-century Internet communication, Yoani Sanchez, a "renegade philologist" as she calls herself, is an average college-educated woman of her generation, a wife and mother. In her transformed identity as a dissident journalist inhabiting a new, self-created space in the blogosphere, she becomes a living reproach to a political system alleged to have eliminated many of the foregoing barriers but in the process having installed new structures of rigid social, economic, and political control, not least among them the silencing of independent civil discourse.

Notably, though separated by nearly two centuries and arising out of vastly different forms of popular-culture representation, the figuring of both women as images of female empowerment also becomes a testament to the complex energies of the textual imagination in its myriad creative evolutions. Indeed, the narratives themselves, existing as they do on one hand in the realm of popular print and on the other in the electronic world of cyberspace, remain oddly but suggestively paired as products in both cases of their own complex histories of textual inscription and evolution. As is well known, Cirilo Villaverde, the author of *Cecilia Valdés*, wrote the novel in at least three distinct stages over a period of nearly fifty years, with an 1839 periodical-length work of popular historical fiction, a melodramatic tale of forbidden love and political conflict set in the historical period 1812–32, followed by a considerably longer 1842 novella, and then a full four decades later—nearly all of which the author had spent, in the circle of José Martí, as a revolutionary expatriate in the United States—by a compendiously rewritten and enlarged 1882 New York edition nearly twice the length of its predecessor. The result, as noted earlier, was a great, panoramic, vastly peopled family romance of the imagined Cuban nation—in its first half capturing life in Havana from the Bohemian artists' balls with their mixing of classes and races to the great glittering mansions, trading houses, and government centers of the colonial economic and political elites; and in the second extending the action into the surrounding exotic landscapes of mountain and tropical forest for dramatic scenes of life on the slavery hell of the vast sugar and coffee plantations of the interior. Yet so closely did the male Cirilo Villaverde identify with his titular female protagonist throughout the long history of textual evolution as to give the two of them the same birth year and the direct, formative political experience of the crucial early anti-Spanish revolutionary upheavals of the 1820s and 1830s. Thus in the ensuing decades of revision and expansion extending over nearly a half century was a legendary heroine of the past made present, an image herself of the nineteenth-century Cuban nation.

In the case of the emergence of Yoani Sanchez as a major cultural icon, the account of textual origin and evolution is more chronologically compressed but no less suggestive as an account of the complex forms and processes of historical and political mythmaking. Again, a distinctive time of political crisis is specified. Here, as imaged in Sanchez's own experience, it is another crucial nexus, the passage of her generation through the breakdown of the newest colonialism, the late twentieth-century end of a Marxist-Leninist era of revolutionary hope and socioeconomic development once underwritten by Russian largesse, with the post-Soviet-era nation plunged into a desperate time of want, shortage, starvation, called at the time el Período Especial, and even now still extending its hardships into the present. Here, as a postindependence, postrevolution successor to Villaverde, a century later Sanchez is a female dissident writer in internal exile in Cuba. She too is a journalist, of the new twenty-first-century online electronic type, generally called a blogger. That is, she maintains a specially constructed personal computer website, a blog (the term a contraction of "weblog") usually devoted to the composition and electronic publication of a personal journal and/or commentary on art, literature, music, popular media, politics, social observation, and the like, installments of which are delivered in a regular series of posts; usually with blogs, as in the case of Sanchez, the site is interactive, eliciting and recording comment and response from readers. Further, as again in the case of Sanchez, other, nonverbal media can be regularly featured: photography, art images, music, voice audio, and video. Beyond this, there are also external connections, via computer link, to other blogs, websites, and interactive media. It is in this rich matrix of virtual Internet culture that Sanchez began in 2008 with her first words of text. Soon, as she discovers, in her attempt to speak to the world of life in today's Cuba, she has become a kind of experimental, electronic, nonlinear, multimedia novelist, creating herself as both the narrator of and the central character of her evolving life history. As quickly, through the new interactive capacities of the electronic medium, her myriad readers with their commentary and response become fellow citizens sharing life in that discursive world.

Soon, in the world of everyday, real life in Cuba on which she reports, she incurs surveillance and harassment. She and a colleague are briefly kidnapped and roughed up by unknown assailants. The outgoing blog is electronically blocked. She continues with the assistance of e-mail couriers who transfer her latest communications to the website. Soon the incoming blog is blocked as well. She is now called a "blind" blogger. Still she writes. Her materials, which she herself has initially had to send through illegal visits to tourist hotels and other public internet sites forbidden to Cubans, continue to go out by e-mail, flash drive, cell phone, or on various social networks. Along the way she receives a number of major overseas freedom journalism awards. She is repeatedly denied the exit visas she seeks to receive any of them. She and others begin traveling the island, giving seminars on blog and personal website construction. After three years, the government stops blocking reception. She is able to read her blog again. Meanwhile, not only has Sanchez maintained her own communication with the world; she is now accompanied by dozens upon dozens of fellow Cuban bloggers and volunteer translators. In creating herself and her world as what we would now call an interactive fiction of fact, she has truly become the voice, the face, the iconic figure, the legendary heroine, if one wishes to call her that, of a whole electronic generation.

Her efforts extending over the crucial first three years of work also result in an internationally acclaimed book. The Spanish title is *Cuba Libre*; the English title is *Havana Real*. The double entitling becomes itself a vivid figure of Sanchez's vision and method, her gift, even in the fixed medium of traditional print, for the telling inflection. In the Spanish of her primary audience, *Cuba Libre* carries its weight of fact under a burden of revolutionary irony. It has been the great historical rallying cry for a free nation under the Spanish, under the US occupation, under the corrupt right-wing puppet dictatorships of the early to mid-twentieth century, and now, by implication, under the Castro regime of the last fifty years. What has changed, it asks. Nothing, it says. For more literalistic Anglophone readers less versed in Cuban history and/or political humor, *Havana Real* means exactly what it says. This is the way things are, it tells us, in the Cuba beneath the slogans. This is a present in which past dreams of freedom remain things of the future. This is the distance between *Cuba Libre* and *Havana Real*, between *Havana Real* and *Cuba Libre*. It is a figurative method as properly measured in the new electronic distance traveled by an ever-lengthening archive of entries and updates, notes from the present toward a new Cuba. Speaking, she says, to all possible audiences in the great world of virtual communication from the island that is her home, "Cuba, at the beginning of the millennium," these posts become "a raft made of binary code."

In this, the book is but a provisional element. To the same degree, for the reader of the larger textual body of the regular Internet posts, it becomes an abstract or epitome of the project. The author herself calls the book a companion to the blog, an interim distillation, the material iteration of a virtual text, with the latter in its endless proliferations something that can be no longer contained on the page, and thereby by conventional censorship, repression—or, as will be seen, legal prosecution. As the latest text of human liberation, it may be said to transcend the very constraints of history, for it is empowered by the newest, technologically self-reifying capacity of the textual imagination itself. Speech, writing, print, themselves now electronically unstoppable, partake further of the supplemental power of the visual image, music, film, audio, video. The discourse of the new cultural imagination in the twenty-first century, the composite creation could not be called by a more appropriate name: Virtual Reality. The etymology is an old one, from the Latin *virtu*: "in essence or in fact, though not in name;" now it has been melded with the new figure of technology: "not physically existing, but made to appear by software." A blog has thus become a great, inspired, political experiment in collaborative cyberfiction in the fullest sense, the discourse of a Cuban nation at once real and imagined.

Accordingly, Sanchez's book, or companion study as she calls it, now takes on an historical, political, and cultural importance of its own, as a meditation in midpassage on how this has been done so far, and, as importantly, on what may yet be accomplished should it continue. At the heart is the figure of a person writing at a computer, the new type and genius of her nation, sitting in her apartment on the fourteenth floor of an apartment building in Vedado overlooking the Plaza de la Revolución. An inhabitant of the political present, at the first keystroke, she has stepped into her own imaginative vision of an emancipatory future.

In just these terms of history, the book begins, with Sanchez, the blogger, now three years into her project, looking back, reimagining herself at just that moment, beginning to write. "I approach the keyboard of my old laptop," she says in her opening sentence "—sold to me six months ago by a rafter who needed money to buy an engine—and start writing." "The scene is simple," she continues: "A weak woman, without dreams sits down to describe what is not reflected on the boring TV or in tedious national newspapers." She interrogates her own doubts and premonitions. Will anybody care? Will she be labeled a puppet of the CIA? An agent of State Security? But there is also already a conversation going between herself and some new avatar of herself of whom she has suddenly become aware. "The guard inside my head is rarely wrong," she says, "but the crazy person who shares that space won't listen to her." She begins to type: "So,

I start circling around my first post, and with it, the empty shopping bag, the tall useless ministry buildings, the gnawing hunger and the raft floating in the Gulf all pass to another plane."

Quickly the crazy voice in the text has found its own narrative line. In that moment, the simple attempt to record small items of simple, everyday truth has already set her free. "I've only written a few lines," she says, "but now I am a blogger." And with the movement of language, the rush of empowerment is dizzying. "I have the vertigo of someone who has just appointed herself publisher and editor-in-chief." She decides on a name for her enterprise. "I christen my new space Generation Y, a blog inspired by people like me, people with names that begin or contain a 'Greek Y,' so unusual in Spanish. We are the generation born in Cuba in the seventies and eighties, marked by Schools in the Countryside, Russian cartoons, illegal emigration, and frustration. So I especially invite Yanisleidi, Yoandri, Yusimi, Youniesky, and all the others who drag their 'Greek Y' to join me and write to me."

With the exotic names—a small gift of political memory from their parents—comes a history. And an attitude. "Our ranks range from political police interrogators to prostitutes chasing tourist dollars. But a thread of cynicism binds us all, the cynicism necessary to live in a society that has outlived its dreams, and seen the future already exhausted before we got there." They are the cohort who came of age, that is, of el Período Especial following the collapse of the Soviet Union. "Without aspiring to utopias, our generation is firmly planted on the ground, inoculated against social dreams." Like her generation, she is quarantined in every sense of the term. Escape must come, she now understands, through a new voyage into speech and writing on the Internet.

Suddenly it is three years later and she has filed, sometimes in ways too strange and ingenious to believe, more than five hundred posts. It is time to compress these materials at least provisionally into a book. Meanwhile, she adds, "there are nearly a million reader comments converting my private, cathartic space into a public square." She knows that she has written and continues to write something profoundly new. "Novels," she says, "are already finished when they reach the page, but the Web, with its hypertexts, hot zones, and interactivity, has barely been touched in literature." The page, she has discovered, is an obsolete, dissolving, evanescent medium. In the invisible language-world of the Internet is the text of infinite possibility and liberation from the constraints of time, place, and even self. "Capturing this virtual world in the form of a book is so hard that I have given up trying." The book, she insists, must be but a kind of portal to the blog. "For the reader who wants more, or who wants to know what happens next, the blog is still there, online, growing like an enormous virtual beast, with more posts and more comments, and in twenty languages."

So the blog itself has become a kind of living, ever-expanding thing, at once a deeply personal and infinitely multivocal web of language and meaning. Sanchez now shows us how one ordinary person can truly invent one's self as a new political individual and find an audience of myriad other individuals to join her in populating the discursive polis thus created. To be sure, even in this post-Gutenberg galaxy, a lot of the features of existence she describes are notably unspectacular: the daily struggle to get along, to find essentials, to buy food, to navigate legal and illegal market systems, the ration system, the black market, the privileged economy of tourists and party elites. There are the frustrations of bureaucracies, petty regulations, endless hours wasted, whole days of one's life, getting something fairly simple done. The Russian elevators in her apartment building finally break down beyond repair. When new ones arrive more than a year later, no one has thought to see if they can be operational with the worn Russian fittings in the shaft. They, of course, cannot. All this is just the point. To undertake the very enterprise of living and reporting on the life of an average Cuban in the first decade of the twenty-first century is to create at once both a quotidian and an existential political identity. Intertwined with the details of everyday existence—shopping for a single meal in two or three market economies, getting turned down in a latest application for an exit visa, wondering if el Comandante's announced resignation will bring even small political liberalizations—we know the honest fears and enlarging braveries of a lone woman facing a future of she knows not what: surveillance, harassment, perhaps arrest, imprisonment, interrogation, torture, death. Apace, as a figure increasingly herself a creation of the verbal and visual media, she begins to come to terms with herself as a public, political character in her texts. At a conference she takes a microphone and begins speaking out. She sees videos of herself on the Internet. She is soon making them herself. She hears herself cited on an official government talk show. She begins to move in political and historical imagination. She visualizes herself, transported in time, back to childhood, young adulthood, forward into old age. Often she is accompanied by her son.

News comes of imprisoned fellow dissidents. One is on a hunger strike; there are rumors of another's impending death. A third is commemorated by an empty chair on Christmas Eve. It is not a game. She confesses to her heinous crimes, what she calls "a mountain of misdeeds: I have routinely bought on the black market; I have criticized, in a whisper, those who govern us; I have nicknamed politicians and I have agreed with pessimists. To top it off, I have committed the abominable offence of believing in a future without 'them' and in a different version of history than what I was taught. I repeated their slogans without conviction, washed dirty laundry in full view and—the greatest transgression—joined together words and phrases without their permission." The last is the one that will get her, she knows; but the words and phrases won't stop coming. "I confess," she says in advance of what is likely to happen, "and accept the punishment for it. I cannot both survive and comply with their law, at the same time."

Somewhere near the middle of the text, the early fears seem to come true in a single episode of terror. She and a male friend are abducted, thrown in an automobile, and given a skilled, police-style beating. It may be "the restless boys" as she calls them of State Security. It may be self-appointed thugs. It may be civilian thugs turning a buck in the hire of State Security. The expert style of beating and intimidating without greatly discernible wounding is described in detail. She appears, visibly needing assistance to walk, in a video where she discusses the incident and describes her injuries. She is accused of staging the episode. Whatever the case, it does not happen again. The moment seems crucial. Somehow the price to the government for public persecution has gotten too high. Somehow she understands that her strange do-it-yourself cyber revolution of one has succeeded in ways she could not have dreamed. In the beginning she impersonated a tourist (after exile in Switzerland, her German is pretty good), paying grossly inflated prices for Internet access at the big hotels. Now there are already too many e-mail and flash drive couriers; too many volunteer translators; too many venues of infinite electronic interconnectivity. A new, free, communal software appears called WordPress. Sanchez and her associates travel out across the island to become techno-missionaries, circuit riders conducting seminars and workshops on blog construction. No longer can every outgoing blog be blocked. No longer can every incoming blog be blocked. Persistence, ingenuity, cooperative enterprise, and collective imagination have taken over. The blog *Generation Y* and its even more expansive companion *DesdeCuba* have become those most Cuban of things: brave, indefatigable, ingenious extensions of the struggle of everyday life on the island; the overcoming of one difficulty, another, another after that; the effort of achieving some small success; one thing done today that at least will not have to be done tomorrow; the individual journey of empowerment into new expression; the voice that will not be silenced; the text that will not be abridged or foreclosed. Sanchez's new novel of the self, of growth of consciousness, of mastering the electronic discourses of infinite connectivity as the newest media of communication between self and world, becomes a fable of the twenty-first-century politics of textual production. It becomes its own engine of power. The officials call it "cyber garbage." Sanchez knows better. She calls it "the virus of expressing ourselves online." Enough, she says, of facile complaints in the developed world about runaway communications technology, the debasing of thought and language. Sanchez puts that conceit to rest: "If there were an altar to technology I wouldn't hesitate to light a couple of candles. These cables, circuits, and chips have brought infinitely much more information, autonomy, and freedom to my life than that generated by the will of politicians or popular movements." Fellow dissidents around the globe, she says, have become "cybernauts." Once she called herself a "renegade philologist." Now she speaks of "us web renegades." The plural pronoun is crucial. It is the category for all those, like herself, guilty of the temerity of "having behaved as a free person in cyberspace."

Meanwhile, beyond "we" or "us," what of "they" or "them"—the authorities? They are still listening, censoring, harassing, intimidating. People still get arrested. They get interrogated and beaten. Some die in prison. Still, the authorities of the state have not been ready for cyberspace. Accordingly, in their clumsy, archaic attempts to exert the usual controls over customary spoken and/or written political discourse, they have fashioned their own undoing. "Digital culture is leaving out in the cold," Sanchez tells us with ever-growing certainty, "those who think revolutions are made of weapons and speeches. For them, these omnidirectional waves are pure child's play. It is better that they think so. By the time they realize their importance, wireless will have managed to reconnect all these threads that have been cut, systematically, between citizens." The ceaseless exfoliations and boundless interconnections of the web are unstoppable. There will always be a new way. "How do you shout on Twitter?" she asks herself toward the end. It is a first test message in opening yet another avenue to the "omnidirectional." She continues: "Today, October 19, 2009, I ask: How do you sing the anthem of a people mobilized on the Internet, how do you broadcast the desire for change that I see in everyone around me? Before it was the sound of bugles, galloping horses, and stanzas that summoned the citizens of Bayamo to 'die for the Fatherland'; now everything is different." That was the old dream of Cuba Libre, she reflects. But now it does not any longer belong to the old ones with their revolutionary shibboleths and hoary patriotic *gritas*. Now there must be "the notes of a new anthem." Suddenly, she begins to realize, she is not only strangely free to write, she is also strangely devoid of fear. In the new universe of a political discourse that cannot be controlled, the conventional fear equation founded on discourses of traditional power relationships, in a strange way, has been reversed. "I will not stop believing," she writes, "that they are much more frightened than I am." It is the year 2010, and, hiding behind their fear, they are the political prisoners.

By the end of the book, three years have passed. Sanchez has gotten international award after international award: the 2008 Ortega y Gasset Prize from Spain; the 2009 Maria Moors Cabot Prize from Columbia University in the United States; the 2010 World Press Freedom Hero Prize from International Press Institute in Vienna; the Prince Claus Award from the Netherlands. With exponentially increasing readership and celebrity abroad, she is refused exit visa after exit visa to go accept them. Her blog, even as it has been blocked in her homeland, has become a regular feature in the Huffington Post. One installment features the account of an exclusive online question-and-answer she has been granted with US president Barack Obama. (Though the blog is officially "blocked" in Cuba, the interview is quickly pilloried as a cyber event, concocted by the self-important author with answers supplied by the United States Special Interest Section in Havana.) She appears as a guest editorialist in the *New York Times* and the *Washington Post*. At home, "the restless boys" just can't help themselves. There are now entire lists of prohibited Internet services and censored websites. On government TV, a talk show panel intones vaguely about "'cyber-terrorism,' 'cyber-commandos,' 'media war.'" The last fumbling totalitarian insult is saved for minions of the postal service. She gets an illegal package notice. It is the shipment of the newly published book by Yoani Sanchez entitled *Cuba Libre*. It is accompanied by written reasons for the interception. Sanchez quotes the operative statement. This is what they have to say. "*The contents of the book* Cuba Libre *are against the general interests of the nation, since it argues that certain political and economic changes are required in Cuba so that its citizens may have more material benefits and achieve personal fulfullment, ends completely contrary to the principles of our society.*"

They are absolutely correct. Only it is not their society any more. They cannot run a world on the principle of "habeas data." Three years have passed in the book. Three years later, she is still writing. With every entry, *Havana Real* gets one step closer to *Cuba Libre*. Digital communication and global networking have released a power of language hitherto unimagined. Virtual discourse, the discourse of the web, the Internet become a cottage industry that cannot be contained by any earthly power. Its great product is nothing less than "the tapestry wherein we attempt to weave the shreds of our own civil society." The result must be for Cubans to see themselves living no longer as comrades, she insists, but as autonomous, individual citizens. "I have committed a systematic and execrable crime," she confesses. "I have believed myself to be free." It is her great act of imagination. In just that belief she has already shown the way: she has become nothing less than the new imaginative creator of both herself and her world. In Susan Sontag's dictum, from Nietzsche, "art is not an imitation of life but its metaphysical supplement, thrown up against it so as to overcome it." In the fullest sense of the phrase, a virtual reality has become fully realized in ways Nietzsche himself could in his wildest moments never have dreamed. Or, to return to the historical parallel with which this chapter began, Nietzsche's Cuban contemporary Cirilo Villaverde, the creator of Cecilia Valdés—though his nineteenth-century enterprise in mining the great historical novel of the Cuban nation as a textual allegory of the revolutionary generation of the 1820s and 1830s and Yoani Sanchez's endlessly evolving twenty-first-century cyber fiction of herself and the new revolutionary cohort she calls *Generation Y* turn out to be remarkably parallel. Cecilia Valdés, a novelistic creation, becomes a heroine in literary space. Yoani Sanchez, a creation of the blogosphere, becomes a heroine in virtual space. Both stand as part and fiber of national myth: the first of a legendary past; the second of a progressive future.

The renegade philologist has come a long way from her University of Havana thesis, *Words under Pressure: A Study of the Literature of Dictatorship in Latin America*. Even as a text of abstract intellectual analysis, it has not, she recalls, been well received by those in authority. A new book now appears: *Word Press: A Blog for Speaking to the World*. They will surely find this one even less satisfactory. It is a practical, concrete, instructional guide for Internet writers in using the titular software as their own free blogging platform. On *Generation Y*, she also conducts video podcast tutorials. Meanwhile, her own textual inhabitation of the blogosphere continues to enlarge. Sanchez continues to publish regular entries every few days. They tell us what we are curious about. Pope Benedict visits and actually says something possibly encouraging. People scavenging in dumpsters begin to cannibalize the dumpsters themselves, with special attention to very useful plastic wheel assemblies. In the marketplaces, the smallest twitch in the price of pork disrupts an entire economy. Among the intelligentsia, a cohort of tame intellectuals continues to reap the rewards of their timidity. But now, five years and more since making her first computer keystroke, now, as then, she is accused of runaway egotism, of obsessive self-involvement with her own cult of geopolitical celebrity. There are recurrent suggestions that *Generation Y* has always been basically Generation Yoani. But by 2012 Sanchez has been joined by myriad others. *Generation Y* continues but has also merged into a plural enterprise called *DesdeCuba*. The latter composite website is headed with a display of photographs of major blog contributors, several dozen of them, most identified by name. Yoani Sanchez is among them. Further bloggers and volunteer translators are now numbered in the thousands. Languages of translation are said to include English, French, German, Portuguese, Italian, Polish, Catalan, Chinese, Lithuanian, Japanese, Czech, Bulgarian, Dutch, Finnish, Hungarian, Korean, Greek, and Russian. The number of bloggers translated regularly into English alone stands at around fifty. A single blog on a given day in a particular translation is likely to attract between fifty or a hundred responses. Built-in forwarding and networking capabilities extend from conventional e-mail to Facebook, Twitter, Linkedin, Tumblr, Digg, Reddit, Friendfeed, Pinterest, Stumbleupon, Technorati, and Google+. The *DesdeCuba* site currently advertises a new *Generation Y* cell phone application. The numbers of participants are exponential. The list of ever-evolving technologies is overwhelming. That is just the point. Here, in a crowning gesture of defiance, the enterprise has even taken over the government's work, keeping tabs on bloggers all over Cuba, indeed all over the world. Their tabulation says exactly what the authorities do not want to hear: there are so many that no one can keep track of them. That, too, is just the point. Virtual writing cannot be stopped. Virtual writing is the new reality. For Yoani Sanchez and her compatriots in the blogosphere, the future has arrived.

CONCLUSION

The Autumn of the Comandante

For a substantial period, the world has now witnessed and wondered at the seclusion of Fidel Castro in what nearly everyone has assumed to be a final decline and slow progress toward the end of life. The Castro deathwatch, as it might be called, began more than a decade ago with rumors of infirmity ranging from Parkinson's disease to pancreatic cancer. In 2006, intestinal surgery to relieve a blockage, perhaps cancerous, perhaps not, was alleged to have resulted in near-fatal peritonitis. In 2008 came Castro's resignation of the duties of the Cuban premiership and/or presidency he had held for five decades, with a transfer of official power to his brother Raúl. Subsequently, in the concluding years of the first decade of a new century, he has made the occasional curious return to the public eye. For a while he achieved modest celebrity in the new world of electronic communications through widely available Internet pronouncements, called "reflections," comprising collected thoughts on various matters of history, leadership, memory, ideology. There have been none since April 2011. Still, he may be seen in the occasional interview, making various pronouncements on current events and appearing fit, energetic, quick witted. He has also made a special appearance to celebrate the first volume of his autobiography, with a second of another thousand pages allegedly to come.

In the geopolitical view, such near-mythic evidence of survivability surely befits a figure who now remains as the last—albeit then as now, least likely—of the Cold War giants of the twentieth century: the handsome, charismatic, young *barbudo* in the green army fatigues and forage cap, known to phrasemakers as "el Caballo," the survivor of the Moncada uprising and then the Granma expedition, along with the martyred heroes Camilo Cienfuegos and Che Guevara, the leader of the valiant guerrilla band in the Sierra Maestra, surviving and eventually winning victory after victory against the hapless US-supplied and supported Batistiano military forces; eventually the conqueror, along with his ragtag army of mountain and jungle insurrectionists, making his joyous, triumphant entry into Havana; the new Latin American dictator in the pantheon of world Communism, with his Soviet patrons, plunging the world into the Cuban Missile Crisis and the threat of global nuclear catastrophe; finally, enduringly, "el Jefe," riding out decades of US embargo, eventual Russian betrayal and abandonment, endless experiences of the Cuban people of hunger, shortage, social and economic deprivation. For all that, he has now outlived, along with a great deal of historical image intact, once-contemporary counterparts including John F. Kennedy, Richard Nixon, Nikita Khrushchev, Mao Tse Tung, and Ho Chi Minh, just to name the most prominent. The survival itself, in all these regards, may be itself reckoned an achievement deserving the term "greatness."

For Cubans, Fidel Castro lives on much more closely at hand—in what is thought to be a largely solitary existence, on the outskirts of the capital, in a compound somewhere on the far edge of Miramar. For them the present era is defined as the long, lingering, mysterious autumn of the Comandante.

The literary reference in the foregoing sentence is purely intentional. It invokes the title and the political content of a famous novel by the Nobel Prize-winning Latin American writer Gabriel Garcia Márquez—himself a lifelong admirer and friend of the dictator, who has often served as an advisor and confidant. The novel, begun in 1968, largely finished (according to Márquez) in 1971, and first published in Spain in 1975, is entitled *The Autumn of the Patriarch*. It is about the long, strange, solitary, much-rumored and discussed death of a Latin American dictator—a caudillo—or, more properly, the death of a dictator amid myriad strange, conflicting, often grotesque rumors and stories concerning the alleged death of the dictator, the impending death of the dictator, the maladies likely to be drawing the dictator toward death, the strange forces of memory and imaginative will somehow keeping the dictator alive.

An antitotalitarian allegory, written from the literary and political left, the novel is also of course about the fate of a country. We never know the country, save that it is in the Caribbean region of Latin America. Geographically it seems to be not an island, though it does have an extensive, valuable seacoast that figures prominently in the geopolitical drama. This last qualification is important but only in a limited way. Márquez as a novelist is invariably called a magical realist. He purports to write, that is, not only of what happened but what might have happened, what could have happened, what should have happened, what could have been kept from happening, what may yet be made to happen. He himself averred that his titular figure derives of a pastiche, a kind of literary-political fantasy-collage of various Latin American strongmen of the era. Márquez was surely not, at the time, writing about his friend and revolutionary Socialist idol Fidel Castro, dictator of the island nation of Cuba. One may now suggest, on the other hand, that at some point the literary and political magic got out of hand. Regarding the long, lingering, mysterious movement toward death of the leader of Cuba, one may be said to witness a kind of grotesque enactment of elements of Márquez's *Autumn of the Patriarch* with prophecy coming full literary and political circle. Fidel Castro now lives out his own latest version of the Latin American dictator novel.

The rise to recognition and permanence of the genre itself constitutes one of the most dubious literary honors of the region—that a dominant fictional form should trace the life and career of the caudillo, the political and/or military strongman, as a fixture in the history and literature of the Latin American nation. Accounts of its origin frequently trace its conventions to the nineteenth century—specifically in most cases to the political novel *Facundo* (1845) by Domingo Faustino Sarmiento, allegedly a representation of the 1835–52 autocratic rule of Juan Manuel de Rosas in Argentina. The classic early twentieth-century model, in turn, is usually considered to be Miguel Ángel Asturias's *El Señor Presidente*, written in 1933, and published in 1946. As with Sarmiento, Asturias's work was historical in basis, centering on the 1898–20 presidency of the Guatemalan autocrat Manuel Estrada Cabrera.

The modern rise in the popularity and literary importance of the genre for the political left would prove concurrent with the increasing twentieth-century upsurge in Latin American resistance to US imperialism in the region, frequently involving the installation and backing of local tyrants at the behest of US business, foreign policy, and military interests. Even a cursory list of twentieth-century US-supported, right-wing Latin American strongmen invokes for inhabitants of the region the chilling memory of decades of remorseless terror and repression: Diaz, Machado, Gómez, Ibarra, Perón, Trujillo, Duvalier, Somoza, Stroessner, Pinochet, Castillo-Armas, Batista. As is well-known, the single democratically elected Socialist head of state prior to the present, Salvador Allende of Chile, was overthrown and killed in a 1973 coup plotted under US president

Richard Nixon and engineered by the CIA. For the next seventeen years, rule would be under the ruthless military dictatorship of Gen. Augusto Pinochet. Meanwhile, elsewhere in the region, with the Cold War waning, new left-leaning political movements would begin to assert themselves against US domination with increasingly frequent success. At present, besides Cuba—now the longest-lived Communist dictatorship in the world save the People's Republic of China—the governments of Venezuela, Brazil, Argentina, Uruguay, Bolivia, Paraguay, Mexico, and Nicaragua may all be said in one way or another to have tilted governments in the hemisphere decidedly leftward.

With regard to such developments, the Latin American dictator novel at mid- to late century may be said to have taken a decidedly postmodern turn, moving into a peculiar visionary dimension through the new techniques concurrently being developed by Latin American literary experimentalists under the heading of "magical realism." Three in particular now seem to have achieved status as both literary and political archetypes, with each exploring the elusive, treacherous, often hallucinatory relations between fact and fiction, reality and illusion, history and imagination. The first, by the Cuban writer Alejo Carpentier, *Reasons of State* (*El recurso del método*, 1974), presents a dictator modeled on several historical figures, most notably the despised Gerardo Machado, dictator of Cuba. The second, Augusto Roa Bastos's *I, the Supreme* (*Yo, el Supremo*, 1974), likewise focused on the fictionalized representation of a specific historical figure, the late nineteenth-century Paraguayan tyrant José Gaspar Rodríguez de Francia.

The third, and best known to this day, is the one of particular interest to us here. It is Gabriel García Márquez's *The Autumn of the Patriarch* (*El otoño del patriarca*, 1975). Here the titular character is an imagined figure, a seemingly eternal Caribbean dictator, called by his people "el macho", who lives to be over two hundred years old. Like his literary cohorts, Márquez at least initially was said to have based his figure on a number of historical models, including the Colombian autocrat Gustavo Rojas Pinilla, the long-serving Generalissimo Francisco Franco of Spain, and Venezuela's Juan Vicente Gómez, with further elements that take the reader all the way back to the Sarmiento depiction of the Argentine Rosas. (A parallel historical Márquez text in this vein, about Simon Bolivar, ironically treats the revolutionary icon, enshrined for the Latin Americans of all political dispositions as "The Liberator," during his last months alive, as he contemplates a final descent into disease, debility, and decay.)

In timing, subject, and style, the Márquez text had much in common with the other classics described. In literary and cultural visibility, as a much-awaited successor to *One Hundred Years of Solitude*, itself an instant classic of the magical realist genre that had won for Márquez instant international literary renown, it seemed to represent a major ideological positioning of the author among contemporary figures of the Latin American revolutionary left—not least among them Cuban dictator Fidel Castro, embarked with the Colombian novelist on what would become a lifelong literary and political friendship. In place of the marvelously imagined, teeming, plenitudinous, intensely human world of *One Hundred Years of Solitude*, that of the new book was dark, claustral, hideously fallen and ridden with decay. In place of the first book's vast rich spectacle of Latin American society and politics, the rise and fall of the family Buendia, the second was a fantasy of horror and moral malediction, a portrait of the endless dying of an ancient, legendary, and universally feared Caribbean dictator amid the rubble of his presidential palace and the hoarded evil and suffering of his infamous regime.

The book is exceedingly involuted—in the fullest sense, labyrinthine. It is divided into six sections. Each tells, and in the process retells over and over again, like a bad, looping movie or runaway computer program, the same sordid story of a lifetime of total power exerted by the titular protagonist over his unhappy people. In his filthy, decayed, ruined palace, endlessly he reflects, remembers, tries to put back together the jumbled details of his life as absolute ruler, now amid the endless chaos and general catastrophe of decline. But what the book is really about, one eventually sees, is about history conceived of as the endlessness of his own dying.

The plot of memory, structurally repeated six times, concurrently repeats itself from within through endlessly unfolding lines, sentences, paragraphs, offered from various points of view, frequently without punctuation or any other design of closure save that of dismal circularity. The events contained, swirling on their own endlessly multiple patterns of dismal occurrence and recurrence, may be briefly summarized. The dying autocrat, named by his adoring people "general forever"—and indeed preceded in "death" by a double, a twin corpse discovered among the ruins, who has inspired a legend of his own immortality—now finds himself ancient, sick, immobile, and imprisoned in his palace and his body, still barely alive as he decays into the human muck of his own mortality. Grotesquely big in the feet, he has been born of a bird woman in a time of flies; worshipping the mother who cannot be made a saint, he has filled the palace with concubines with whom he capriciously ruts and inseminates, with all his bastards having the same gestation of seven months. Now he pays for the stud work with an old man's groin rupture, an endlessly aching herniated testicle swelled to the size of a fig. The nation pays for his autocracy and cruel, tyrannical, and stupid misjudgments. He has changed the hour of dawn to suit his own rising; he has advanced the bloom of favorite roses. Where his nation borders on the sea, he has sold the ocean to the gringos. To replace the breezes, they have given him wind machines. He rigs the national lottery so he always gets the three winning numbers. He uses little children to draw the numbers. To guarantee their silence, he eventually banishes them all and disposes of them in the ocean. He has cooked one of his generals and served him to other members of the junta. In the palace, wandering cows have eaten the carpets and curtains. They too lie down in their own body effluvia to die and decay. The country waits and lives on rumors.

At the time of writing, as noted, a number of historical candidates were set forth as possible models. Above all, with the novel mainly written during Spanish exile in Madrid, there was the interminable dying of Francisco Franco. Meanwhile, on the other hand, as revealed by various commentators, in Latin America there was no shortage of contemporary candidates. Venezuela alone offered two, Marcos Pérez Jiménez and Juan Francisco Gómez. In Márquez's own Colombia, there was the '60s and '70s regime of Rojos Piniella. And then there were all the other legends of horror, mostly US-supported. Batista, Somoza, Trujillo, Duvalier, Stroessner, Pinochet. Any and all this certainly fit the bill as blazoned in ads by Harper, the novelist's US English-language publisher: "A brilliant tale of a Caribbean tyrant and the corruption of power." The commercial accolade was critically seconded at the time by the novelist William Kennedy in the *New York Times* on 31 October 1976. "The book is a supreme polemic, a spiritual expose, an attack against any society that encourages or even permits the growth of such a monstrosity." The certainty at the time was of course that Márquez was writing in the long tradition of the dictator novel as it had become an instrument of the literary and cultural international left—a liberal Socialist indictment of American hegemonics, the complicity of American military, political, and business interests in the greeds, cruelties, atrocities, of right wing client anti-Communist Neanderthals and thugs.

Then and now, one searches vainly for a dictator novel about a leftist totalitarian figure. A half century into the longest-lived Communist dictatorship in the Americas, this may be no longer the case. In life—I would propose—now appears before us just such a critique of history as a self-reflexive, postmodern fable of autocratic decline and decay that materializes itself before our very eyes. Of Márquez's novel has come the prophecy of his beloved Fidel Castro, and of his beloved Cuba. People wait and talk in the autumn of the Comandante. The fictional particulars blur into strange correspondences: "The leader, 'el macho,' has a terrible, herniated swollen testicle; the leader once sold the ocean to the gringos and took wind machines in return; the leader once changed the hours of the day to advance the bloom of his own roses." Or, "He suffers from this illness; know that." "He has lost his senses; he still seems as sharp as ever." "He is dying. He is already dead."

One is familiar in literary reading with such laws of unexpected outcomes. At the far extreme of such readings as that above is the critical law of literary indeterminacy. There are no authors; there are no readers; there are only texts. Closer to the living world are the politics of literary-cultural coincidence and/or proleptic statement associated with particular texts. In the years of the autumn of the Comandante, the Márquez novel now seems to reify itself, however unintentionally, into something like existential fact.

As if to make the historical reality-picture so described even more complex, the same strange laws of cultural coincidence and/or prophecy seem now to have been in operation with regard to a text of a once-contemporary satire. The text in this case turns out to be a 1971 movie by the American filmmaker Woody Allen—by queer coincidence, it turns out, almost precisely contemporary with the Márquez novel. The title is *Bananas*. The genre is vintage early Woody Allen existential slapstick. The mode is self-reflexive satire both of Latin American revolutionary politics and of its own cinematic mock-experimentalism. The plot centers on a nebbishy urban American everyman, Fielding Mellish—played by Allen himself—who blunders into the endless ongoing political upheavals of a Latin American nation and eventually gets himself made dictator or *presidente*, if not for life, for as long as it takes until the next dictator or president for life comes along. The title makes its point obvious long before there was an upscale clothing store supplying its own unintended gloss. The place is a Banana Republic. Again, the ostensible theme is the long sordid history of American imperialistic intervention in the politics of Latin American nations, frequently the installation and maintenance of right-wing dictatorial regimes friendly to, and above all, profiting from American business, military, and foreign policy interests. The origin of the term itself seems to have come from a well-known American company, among the earliest monopolistic US economic giants to plant a footprint in the region, United Fruit. The chosen fruit was bananas—in this case not pineapples, sugar, coffee, coca leaves. In Allen's title, the economic meanings are extended into Yiddish humor. The Marx Brothers gave us *Coconuts*—a world where everyone is nuts. Woody Allen gives us a place where people are all bananas.

Given the times and the headlines, it is hard not to miss the proximate focus of the satire, such as it may be termed amid the more general zaniness. The locale of the action is some representative Latin American stew of political upheaval, in this case an island republic named San Marcos. The identity of the revolutionaries is completely and unmistakably dictated by makeup and wardrobe. They all have long, bushy beards. They all wear olive drab military fatigues. They act as if they all just wandered out of the jungle. They do a lot in the way of firing squads.

The American intruder is a scrawny, hapless New York type named Fielding Mellish, politically and emotionally blackmailed into journeying to San Marco and joining the revolution after he has fallen hopelessly in love with a fellow New York liberal-activist-intellectual, in this case a feminist-Marxist going door-to-door collecting signatures for the rebel cause. Her line: "Would you like to volunteer for the Volunteers for San Marcos?" He is a mild-mannered, decidedly unadventurous product-tester for a US corporation marketing an array of consumer goods. Before giving herself to him romantically and sexually, she demands that he somehow give palpable evidence of his commitment to the revolution. He duly travels to the island, where, unlike many Americans in similar positions before him, he survives the common perils and vicissitudes of the filibustero. Winning the trust of the revolutionaries, he assists them in the overthrow of the US-backed tyrant. His popularity is parlayed into getting himself eventually acclaimed presidente—largely, it seems, on condition he keep wearing his geeky 1960s black-framed eyeglasses but now augmenting them with a proper revolutionary beard—in his case, a fake red one. The glasses, of course, make him look like Fidel Castro. The beard, of course, makes him look silly. Sent to New York City on a Castro-like fund-raising and public relations excursion, he is identified by the CIA as himself, Fielding Mellish, a representative of the San Marcos government, and thereby arrested and subjected to trial for illegal political activities. Subjected to courtroom hectoring and denunciation, he barely escapes jail. Reunited with the object of his love, he can now barter sex for political credibility. The consummation of the bargain, so to speak, is unfortunately very quick and unsatisfactory. The end.

As one may infer, the story from start to finish is largely framed in silliness, albeit at times of a very high, absurd order. The opening involves a typical San Marcos, banana-republic–style assassination scene, covered on radio or television play-by-play style by an American sportscaster. The sportscaster is Howard Cosell. "Good afternoon," he intones, in full nasal pomposity. "Wide World of Sports is in the little republic of San Marcos where we're going to bring you a live, on the spot assassination. They're going to kill the president of this lovely Latin American country and replace him with a military dictatorship."

From there, things improve little. The adventures of the soon-to-arrive Fielding Mellish seem pretty much covered by the title of the book from which the concept was derived, *Don Quixote U.S.A.*, written by popular novelist Richard Powell and excerpted for Reader's Digest Condensed Books. In the Allen transformation to his island avatar, he is accorded his own heroic epithet: "El Weirdo." Further muggings, cameos, sight gags, terrible one-horse jokes attend a film drenched in political murder and assassination. It is all accomplished, however, with no fake blood. In an execution scene, victims stand in a waiting line, with Mellish issuing order-number slips as in a delicatessen. In various fake-auteur movie references, a baby carriage careens down a long flight of steps as in the *Battleship Potemkin*; a dream sequence pays homage to Ingmar Bergman's *Wild Strawberries*; bits from the Marx Brothers in *Duck Soup* mix with others from Charlie Chaplin in *Modern Times*. An eating scene with Mellish faced off against a rebel woman recalls the classic one from *Tom Jones*. Background music includes the *1812 Overture*. Cosell manages to remind us of Sunday Night Football, Wild World of Sports, and Muhammad Ali. Brand placements include New Testament cigarettes. A band at a general's military dinner mimes their instruments (apparently the inspired result of a failure of the real ones to arrive in time for the filming).

Stupid one-liners abound. "When is the revolution?" Mellish asks one revolutionary comrade-in-arms. "Six months," is the answer. "Six months?" he expostulates. "I have a rented car." The disguise for Mellish's return to the United States involves easily the silliest fake beard in the history of movies. The question at trial becomes an inventory of McCarthy/HUAC bloviation. The consummation of the marriage at the end again features play-by-play coverage by Howard Cosell with an exclusive follow-up interview.

In Gabriel Garcia Márquez's *Autumn of the Patriarch*, the titular figure now nearly four decades later turns out to look strangely like Fidel Castro. In Woody Allen's *Bananas*, the figure looking strangely like Fidel Castro turns out to be an American named Fielding Mellish played by Woody Allen. Without pressing too hard on literary-cinematic conceit, a third scenario still remains worth inquiring about. In the long autumnal movement toward death, how does Fidel Castro try to put together the story of his life? Who was he in the beginning? Who is he now? How will a remembered Fidel Castro wind up being mythologized? How will a mythologized Fidel Castro wind up being remembered?

He himself must look back on a life that now seems in and of itself a book or a movie. Moving from a relatively affluent family in Santiago de Cuba, the second city of the island, to a Jesuit seminary and an early career as a political instigator and enforcer amid rival factions while doing law studies at the University of Havana, back in Santiago, he culminated a quick apprenticeship in revolutionary violence with the 26 November 1953 attack on the Batista garrison at the Moncada Barracks. A disaster from its very inception, the affair resulted in the killing or execution of most of the attackers. Castro barely escaped with his life. At a show trial, he delivered his famous "History Will Absolve Me" speech. Imprisoned on the Isle of Pines, he was given fortuitous release in a showpiece Batista amnesty.

In Mexican exile, he became a student of military revolution under the renowned revolutionary colonel Alberto Bayo. A hastily purchased pleasure cruiser, the *Granma*, packed with insurgents, in 1956 became an invasion scow, with bands of fugitive rebels quickly dispersed by Batista forces to the wilds of Oriente. Again Fidel Castro—once more with his brother Raúl, but this time with the revolutionary genius Che Guevara as well—was somehow inexplicably, almost miraculously, spared. In the mountains, the revolutionaries learned survival and military discipline. Building to a force of perhaps three hundred immediately surrounding Castro himself, and never numbering more than three to four thousand overall, over a period of two years they steadily went about defeating Batista's forces, usually reckoned at around thirty-five to forty thousand.

Meanwhile, as in novels and movies, legends began to grow. To a certain degree, in Castro's case popular-culture mythologizing itself became a kind or reality. Reporters infiltrated for stories, offering a frequently oddball publicity in story and picture. Interview exclusives portrayed the leader as a *guerillero* media idol, a kind of jungle commando rock star, coyly marking political time on Marxism-Leninism, playing to image with his signature beard, fatigues, glasses, cigars. The final military "offensive" completing the Fidelista military advance across the island consisted of wings of battalion-sized units. At the time, American planners speculated that a couple of US divisions, the Eighty-Second Airborne, perhaps the First Marine, with artillery and air support, could have cleaned the place up in a matter of months. Before they knew it, the ragged guerillas with beards, cigars, and green fatigues were in Havana. An impulsive, ironic, intellectual interloper had become president of a new revolutionary nation.

Havana and rebel victory became pictures of complete chaos. The leader's comic opera travels perpetuated the circus atmosphere. He showed up, always in costume, always in character, in New York, Moscow, at the UN. US secret agencies countered with goofy assassination plots. A US-supported Bay of Pigs invasion by Cuban exiles and American mercenaries foundered of its own military halfheartedness and ineptitude. The Cuban Missile Crisis became Fidel Castro's great moment in the geopolitical sun, as the mighty United States faced off against the mighty Soviet Union. Even here, histories of the event suggest that Castro was the original loose cannon, thwarting Russian attempts to resolve the missile impasse as readily as he scotched the Americans. Here, as with African military adventures involving costly US-style "advisory" missions in Angola and

Eritrea, his egoistic, impulsive, mercurial showboating and dice rolling seemed to put him out of his geopolitical league. The same may be said about domestic policies that have plunged the island into social and economic crisis after crisis. The judgments of el Lider have frequently seemed heedless, ill-considered, eccentric—in a word, bananas. The people have paid the price.

How will this be reckoned according to history's accounting? How will the release of Cuba from former US domination and the tyranny of a right-wing client dictatorship be weighed against the sufferings of those on both sides who underwent the Cuban Revolution? How will the genuine domestic accomplishments of the Castro era—including comprehensive public education, nearly universal literacy, and uniform, free health care—weigh against the suppression of individual rights and the legacy of the last fifty years of failed economic and foreign policy experimentation, much of it catastrophic? Out in Miramar, moving into the final passages of a death long rehearsed, does he think on all this and more?

We speak here of a figure himself now historically astonishing to the point of the surreal. He has been an absolute dictator for fifty years. Hitler made it twelve; Mao twenty-seven; Stalin thirty. Bolivar made it four—as noted earlier, prompting another well-known Márquez dictator fiction, *The General in His Labyrinth*, in many ways apposite here as well, where the dying liberator reflects over the events of his life. Fidel Castro has been the absolute ruler of his nation for five decades. He has been a military revolutionary for six decades. What does he choose to remember? What does he wish to forget? What will be his last thoughts?

What will be ours of him? One of the last popular media resurrections of Fidel Castro may supply a kind of parable, if an eccentric and personal one. It occurred for me in a video of his last recorded outing, a visit to the new National Aquarium in Miramar. Cuba's shining attempt at a new, deluxe, SeaWorld-style tourist attraction, it includes a restaurant where diners may enjoy a dolphin show. There, pictures were taken of the Comandante, sitting at one of the best tables, closely facing the dolphin tank built into the restaurant wall, and later with the wet-suited trainers. He apparently found the show quite entertaining.

So did I, as it turns out, a few months earlier, sitting more or less exactly where he did. On a research trip from the US university where I work, several of us had invited a group of Cuban associates for a customary meal at a good restaurant—a *paladar*, perhaps, one of the first experiments in free enterprise, quite splendid restaurants with limited numbers of seats run out of people's residences; or some larger commercial place frequently, by local standards, quite expensive, or for a large group, downright unaffordable. It is invariably repaid many times over by a lovely home-cooked meal at someone's house or apartment.

Our friends seemed enthusiastic about the new aquarium restaurant. The food was good, and there was also a terrific dolphin show. The evening walk to get there, it turns out, took us past the darkened monolith of the former Soviet embassy. We were not disappointed on arrival. The dining room was very chic and snazzy, painted in underwater shades of blue with an entire wall devoted to the dolphin tank. The waitresses were costumed art deco style, in blue and gold tuxedos, as stewards from a 1930s cruise ship. The menu specialized in seafood. Well into the process of making orders, with a dozen or so in the party, came an embarrassing revelation. There was no seafood—no fish, no shrimp, no squid, no octopus. They had some chicken and pork, eggs, rice, cheese, and vegetables. We ordered and made a meal of it.

The restaurant story—about the night I sat where the Comandante would be photographed three months later on one of his rare public appearances—is a real story about Cuba today. To be sure, things are not nearly as awful as in the Special Period, about which almost no one talks, apparently because the memories are too hard to revisit. The fact remains that shortage and unavailability are still part of life everywhere, even in the simplest details. In groceries, you go for peanut butter and they have some cheese. You go for crackers and they have bread. People eat what's for sale.

Here the autumn of the Comandante is also the winter of the Revolución. The country goes on. Despite stern recent cutbacks—allegedly to encourage private initiative—immense numbers of Cubans have some form of government employment: teachers, medical staff, government workers, docents, street cleaners; by uniforms alone, there seem to be at least fifteen different kinds of police and/or security forces. To be sure, under the stewardship of Raúl Castro, there is a new, official emphasis on individual entrepreneurial projects, with special encouragement of small business. For the first time, private citizens may buy and sell cars and residential properties. On the streets and highways, the old signature 1940s and 1950s American Detroit behemoths and the smoking, wheezing 1980s and 1990s Soviet-era Ladas and Fiats are gradually augmented with largely Latin American–produced US, German, Japanese, and Korean makes.

Such accelerated modernizations notwithstanding, the distinct impression remains that everyone is mostly just doing whatever it takes to keep the country running for another three days or so. Two, three, four economies run simultaneously: the official one, the black market, the barter, and the one for the tourists and the local elites. With a ham-handed repressiveness exceeding even that of the Chinese, Internet access is tightly controlled; blogs and personal websites are monitored. People travel to the United States and bring back enormous foam-wrapped parcels of capitalist goods—electronics, bedding, housewares. The people live on what they can get their hands on. Things begin to change. Enormous cutbacks are made in state-supported employment. People are legally allowed to run certain kinds of small businesses as independent entrepreneurs. It becomes possible for Cubans who own automobiles to sell them to other Cubans. It becomes possible for Cubans who own real estate to sell their homes to other Cubans. Thus life goes on in the autumn of the Comandante.

Once upon a time for Fidel Castro, in the first days of the triumph of the revolution, the future must have seemed as if it would go on forever, much as it did for me, a fourteen-year-old boy in the United States with an interest in "current events," devouring a weekly issue of *Life* magazine. The date on this one was 12 January 1959. On the cover was the subject of a feature article, Hubert Humphrey, senator from Minnesota, in a Russian winter hat. He was just back from a Cold War visit to the Soviet Union, and, as blazoned on the top right cover headline, "Eight Hours with Khrushchev." Inside, the lead item was a related, late-breaking story rushed into production on events in Cuba, the end of a thrilling two-year guerilla revolution, culminating in the victory of rebel forces under Fidel Castro and the flight of the hated dictator, Fulgencio Batista. Headlined "Jails Open, Cubans Cheer as Castro Does Batista In: Dynamic Boss Takes over a US Neighbor," the opening featured a picture of Havana citizens standing atop the walls of a city prison they have just stormed, greeting political inmates; it was flanked by one of Castro barking out an order at his military command headquarters. Battle photos were provided from the final Western offensive. Also shown were almost Viet Cong–style jungle schools, clinics, field hospitals. Individual pictures of revolutionary fighters included a girl guard, veteran rebel, patrol leader, bomb builder, field commander—and one young volunteer American combatant. A spread on the last days of Batista showed street mobs wreaking destruction on gambling palaces and fancy hotels and gave a profile of the new president, Manuel Urrutia. The section concluded with a group portrait of tough jungle fighters entering Havana, and then a solo shot of a black irregular, in civilian clothes, finished off with a US-style helmet liner and an American M-1 rifle, likely from Batista army stores. He was walking proudly. The rebels all looked incredibly young, brash, cocky. Castro himself was described as "a young diehard idealist." His age was listed as thirty-two.

Having begun back in the Sierra Madre with the adulatory reporting of Herbert Mathews of the *New York Times* and others, the new global media idolization of Fidel Castro as el Comandante had been launched. (The title itself was initially meant to be a gesture of revolutionary humility. It indicates the rank of major, above which no leader was allowed to rise.)

Meanwhile, Castro set about creating himself in the new role. Accounts of a 1960 trip to the United States to attend a UN meeting spotlighted his choice of lodgings at the Hotel Theresa in Harlem, where he was visited by Nikita Khrushchev and held meetings with African American leaders, including Malcolm X from the Nation of Islam and the poet Langston Hughes. (He had made a less-publicized earlier visit, in the spring of 1959, when he had stayed at the New Yorker and met with Vice President Richard Nixon.) At the UN, on 26 September, he delivered a searing, stemwinding four-hour indictment of American "aggression" and "imperialism," including the explicit accusation of the US government having already "decreed the destruction" of his revolutionary government.

There exists from the period a newsreel of Fidel Castro's arrival at Idlewild Airport—now John Fitzgerald Kennedy Airport—on that trip. He appears perceptibly awkward, immature, inarticulate, suddenly somewhat comic looking in his beard, fatigues, and billed cap. Further, in the newsreel, he is just one of a number of Communist Bloc leaders shown as attending the fifteenth annual UN General Session. There is the headliner, Nikita Khrushchev, and also Czech Anton Novotny and Polish Ladislaw Gomulka. The flashpoint issue of the session was the situation in the Congo. During the trip, Castro had hoped to gain a meeting with the US president, Dwight D. Eisenhower. He was refused, as if he or his revolution could hardly be taken seriously. The world shortly learned otherwise: John Kennedy, with an inherited invasion plan and overthrow plot, eventuating in the disastrous 1961 Bay of Pigs debacle; Castro, with the announcement that he planned a Socialist republic; the 1962 Cuban Missile Crisis; the US embargo; ludicrous CIA overthrow schemes—exploding cigars, depilatory shoe powders, airborne hallucinogens; the breakdown of the Soviet Union; el Período Especial. All this is somewhere back in time now. How could the Comandante have ever gotten so old? How could the revolution ever have managed to put the beloved nation and people though so many decades of failure, repression, poverty, and misery?

How does one outlive one's own history, somehow moving beyond both prophecy and parody? The answer is, of course, that one outlives nothing. Here we may go instructively all the way back to Herbert Matthews of the *New York Times*, infiltrated into the fastnesses of the Sierra Maestra for a world famous three-hour interview with Castro after Batista-regime claims that the seemingly unkillable young revolutionary leader—who should have died at least twice before, at Moncada, and then again with the *Granma*—had finally been eliminated. A series of articles appeared in the *Times*. In the words of Anthony de Palma, Mathews became "the man who invented Fidel." The first included a photo of Castro holding a rifle, in fatigues, the bearded, handsome, embattled, romantic, young revolutionary. The headline read, "Cuban Rebel Is Visited in Hideout," with subhead, "Castro Is Still Alive and Still Fighting in the Mountains." In his notebook, Mathews gave a two-word general characterization of the band of revolutionaries he recalled meeting that day: "How young!" Now Fidel Castro, in his long dying, must surely know that even for el Jefe history cannot be outlived. He is late in the autumn of the Comandante, where he too has surely come to know that a life, be it measured in the ages of men or of nations, is finally but a death waiting to happen.

Source Notes and Reading Suggestions

Introduction: Cuba and the Imagination
Carlos Eire includes the "paradise" anecdote early in his account of growing up in Vedado during the years just before the Castro revolution, *Waiting for Snow in Havana* (New York: Free Press, 2003). A video of the Kennedy Cuban Missile Crisis speech can be viewed in its entirety at http://www.youtube.com/watch?v=bOnY6b-qy_8. The Hatuey response to the Spanish priests is a ubiquitous part of national mythology. When the famed Bacardi Rum family of the eastern island branched into beer production, they chose the name Hatuey. It is still thought of as the national brand. For the definitive recent history of the Bay of Pigs Invasion, see Howard Jones, *Bay of Pigs* (New York: Oxford University Press, 2008). The photo volume by Chip Cooper and Nestor Martí is *Old Havana/la Havana Vieja* (Tuscaloosa: University of Alabama Press, 2012).

1. Romancing *Cecilia Valdés*
A 2005 English translation by Helen Lane is available from Oxford University Press in the Library of Latin America Series. A comprehensive introduction and notes are supplied by the volume editor, Sibylle Fischer. While the novel has been the subject of a vast body of Spanish-language scholarship, it has not been much addressed by US scholars. An exception is Rodrigo Lazo, whose "Filibustering Cuba: Cecelia Valdés and a Memory of Nation in the Americas," *American Literature*, 74, 1 (March 2002): 1 –30, remains an indispensable introduction to the novel for Anglophone readers interested in Villaverde's long and complex political investment in his imaginative project. The zarzuela, commonly regarded as the greatest Cuban example of the form, has been written about in numerous musicological studies, the most recent and notable of which is Susan Thomas, *Cuban Zarzuela: Performing Race and Gender on Havana's Lyric Stage* (Urbana: University of Illinois Press, 2008).

2. *Un Militar Español de Origen Venezolano*
Though López was not much commemorated in Cuba, probably because of both his proslavery US associations and his sponsorship by the wealthy Club de la Habana, his indefatigable efforts at invasion and insurrection are detailed in all US histories of the filibustero era. Of particular interest to US scholars are his multifarious recruitment and finance activities, involving, as noted in the chapter, a veritable who's who of prominent US military and political figures, during the slavery crisis of the 1830s and 1840s. The standard

study in English of López's military adventuring is Tom Chaffin's *Fatal Glory: Narciso López and the First Clandestine U.S. War against Cuba* (Charlottesville: University of Virginia Press, 1996).

3. Mambises in Whiteface

While relying on many photographic and popular history sources currently unavailable to US researchers, as to racial iconography this chapter owes much to the work of Luis A. Pérez Jr., most notably his *Cuba in the American Imagination: Metaphor and the Imperial Ethos* (Chapel Hill: University of North Carolina Press, 2008). Also useful is the work of Aline Helg, whose scholarly work is published both in the United States and Cuba. See, for instance, *Lo Que Nos Corresponde: La Lucha de los Negros y Mulatos por la Igualdad en Cuba, 1886–1912* (La Habana: Imagen Contemporanea, 2000). The "whitened" US images in war photography may be viewed on the Internet at http://www.havanajournal.com/gallery/image. The early newsreel footage described may be viewed at http://www.memory.loc.gov/ammem/sawhtml/sawhome.html. The *Cátalogo de Fotos de la Guerra de Independencia de 1895*, taken from the records of the official *Fototeca del Archivo Nacional de Cuba*, was a gift of the eminent Cuban photographer Julio Larramendi.

4. The Ghost of Walker Evans

A text-specific version of this essay appears in the 2012 University of Alabama Press photo-volume cited above. The original collection of the Havana photos was in Carlton Beals, *The Crime of Cuba* (Philadelphia: J. P. Lippincott, 1934). An enlarged edition, *Walker Evans: Cuba*, with introductory essay by Andrei Codrescu, was published by the Getty Museum in 2011. The standard biography of Evans is James Mellow, *Walker Evans* (New York: Basic Books, 1999). Eric Jose Estrada details the Evans-Hemingway meeting in *Havana: Autobiography of a City* (New York: Palgrave-Macmillian, 2008). Many of the Havana photos are available through Google images. A lively 2004 account of the 1933 Evans-Hemingway encounter in Havana, by Cara Buckley of the *Miami Herald*, may be found at http://www.cubanet.org/CNews/y04/jan04/15e9.html. In 2004–6, the photos also became the subject of a touring exhibit, "Ernest Hemingway and Walker Evans: Three Weeks in Cuba," featured at various art museums around the country.

5. Ignacio Piñeiro, George Gershwin, and the Schillinger System

The standard biographical/critical study of Gershwin is Howard Pollock's *George Gershwin: His Life and Work* (Berkeley: University of California Press,

2006). A lively account of the Cuban sojourn appears in Bennett Cerf's autobiography, *At Random* (New York: Random House, 1977).

Regrettably, the particular focus of this essay does not do justice to the vital, exuberant popular music culture of Cuba in the first half of the twentieth century. Beyond Pérez Prado, Xavier Cugat, Desi Arnaz, Tito Puente, and Don Apiazú, the performer of the original "*el Manicero*," major musicians well known on the island and throughout Latin America included groups such as the Trio Matamoros and the Lecuona Cuban Boys (formed by classical composer Ernesto Lecuona). In recent decades, much publicity has also been devoted to pioneering members of the Buena Vista Social Club. As to individual performers, Benny Moré is still regarded by many as the greatest Cuban popular singer and bandleader of all time. More recently, Celia Cruz came to occupy the role of Cuba's national musical performer of the twentieth century. Fortunately, countless period videos of major twentieth-century figures and bands may now be found on the Internet.

6. The Secret Life of Ricky Ricardo

Several full scale biographies of Lucille Ball include copious biographical information on Desi Arnaz. The most recent and reliable is Stefan Kanfer, *Ball of Fire* (New York: Knopf, 2003). For his own direct account of his life and career, see Desi Arnaz's autobiography, entitled, simply, *A Book* (Cutchogue, NY: Buccaneer Books, 1976). For the US Mob era in Cuba, see T. J. English, *Havana Nocturne* (New York: William Morrow, 2008). *The Mambo Kings Play Songs of Love* is readily available on CD/DVD. The segments featuring Desi Arnaz Jr. as his father and integrating materials from the Lucy Show can be viewed on YouTube at http://www.youtube.com/watch?v=35DbrCPuf-H4&feature=endscreen&NR=1.

7. Good Neighbor Batista

The Volusia County Museum of Art and History is located just off I-95 South near the Daytona Beach airport. An illustrated catalog of the museum's holdings in Cuban art, including the Batista collection, is entitled *Two Centuries of Cuban Art: 1759 –1959*. The 1948 *Time* magazine account of Batista's life as a resident of Daytona Beach is of particular interest, revealing US popular culture perceptions of Cuba and the Batista dictatorship—as guided by the friendly conservative hand of Luce, Inc.—but also serving as a reminder of the frequently breezy style of post–World War II American popular-magazine journalism generally.

8. The Two Ernestos

Images of Che Guevara alone, frequently taken from the Solas photograph—shot on the day of the explosion of the French ammunition ship *Cobre* in Havana Harbor, usually reckoned an American CIA act of sabotage and/or terror—are ubiquitous on commercial items: flags, shirts, posters, bandanas, and the like. In official iconography, he is frequently joined by Camilo Cienfuegos and Fidel Castro in a kind of revolutionary trinity. Hemingway is remembered at all his favorite drinking and socializing spots in the city. Literary associations are emphasized at preservation sites such as the Hotel Ambos Mundos, the Finca Vigia, and the marina at Cojimar. As to the Havana atmospherics of his works, the Plaza San Francisco and the harbor terminal still evoke a particular sense of the Cuba of his early work, such as *To Have and Have Not*.

9. Steverino in Gangsterland

Here again, on the entertainment and gambling culture of the Mob era on the island, *Havana Nocturne*, by T. J. English, is essential background reading. Most of the information in this account is taken from US news magazine reporting of the era. Again the *Time* account of the show's visit is revealing both of US popular-culture perceptions of Cuba and of the style of 1950s popular magazine entertainment journalism. In much the same vein, the current Riviera Hotel website features a 1950s style brochure as its guide to prospective visitors.

10. Why No One in Havana Speaks of Graham Greene

The biographical information in this chapter derives from the standard two-volume *Life of Graham Greene* by Norman Sherry (New York: Viking, 1989, 1995), combined with Greene's autobiographical reflections in *Ways of Escape* (New York: Simon and Schuster, 1980) and his introduction to the 1977 Bodley Head edition of *Our Man in Havana*. In the case of Greene's account of the pleasures he enjoyed during his time in Havana, as with elsewhere in his autobiographical reflections, one has to discount a tendency to provocation, a certain kind of louche grandstanding.

11. Inspector Renko on the Malecón

The Arkady Renko series includes five novels, beginning with the acclaimed *Gorky Park* (New York: Random House, 1981), all set in the post-Soviet era. The Jacqueline Loss comment on the choice of Special Period Cuba for *Havana Bay* appears in "Wandering in Russian," *Cuba in the Special Period*, edited by Ariana Hernandez-Reguant (New York: Palgrave, 2009), (105–22). As Loss observes, information on common life during the era is notably scanty, both in academic and popular culture study. As will be seen just below, it has become a subject of recollection in recent electronic venues, such as the website *Generation Y*, named by the blogger Yoani Sanchez for the young Cubans who came of age during the economic collapse.

12. The Example of Yoani Sanchez

The two books published to date by Yoani Sanchez are *Cuba Libre* (Debate Editorial, 2010), translated as *Havana Real*, translated by M. J. Potter (New York: Melville House, 2011); and *Word Press: un blog para hablar al mundo* (Anaya Multimedia, 2011). Her electronic postings appear regularly on the *Generation Y/DesdeCuba* website www.desdecuba.com/generationy/. In her newly acquired prominence as a celebrity dissident, she has her detractors, to be sure, and they are numbered not just among the official representatives of the regime. As a US academic who has traveled to Cuba for extended stays, and who has spent much time in the streets and the markets, I certainly find Sanchez's passionate honesty inspiring and her candor about day-to-day life consonant with the experiences of my friends and associates there.

Conclusion: The Autumn of the Comandante

As noted, I acknowledge my borrowing of the title of Márquez text, and the idea of reading as context and prophecy in relation to the last years of the Castro regime, as far from the author's original literary and/or political intentions. A different kind of retrospective caveat applies to the Woody Allen movie: it may be a satire of dictatorships, but for Cubans especially there is nothing funny about firing squads. As noted in the essay, my point in both cases is that Fidel Castro, as the last of the great twentieth-century geopolitical figures, has now managed to outlive both prophecy and parody. As with the concluding section, going all the way back to the pioneering US reporting and photojournalism on the revolution in Oriente by Herbert Matthews and others, they just seemed appropriate to me as part of final meditations on current life and history in a book on Cuba and the imagination.

Index

ABC *(abecedarios)*, 58
Abela, Eduardo, "Promenade," 94
Afra, Tybee, 119, 121
African-soldiers, , 37, 40
Agee, James, *Let Us Now Praise Famous Men*, 52–54, 55, 56
Afrocubanismo, 14, 25, 64, 72
Albert, Eddie, 78
Alda, Robert, 68
Allen, Steve, 12, 120, 121, 122
Allen, Woody, *Bananas*, 170–73
Allende, Salvador, 167–68
Anastasia, Albert, 2, 122–23
Annexationism (US), 7, 18, 22, 23, 29, 31, 32, 33, 36, 37
Apiazu, Justo ("Don"), Havana Casino Orchestra, 64, 183
Aponte uprising, 8
Arciaga, Lorenzo Romero, "The Cup of Coffee," 95
Arenas, Reinaldo, 15
Arias, Miguel, 94
Arnaz, Desidero y la Acha, 2, 12, 70–85, 183
Arnaz, Desi, Jr., 81, 84, 183
Assante, Armand, 83–84
Asturias, Miguel Ángel, *El Señor Presidente*, 166
Augie and Margo, 119, 121
Avila, Jose Sanchez, 14

Babalu (deity), 74; (song), 74–76, 81, 85
Babalú—A Tribute to the Music of Desi Arnaz, 84
Bacardi (distillers), 6, 71, 72, 73, 181
Badue, Daniel Serra, "Cuban Sweets," 94
Baker, Josephine, 116

Ball, Lucille, 70–71, 76–80, 183
Banderas, Antonio, 83, 84
Bank for Economic and Social Development (BANDES), 118
Basto, Augusto, *I, the Supreme*, 167
Bataan (movie), 77
Batista, Elisa Godinez Gomez, 87
Batista, Fulgencio, 2, 4, 5, 7, 8, 12, 71, 73, 86–98, 101, 104, 112, 115, 117, 118, 127, 128, 129, 132, 134–38, 147, 164, 166, 169, 173, 174, 177, 178, 179, 183; *Sombras de América (Shadows of America)*, 87–88
Batista, Fulgencio (son), 92
Batista, Jorge, 92
Batista, Marta, 87, 91, 98
Batista, Roberto, 92
Batista, Ruben, 92
Bay of Pigs Invasion, 5, 9, 10, 174, 179, 181
Bayo, Alberto, 175
Beals, Carleton, *The Crime of Cuba (El Crimen de Cuba)*, 51, 52, 56–57, 58–59, 182
Bergen, Edgar, 119, 120–21
Benjamin, Walter, 27–28
Bermudez, Cundo, "The Balcony," 94; "Barbershop," 94
Bodeguita (bar), 71, 110, 111–12, 124, 139
Bogart, Humphrey, 101, 109, 127
Bolero, 61, 62
Bolivar, Simon, 30, 167–68, 175
Brent, William Lee, 148
Brooks, Paul, 38
Brouwer, Leo, 15
Brown, William Wells, *Clotel*, 24
Buena Vista Social Club, 183

Calhoun, John C., 32
Campos, Arsenio Martinez, 2, 39
Campbell, Robert, 31
Canosa, Raul Izquierdo, *Dias de la Guerra Chronologica*, 43
Capone, Al, 74
Capone, Albert Francis ("Sonny"), 174
Capri (hotel), 71, 115, 116, 117, 124, 136, 138
"*carga al machete*," 43, 44
Carpentier, Alejo, *Reasons of State*, 167
Carreno, Mario, 94
Carta, Valentin Sanz, "Landscape and Seascape," 94
Casablanca, 109
Casa Marina, 117
Castaneda, Jorge, 103
Castillo de las Tres Reyes del Morro, el ("Morro Castle"), 3, 29, 51, 145
Castillo de San Salvador de la Punta de Havana, el ("la Punta"), 29, 51, 142
Castro Brothers Orchestra, 64
Castro, Fidel, 2–5, 7–10, 12, 45, 70, 73, 89, 90, 92, 98, 100, 103–109, 112, 113, 122, 128, 129, 132, 134, 135, 148, 154, 164–79, 181, 184, 185
Castro, Raul, 2, 3, 89, 104, 106, 112, 148, 164, 174, 176
Catálogo de Fotos de la Guerra de Independencia de 1895, 45
Cecilia (film), 14–15, 24–25; (ballet), 15
Cecilia Valdes (zarzuela), 14, 25
Central Intelligence Agency, 5, 10, 167–68, 184
Cerf, Bennett, 61, 183
Cespedes, Carlos Manuel de, 2, 8, 38, 72, 114
Chabrier, Jacques, *Espana*, 61
Chaivano, Daina, 15
Chartrand, Esteban, 94

Cienfuegos, Camilo, 2, 31, 45, 104, 107, 164, 184
Ciro's (Los Angeles), 78
Cleveland, Grover, 38
Club de la Habana, el, 31, 32, 35
Coello, Marrana Grajales, 45
Cojimar, 106–107, 111, 183
Cole, Nat "King," 116
Columbus, Christopher 1, 2, 6, 26
Contreras, Felix, 84–85
Copacabana (New York), 78
Cortes, Hernan, 6
Cosell, Howard, 172, 173
Costello, Lou, 119, 121, 122
Coward, Noel, 133
Cowley, Malcolm, 108
Crane, Hart, *The Bridge*, 55
Crane, Stephen, 46, 126; *The Open Boat*, 35
Crittenden, John J., 34
Crittenden, William L., 2, 34
Crucet, Enrique, 95
Cruz, Celia, 183
Cuba—A History in Art, 92
Cuban Foundation, 90, 92, 95, 97, 98
Cuban Missile Crisis, 2–5, 9, 10, 12, 103, 123, 138, 165, 174, 179, 181
"Cuban Pete" (song), 78, 81
Cugat, Xavier, 70, 71, 76, 81, 183

"Dance of the Millions," 8, 50, 62
Davis, Jefferson, 32
Davis, Richard Harding, 39, 45, 68
Daytona Beach, Florida, 12, 84–96, 96–98, 183
De las Casas, Bartolome, 7–8
del Toro, Benicio, 107
de Palma, Anthony, 179
Desilu Productions, 74, 78, 80; *The Untouchables*, 74, 80

De Soto, Hernando, 6
Dupuy de Lome, Enrique, 38

Eire, Carlos, *Waiting for Snow in Havana*, 1
Eisenhower, Dwight D., 10, 178
English, T.J., *Havana Nocturne*, 71, 115
Enriquez, Carlos, "Harlequins," 94
Escalera conspiracy, 8
Escalera, Jose Nicholas de la, "Coronation of the Virgin by the Trinity," 94
Escobar, Vincente, "Portrait of Don Tomas Mateo Cervantes," 94
Estorino, Abelardo, 15
Estrada, Alfredo Jose, 56–58, 182
Evans, Walker, 2, 11, 12, 50–59, 124, 143, 182; "Havana Citizen," 57; *Let Us Now Praise Famous Men*, 52–54, 55, 56

F.B.I., 74
filibusteros/filibustering, 2, 11, 18, 23, 31–35, 39, 171, 181
Fillmore, Millard, 34
Finca Vigia, 104, 108, 110, 111, 184
First War of Cuban Independence (1868), 8, 29, 72
Fitzgerald, F. Scott, *The Great Gatsby*, 68
Flaubert, Gustave, 54
Floridita (bar), 71, 110–12, 124, 139
Fortaleza de la Cabana ("la Cabana"), 51, 104–105, 142, 145, 149
Franco, Francisco, 167, 169
Frawley, William, 78
Fuentes, Grigorio, 110, 111
Fuller Brush Girl (movie), 78

Garcia, Calixto, 2, 8, 39, 44, 45, 72, 114
Genovese, Vito, 2, 121

Gershwin, George, 2, 12, 60–69, 81, 126, 182–83; *An American in Paris*, 61, 63, 66; *Concerto in F*, 61, 62, 63, 66; *Cuban Overture*, 60–69, 81; *Porgy and Bess*, 65, 66; *Rhapsody in Blue*, 62; *Second Concerto*, 66
Gitelson, Henry, 61
Glazounov, Alexander, 67
Godfather II, 133, 138
Gomez, Maximo, 2, 8, 39, 44, 45, 72, 114
Good Neighbor Policy, 86
Granado, Alberto, 99–100
Granma Invasion, 73, 90, 104, 110, 113, 135, 169, 174, 179
Greene, Graham, 2, 12, 111, 126, 127–39; *The Comedians*, 135, 137; *Our Man In Havana* (novel), 126–27, 129–32, 134, 135, 136, 138, 141, 184; (movie), 129–34, 135–36, 138; *The Quiet American*, 128–29, 134; *The Third Man*, 129
Grenet, Eliseo, 14
"Grito de Yara," 8
Guevara, Ernesto "Che," 2, 12, 45, 90, 99–108, 112–14, 122, 164, 174, 184; *Reminiscences on the Cuban Revolutionary War*, 105; *Motorcycle Diaries* (book), 105, 107; (movie), 107; *Bolivian Diaries*, 105
Guinness, Alec, 132, 133

Haiti, 8, 37, 63
Hambitzer, Charles, 67
Hansen, Liane, 71, 76, 78
Hatuey, 2, 7–8
Havana, 1, 3–4, 7, 11, 12, 14, 16, 18, 24, 26, 50–53, 56, 71, 72, 91, 107, 109, 110, 117, 120, 127–30, 132, 136, 138–39, 142–43, 152, 184; "Living City" (*Ciudad Viva*) Project, 11, 26–27, 181
Havana (movie), 138

Havana Hilton Hotel (*Habana Libre*), 7, 71, 115, 122, 133
Hearst, William Randolph, 39, 40
Helg, Aline, *Los Que Nos Corresponde: La Lucha de los Negros y Mulatos por la Igualidad en Cuba 1886–1912*, 43
Hemings, Sally, 24
Hemingway, Ernest, 2, 12, 52, 58, 59, 71, 99–104, 107–113, 116, 124, 126, 127, 139, 143, 182, 184; *Across the River and Into the Trees*, 110; *For Whom the Bell Tolls*, 109, 110; *The Garden of Eden*, 110; *Islands in the Stream*, 110, 127; *A Moveable Feast*, 111; *The Old Man and the Sea*, 102, 108–11, 126; *To Have and Have Not*, 109, 127, 184
Hemingway, Valerie, 112–13
Henderson, John, 33
Henderson, Skitch, 122
Hijuelos, Oscar, *The Mambo Kings Play Songs of Love* (novel), 81, 83; (movie), 83
Historia de Cuba, 43
"History Will Absolve Me" (Castro speech), 89, 173
Ho Chi Minh, 10, 165
Hope, Bob, 78
Hotel Almendares, 61, 64
Hotel Ambos Mundos, 52, 111, 124, 139, 184
Hotel Inglaterra, 51
Hotel Nacional, 51, 64, 71, 88, 111, 115, 116, 117, 132
Hotel Telegrafo, 51
Hoover, J. Edgar, 74
Huffington Post, 160
Hughes, Langston, 178
Hulme, Peter, 136
Humboldt, Alexander von, 6
Humphrey, Hubert, 178

Iglesia de Paula, la (Havana), 14
I Love Lucy, 78–84
Intervencion, la, 2, 8, 35, 47, 50, 72, 73
Isle of Pines, 173
Ives, Burl, 133

Jacobs, Harriet, *Incidents in the Life of a Slave Girl*, 24
Jefferson, Thomas, 24
Jobabo uprising (1533), 8
Johnson, Lyndon B., 9
Johnson, Philip, 118
Jolson, Al, 68

Kilyeni, Edward,
Kennedy, John F., 5, 9, 165
Kennedy, William, 169
Khrushchev, Nikita, 10, 165, 178
Knotts, Don, 119, 121–22
Korda, Alexander, *El Guerrillero Heroico* (photo), 101, 105, 106, 108
Kovacs, Ernie, 133–34
Kundera, Milan, *The Book of Laughter and Forgetting*, 97; *La Comida in el Monte: Cimarrones, Mambises, and Rebeldes*, 42–43

Lam, Wilfredo, "Zambesia, Zambesia," 93–94
Lansky, Meyer, 2, 88–89, 91, 115–20, 122–24
Lawrence, Steve, 119, 120, 121
Lazo, Rodrigo, 17, 22, 23
Leal, Dr. Eusebio, 11, 26–27
Leante, Cesar, 26
Lecuona, Ernesto, 14, 15, 25, 183; Lecuona Cuban Boys, 183
Lecuona, Margaret, 85
Lee, Fitzhugh, 2, 39

Lee, Robert E., 32
Levant, Oscar, 67, 68–69
Life magazine, 108, 177
Llinas, Guido, "Composition," 95
Loma del Angel, la (Havana), 14, 26
Lopez, Narciso, 2, 11, 18, 22, 23, 29–38
L'Ouverture, Toussaint, 8, 37
Luce, Henry, 89
Luciano, Lucky, 2, 88, 115, 116, 117
Luening, Hans, 129
Lukacs, Georgy, 27

MacAllister, Wayne, 118
Maceo, Antonio, 2, 8, 39, 43,
  44, 45, 48, 72, 114
Machado, Gerardo, 2, 50, 52, 57, 58,
  62, 73–74, 84, 109, 127, 166, 167
Maine, U.S.S., 39, 113
Malcolm X, 178
Mambises, 11–12, 37–49
Manuel, Victor, "Landscape
  with Figures," 93
Mao Zedong, 10, 165
Marina Hemingway (Havana),
  112, 142, 148
Marquez, Gabriel Garcia, 2, 12, 165; *The
  Autumn of the Patriarch*, 165–70, 173;
  The General in His Labyrinth, 175;
  One Hundred Years of Solitude, 168
Marti, Jose, 2, 3, 8, 18, 23, 26, 39,
  49, 56, 72, 90, 111, 114, 152
Marx Brothers, 171
Matacena, Orestes, 43
Mathews, Herbert, 178, 179, 185
McCarran Act, 135
Melero, Miguel, "Portrait of
  Aurelio, Son of the Artist," 94
Menocal, Armando, 44; "Caballaría
  Mambisa," 44; *Death of Maceo*,

44; *Maximo Gomez en Campana*,
  44; "Peasant Child," 93
Moncada Barracks, 7, 73, 89, 104,
  110, 135, 164, 173, 179
*Monumento des Estudiantes de
  Medicina* (Havana), 29
Montalban, Ricardo, 77
Montejo, Esteban, 47
More, Antonio Rodriguez,
  "Symphony in Green," 93
More, Benny, 183
Morrow, Jo, 133
Museo de la Revolucion, 26, 90,
  103, 105, 110, 113, 142
*Museo Nacional de las Bellas
  Artes*, 44, 91, 93, 98
My Favorite Husband (TV show), 78

Navarro, Jose Canton, 43
New York Times, 56, 160, 169, 178, 179
Nietzsche, Friedrich, 161
Nixon, Donald, 148
Nixon, Donald, Jr., 148
Nixon, Richard, 10, 148, 165, 167–68, 178
Nye, Louie, 119, 121, 122

Olney, Richard, 38
O'Donnell, Leopoldo, 2, 31
O'Hara, Maureen, 133, 134
O'Sullivan, John L., 32
Oswald, Lee Harvey, 9

*Palacio de los Capitanes
  Generales*, 44, 51, 73, 113
Palau Brothers Hollywood Orchestra, 64
Parece Blanca (She Looks White), 15
"Peanut Vendor" ("el Manicero"), 61, 64
Pelaez, Amanda, 93
Perez, Louis, 38, 182

"*Periodo Especial*" ("Special Period"), 103, 106, 140–42, 153, 176
PhotographicHistory of the Spanish-American War, 41
Pidal, Pedro, 32
Pineiro, Ignacio, 60, 63, 64, 65, 68, 69, 182; "Echale Salsita," 62–65
Pinochet, Augusto, 168, 169
"Placido" (Gabriel Concepcion Valdes), 2, 17, 22
Platt Amendment, 8, 62
Plaza (hotel), 51, 64, 111
Pogolotti, Marcelo, 94
Polevitsky, Boris, 118
Polk, James K., 31, 32, 33
Portacarrero, Rene, "Figure in Grey," 94
Poston, Tom 119, 121
Powell, Richard, *Don Quixote U.S.A.*, 172
Prado, Perez, 71, 81, 116, 183
Puente, Tito, 183

Quitman, John, 2, 33

Ramos, Carlos and Roberto, *Art of the Cuban Republic, 1902–58*, 92
Raft, George, 117
Ravel, Maurice, 67; *Bolero*, 61, 62
Rayburn, Gene, 120
Rebozo, Bebe, 10
Reconcentrado (concentration camp) program, 39, 41, 42, 48
Reed, Carol, 129
Remington, Frederic, 40
Resik, Magda, 11
Richardson, Ralph, 133
Rivero, Emilio, *Corner in a Cuban Garden*, 94–95
Riviera (hotel), 71, 91, 115–25, 184
Rockefeller, John D., 96–97
Rodriguez, Agustin, 14

Rodriguez, Paul, *Heroes de la Independencia de Cuba*, 43
Rogers, Ginger, 116
Roig, Gonzalo, 14, 15, 25
Romanasch, Leopoldo, "Italian Peasant," 93; "On the Way to Mass," 93
Roosevelt, Franklin, 52, 101
Roosevelt, Theodore, 2, 39, 45, 73
Rough Riders, 39, 40, 44
Rowan, Andrew S., 39
Ruby, Jack, 9
Ruiz, Pedro, 15
rumba, 8, 60, 61, 63, 64, 65, 81; "Rumba" (Gershwin title), 61, 69

Sanchez, Yoani, 2, 12, 151; *Desde Cuba* (blog), 159, 162, 185; *Generation Y* (blog), 159, 162, 185; *Havana Real/Cuba Libre* (book), 154–61, 185; *Word Press: A Blog for Speaking to the World*, 162, 185; *Words under Pressure*, 162
San Juan Hill, 39, 40, 73
San Martin, Ramón Grau, 87, 88
Santa Clara, 105
Santeria, 25, 72, 74, 85
Santiago de Cuba, 2, 6, 7, 46, 70–74, 84, 89, 135, 173
Sarmiento, Domingo Faustino, *Facundo*, 166
Saturday Night Live, 81
Schillinger, Joseph, 60, 66–69, 182–83; "Schillinger System," 60, 66–69, 182–83
Schoenberg, Arnold, 67
Septeto Nacional, 64–65
Sevilla-Biltmore (hotel), 51, 71, 111, 115, 117
Silberberg, Daniel H., 61
SIM (*Servicio de Inteligencia Militar*), 90

Simons, Moises, 64
Sinatra, Frank, 116
Smith, Martin Cruz, 2, 12, 141–50; *Havana Bay*, 141–50
Smith, William L., 35
Solas, Humberto, 14, 24–25
son, 64
son pregon, 64, 65
Sorrowful Jones (movie), 78
Spanish-American War, 8, 32, 37–49, 50, 72–73
Spanish Civil War, 93, 100, 110
Steve Allen Show, 115, 119–22, 125
Stowe, Harriet Beecher, *Uncle Tom's Cabin*, 24–25
Sullivan, Ed, *Talk of the Town*, 115

Taino, 6, 7
Taylor, Zachary, 32, 33
Tchaikovsky, Peter, *Capriccio Espana*, 61; *Capriccio Italien*, 61
Ten Years War (1868–78), 8
Third War of Cuban Independence (1895–98), 8, 35, 37, 72
Thomas, Susan, 25–26
Time (magazine), 87, 120, 121, 183
Too Many Girls (stage musical), 76; (movie), 76–77
Tracy, Spencer, 109, 127
Trafficante, Salvador, 2, 115, 117
tragic *mulata*, 24, 25
Trio Matamoros, 183
Tropicana (nightclub), 116, 117, 124, 132, 133, 134, 139
Two Centuries of Cuban Art: 1759–1959. 92

University of Havana, 10, 162, 173

Vance, Vivian, 78

Van Doren, Mamie, 119, 121, 122
Vanguardia Cubana, 92–94, 95–96
Varela, Felix, 22, 26
Vesco, Robert, 148
Vietnam War, 3–4, 9
Villaverde, Cirilo, 2, 14, 18, 23, 25, 31, 32, 143, 152, 153, 161, 181; *Cecilia Valdes* (novel), 11, 14–28, 151–52, 161
Vietier, Jose Maria, 15
Vives, Dionisio, 2, 22
Volusia County Museum of Art and Sciences, 90, 93, 96, 97, 183

Walker, William, 35
Watergate, 10
Weyler, Valeriano, 2, 39
Wheeler, Joe, 2, 39
Whiteman, Paul, 68–69
Winchell, Walter, 76
Wizard of Oz, 137
Wood, Leonard, 2, 7, 8
Worth, William L., 31, 32

Yara, 7
Yoruba, 6

Zarzuela, 14, 15, 25, 181
Zayas, Carlos Saladrigas, 87